PENGUIN CANADA

OUR LIFE WITH THE ROCKET

Roch Carrier is the author of such celebrated works of fiction as *La Guerre, Yes Sir!*, *The Hockey Sweater*, *Heartbreaks along the Road*, *The Man in the Closet*, *The End*, and *Prayers of a Very Wise Child*, which won the Stephen Leacock Award for Humour in 1991. Since 1999 he has served as National Librarian of Canada. Roch Carrier lives in Ottawa.

OUR LIFE WITH THE
ROCKET

THE MAURICE RICHARD STORY

ROCH CARRIER

Translated from the French by
SHEILA FISCHMAN

PENGUIN
CANADA

PENGUIN CANADA
Published by the Penguin Group
Penguin Books, a division of Pearson Canada, 10 Alcorn Avenue, Toronto, Ontario,
Canada M4V 3B2
Penguin Books Ltd, 80 Strand, London WC2R 0RL, England
Penguin Putnam Inc., 375 Hudson Street, New York, New York 10014, U.S.A.
Penguin Books Australia Ltd, 250 Camberwell Road, Camberwell, Victoria 3124,
Australia
Penguin Books India (P) Ltd, 11, Community Centre, Panchsheel Park,
New Delhi – 110 017, India
Penguin Books (NZ) Ltd, cnr Rosedale and Airborne Roads, Albany,
Auckland 1310, New Zealand
Penguin Books (South Africa) (Pty) Ltd, 24 Sturdee Avenue, Rosebank 2196,
South Africa

Penguin Books Ltd, Registered Offices: 80 Strand, London WC2R 0RL, England

First published in Viking by Penguin Books Canada Limited, 2001
Published in Penguin Canada by Penguin Books,
a division of Pearson Canada, 2002

Printed in Canada
1 3 5 7 9 10 8 6 4 2

Copyright © Roch Carrier, 2001
English translation copyright © Sheila Fischman, 2001

All rights reserved.

NATIONAL LIBRARY OF CANADA CATALOGUING IN PUBLICATION DATA

Carrier, Roch, 1937-
Our life with the Rocket : the Maurice Richard story / written by Roch Carrier ;
English translation by Sheila Fischman.

Includes index.
Translation of: Le Rocket.
First published: Toronto : Viking, 2001.
ISBN 0-14-028007-3

1. Richard, Maurice, 1921-2000. 2. Montreal Canadiens (Hockey
team)—History. 3. Carrier, Roch, 1937-. 4. Hockey players—Quebec
(Province)—Biography. I. Fischman, Sheila II. Title.

GV848.5.R5C3713 2002   796.962'092   C2002-903266-0

Visit Penguin Books' website at **www.penguin.ca**

CONTENTS

LETTER TO MY PUBLISHER

March 1998. No, I won't write a book about Maurice Richard. You've invited me to tell the story of my childhood hero, the greatest hockey player of all time. I've thought it over as you suggested. My answer is still no.

At the closing of the Forum on March 11, 1998, when Maurice Richard appeared on the ice the Montreal crowd gave him a standing ovation that went on for more than eleven minutes. There wasn't a dry eye in the house. The Rocket had played his final game in 1960. Three-quarters of the people who were cheering the former champion hadn't been born when he scored his last goal.

Then an announcement came that shattered all of Quebec. It made the front page of all the papers: Maurice Richard had cancer. I'd seen many people destroyed by cancer but I was not desperately sad. Maurice Richard won't let himself be pushed around by cancer. He'll either outsmart it or he'll knock it out. Maurice Richard has never backed down before an attacker. Maurice Richard can't lose. The old child I've become still needs his hero. A hero who is fearless can wipe out the fear of a child. If his hero is fearless the child will walk through life with confidence.

Four years ago, on July 18, 1994, Maurice Richard's wife, Lucille, passed away. On Saturday night a few days later, it was like the good old days of hockey on the radio. Several friends, grey-haired men who'd become a lawyer, a financier, a politician, an economist, were swapping memories of the time when the Rocket was the emperor of the ice. When it was over, we all agreed that we'd shed tears on the day when the Rocket flies away towards the skating rink in the sky.

No, dear publisher, I can't write a book about Maurice Richard.

DID YOU RECOGNIZE MAURICE RICHARD ON THE MAIN STREET OF THE VILLAGE?

1945. Winter at last. The ice on the rink is as smooth as a blue sky. At the bottom of the hill the fields are now as white as they were green last summer. The houses are wearing white bonnets. The smoke from the chimneys is white. The street is white. In my village we don't drive the snow away with a plough. We let it pile up. When it has finished falling, a big wooden roller drives by, drawn by horses with icicles clicking in the hair of their hocks. The roller flattens the snow the way our mother's rolling pin flattens the dough for her pie crusts. Everything is so white. Everything is so calm in this beautiful sparkling cold.

Monday. We're five schoolboys wearing aviators' helmets with the fur-lined flaps pulled down, parkas with fur-lined hoods and felt boots. Our bags are crammed with books and scribblers. We're seven, eight, nine years old. Of course we know that there's a war being fought in the old countries. Our parents listen to the bad news on the radio as if it were a prayer in church. If we make a sound we set off the anger of father and mother alike. We schoolboys are happy. Last Saturday the Canadiens won their game against Toronto.

This morning we're listening to our friend Jacques. He's the worst pupil in class. He can't remember a thing that the nun teaches us. The shortest answer in the whole catechism is the one to question number thirteen: "Where is God?" The correct answer is: "God is everywhere." Jacques can't remember that. Three nines are twenty-seven: Jacques can't remember that. Or two nines are eighteen. He doesn't even know what one nine is. He doesn't know the capital of Canada. He can't remember anything the nun teaches us in class but on Monday morning he gives us a description of the Saturday night hockey game. Not only does he remember every word of Michel Normandin, who describes the match on the radio, but he also imitates his voice. He makes his voice vibrate in his nose like Normandin and he rolls his *r*'s: "Maurrrice RRRichard takes the puck and slams it at Turrrk Brrroda; the Canadiens are back on the rrroad to victorrry against Torrronto!"

We climb the hill. Nothing is impossible. Maurice Richard has won. The Canadiens have won. We have won. Under the blue sky we're taller now, stronger, more important. Maurice Richard has scored two goals. We have scored two goals. The new school week weighs lightly on our shoulders. We're all Rockets. When we meet adults they can see that we are champions.

=====

1944. Another memory. At our house, Saturdays are chaotic. We're rushed, shoved, pushed. Everything has to be finished before the start of the Canadiens game on the radio. Our mother is the commander-in-chief of operations.

It begins in the afternoon. First of all our mother, like all the other fastidious mothers in the village, washes the floor. When we see her on her knees with a bucket of soapy water and a brush, we know it's Saturday: there will be a Canadiens game on the radio, Maurice Richard will score goals. After that will come Sunday. Instead of going to school we'll go to church to hear the priest shout himself hoarse from the pulpit, scaring us with the flames of hell and the devil's pitchfork.

After she washes the linoleum our mother, still on her knees, will wax it. Then it's our job to make it shine like a new penny. Our grandmother will come and inspect it and our mother doesn't want to be reproached for neglecting her floor. So the floor becomes our rink. We pull on our woollen socks and we slide, we chase, we hunt one another, we swivel, we push and shove. It always ends in a squabble. The referee, our mother, sends one of us to the penalty box.

And then our father comes home from his expeditions. Inevitably he leaves boot marks on the clean floor. Our mother grows impatient at always having to level the same criticism at him. The previous Saturday he also left marks. The Saturday before that too. And every other Saturday. Our mother is as anxious to see him as we are. All at once she's angry: "I scrubbed this floor on my hands and knees!" Every time, our father is amazed at all this noise for nothing. He looks around him as if he's landed on the moon. And offers his apology, as he does every Saturday: "I wasn't thinking." Suddenly our mother isn't angry any more. She has a smile for my father that we only see on Saturday. "You weren't thinking . . . I'm well aware of that . . . You weren't thinking . . . When men think it doesn't go on for very long . . ." So then we boys watch our father pull off his boots. We feel proud: one day we'll be men like our father. "It's Saturday. Tonight, youngsters, we listen to Maurice Richard!"

Supper. We bolt it. We won't have time to do everything before the game. Our father came home late, so now the meat is overcooked, the potatoes come apart like flour, the bread has baked too long and the pies that our mother had to take out of the oven are cold.

To our mother's lament our father replies, as he does every Saturday, that he'd have liked to come home much sooner. Unfortunately, earning money is hard work. Business has become impossible. With this war on, nobody knows what the future will be. Lumber isn't selling because, on account of the war, everything is iron now. On account of the war the price of everything we have to buy is going up. If the war goes on, the government will ruin the French Canadians.

I listen to this economics lesson. We've got just one hope. Maurice Richard will give the Canadiens a victory.

"Hurry up and eat!" Because our father wasn't home when he was due, according to our mother's timetable we're already late for saying the rosary.

That's a religious exercise which requires us to repeat the same prayer fifty times. Isn't the good Lord smart enough to understand it the first time? We whimper rebelliously; we don't feel like getting down on our knees. Our mother used to be a schoolteacher: "For the love of Jesus, behave yourselves like proper Catholics! If you keep pushing like that, you're going to turn into little Communists."

The hockey game is about to start. The rosary hasn't been recited yet. We haven't had our baths. Like a person who doesn't intend to lose a race, she rattles off the pious words: "Our Father who art in Heaven, hallowed . . ."

We little soldiers of Christ know that time is short. We hurry the words, we stammer, we stutter. We aren't kneeling properly. Our backsides are sticking out too far, we're resting on our elbows too much, our backs aren't straight, our knees aren't touching the floor, our eyes aren't focussed on the crucifix on the wall. With our grins, we don't look pious enough; our mother interrupts, corrects our imperfections. The recitation of the rosary is bumpy and arduous.

At one point our young brother, the clown, says: "Maurice Richard, who art in Heaven . . ." Our father, who likes kid brother's humour, covers his face with his hands. We know he's laughing; we can see his shoulders shake. We boys hold back for as long as we can, but then we burst out too. Our mother can't stand this resistance to prayer. She stands up, rubbing her tired knees. The rosary is over before it's finished. We're happy. Our mother is not: "You, old man, you're a worse Communist than your sons." And desperately: "That Maurice Richard of yours, I don't see what's so special about him."

And then we have to go and take our baths. A while ago we got a bathtub with hot water, cold water and lukewarm water, just like they have in town. We're proud of it. Every week someone comes to visit our bathroom. The war has brought us modern progress. Often farmers come and talk about progress with our father, on the veranda that wraps around our house. The war has also brought tractors to the farmers who've given their horses a vacation. So many cars drive through our village that nobody bothers to count them any more. There are even some women who drive. And women dare to smoke. Life is changing. Our mother doesn't sound off against change, unlike many other mothers who don't want to be torn away from the good old days.

The bath is another ordeal to be got through. We have no choice. It's like the family rosary. We clean ourselves off in three licks of a washcloth. What we don't wash tonight, we'll wash some other time. But our mother is watching. If we don't scrub, she does; and she soaps if we don't.

At last, clean and smelling of Ivory soap, we're ready to press our ears to the radio for the Canadiens game.

Our mother, who's not allowed to speak now, is bored. She's anxious for Maurice Richard to win the game so that life in the house can resume. Everyone has to be absolutely silent, like when our parents listen to the war news. To help pass the time, she leafs through the family photograph album.

There are all the faces of old dead people I've never met. And there are photos that I hate of us, the children, when we were babies. There are ridiculous pictures of our parents before they were parents, trying to look gorgeous in their Sunday best. And there are some very old photos of hockey players in ancient uniforms.

How can it be that my mother, a *mother*, has photos of hockey players in her album, along with those of ancestors, cousins and children? Hockey photos among pictures of weddings, funerals and religious processions? Sometimes she'll point at one of the players sitting in rows: "That one moved like a deer on skates."

When my mother was a young girl she must have got all dressed up and pulled a woollen hat over her curly hair to watch the boys play hockey. While she waited for her team to win, her feet would freeze in the snow. She hasn't forgotten the exciting times when her heart would beat a little faster if her favourite player was brutally checked or when he scored a goal. She hasn't forgotten those moments of her youth and she doesn't want to forget them. In their coloured uniforms those young men were handsome; they stood tall in their skates, they were proud, they weren't afraid of anyone or of getting hit or injured.

Hockey was introduced into my village in 1928, by the *curé*. My mother was eighteen years old at the time. A new game, a rink like they had in town, a place where the boys could strut and the girls could watch the boys. That must have been a significant occurrence in a village so quiet that the wind was an event to be noticed. Like all the young girls her age and all the boys, my mother must have been excited. Very early on, our team enjoyed victories. The young girls were proud to see their players beat the show-offs from the other villages. It wasn't long before our team, Jeune Canada, was invincible.

In those very Catholic days dancing was forbidden; the priests had made it a mortal sin. Now, suddenly, in the shadow of the church, boys and girls had permission to skate with their arms around each other's waists. Some years later a new *curé* arrived. Seeing young girls enticing boys onto the ice and then seeing boys and girls skating close together, the new *curé* cursed the rink. For some years there was no ice in the shadow of the church.

Is our mother thinking about those days as she turns the pages of the album while we follow every move of Maurice Richard, Toe Blake and Elmer Lach?

So much has happened since that time when, all agog, she'd go to the village rink. Since then electricity arrived, then the radio and lights in houses; she got married, she had children. Automobiles took over the roads.

With my ear pressed up against the radio, I don't allow my mind to wander. I pay attention. Something important is going on. I want to have something to say at school on Monday when we gather near the big willow tree to talk about the Canadiens game.

Maurice Richard, despite his speed, takes his time, analyzes the situation, finds the weak point, takes aim, then drives the puck between the pads of the goalie, who seems to be wondering if it's Saturday, Sunday or Monday.

"Stop jumping up and down, Roch, you'll break the floor!"

"Maurice Richard scored a goal with a Black Hawk on his back!"

"Maurice had *what* on his back?"

"A Black Hawk."

That's one of the things a mother can't understand.

===

May 13, 1998. I turned sixty-one today. This afternoon I put on my in-line skates. I haven't skated since . . . since . . . Is it some loathsome form of vanity that's made me take up skating again? People make fun of me, pleasantly. They tease me about being vain. I take it all with Olympian composure. I fasten my skates as if I won a race yesterday. In fact I'm nervous, terrified, to be honest. I feel light-headed before I stand up. Could I have forgotten everything I've learned—I who spent my childhood on skates? I'm gripped by fear. Fear of falling. Because of the wheels under my feet, fear that I won't be able to stand up. Fear that my speed will sweep me away. Fear that I won't be able to stop. I'm afraid but I know what I'm doing.

Do I want to write a book about Maurice Richard? I try to relive the terror that used to make my heart pound when I was four or five and our mother tightened the laces of my first pair of skates. If I can recreate that excitement I'll be able to talk about hockey. I have a hunch that when Maurice Richard took flight on the ice to the shouts of the crowd, he became again the young Maurice, proud to show his mama how fast he could go on his skates.

I'm not a champion yet and I'm mindful of everything that will go on inside me. I get up on my wheels, wobbly. The earth moves under my feet; my hands try to clutch at the air. I'm going to collapse. No, I'm still on my feet. The earth stops moving. Ah, the joy of being a man who hasn't fallen! On my skates I'm taller. That's another of the hockey player's joys, being taller than others. Humans like to make themselves bigger, to perch on high boots, on heels. It's a delectable pleasure for humans to perch. I'm cautious, so I'm wearing a helmet, I'm decked out with knee pads, elbow pads, wrist protectors. And I'm experiencing that old well-being: that of being taller, of belonging to the superior tribe, the tribe of those who have skates on their feet and access to the sacred territory of the rink. It must be the same kind of pleasure people get from wearing a theatrical costume, a uniform or a suit of armour. In my book on the Rocket I'll remember that delightful shiver of the soul a child experiences when he puts on skates.

Hardly more confident than when I first started skating, today, fifty-six years later, I rush forward, but cautiously; one thrust of the skate, go forward, farther, farther, a second thrust of the skate. I'm another man now: I'm not walking, I'm flying! Skating is flying. Skating means rising up above those who walk, those crawling creatures. Skating means having wings. I glide along Maisonneuve Boulevard. I feel all the muscles that work when I push on my skate, when I take a curve, when I brake, when I take off again. Of course I notice how slow I am, too, but that's not what I want to remember. To write about the Rocket I want to remember the emotions I felt as a child, because a great hockey player is always playing his first game.

Without a break I come back to the house in triumph. Do I still have enough breath to blow out my sixty-one candles?

═══

As one of my teachers instructed me, "The world was created long before the creation of the world." Sports historians have identified as the origin of hockey certain games in which the Egyptians and the Persians used rudimentary sticks and balls. Others maintain that hockey originated with *gouret*, a game that the Romans at the time of Julius Caesar taught the Gauls when their land was under Roman occupation: this game was played on ice, snow or grass.

Whenever I'm in a foreign city, after I visit the market, where the everyday face of the city is to be found, I hurry to the museum to plunge into its memory. Of course I also meditate before the dreams

painted by geniuses, but I'm no less curious to find chilly scenes in
which minor artists have tried to fix on canvas the winter with its
grey skies, bare trees, white fields, frozen ponds and brisk flights of
birds. In these landscapes I always try to spot hockey players.

I like those fat burghers in the baggy pants skating with their
ladies dressed in velvet. They are celebrating winter. I feel as if I can
hear laughter, conversations. Little girls. Grandmothers. These fine
folk have skates attached to their shiny shoes. Ruddy-faced boys sitting on huge plates push themselves along with two short sticks.
Among the skaters there are prosperous merchants treating themselves to a game that looks like golf. In *Hunters in the Snow*, painted
by Brueghel in 1565, in the left-hand corner of the rink which has
been built next to the church, a boy is playing with a stick and a
ball. He's not wearing skates. Often when we practised our shots to
be more like Maurice Richard, we didn't bother with skates either.

For anyone who spent his childhood in a village, winter scenes
by the modest Hendrick Avercamp provide lots to dream about.
Portly burghers, plump ladies in high collars of starched lace, scurry
across a frozen pond next to a castle. A young hockey player on
skates and holding a stick is indifferent to the crowd. If I study this
moment, set in 1615, I spot among the people crowded onto the ice
two players on skates who are wielding sticks, playing near a small
boat that's run aground on the ice. Is it golf on ice? Is it hockey?

In 1658, another little-known artist, Jan Beerstraalen, painted
Le Château de Muiden, a few miles from Amsterdam. In the fore-
ground are some players on skates with turned-up ends who are
holding curved sticks. One player is looking into the distance like a
golfer who's just completed a powerful shot. Is it golf on ice? Is it
hockey? In the face of the disasters of this world, the question is
unimportant. Hockey is derived from a long tradition of fundamental games that humans invented in peacetime to mimic war and
maybe to avoid it.

Hockey came to Canada with the British. During the long winters, soldiers billeted in Kingston, Halifax, Quebec City or Montreal

needed to amuse themselves. They learned to skate. As soon as they were able to move around they took to playing games that were familiar to them. In 1843, an officer named A.H. Fielding recorded in his journal the pleasure he had playing hockey on ice. Was it really ice hockey? It's unlikely. On Canadian ice, these young uniformed Britons played games that they'd played on grass at home: the Scottish shinty, the Irish hurling, the English field hockey or the golf played by the Dutch and the Scots. No doubt the officers strongly encouraged their troops to play "hockey." Is there any better exercise to prepare for war?

French Canadians came late to the sport. Our game was survival. In Montreal on March 3, 1875, *The Gazette* ran an ad for a hockey match. The population of Montreal at the time was 55 percent French-Canadian. The journalist explains that the game consisted of placing a rubber ball between two flags. The match was played at the Victoria Skating Hall on Drummond Street, a wealthy English neighbourhood where French Canadians only ventured as housemaids or coachmen. The journalist wanted to reassure the spectators: hockey is played with a rubber ball but that evening, to avoid accidents, they would use a wooden disc which would slide across the surface of the ice rather than bounce.

At the end of the nineteenth century there were no French Canadians on a senior-level team. This fact led a journalist from *La Presse* to launch a *cri de coeur*: "We must demonstrate that in sports as in all other branches of human activity, French Canadians are not inferior to the other races."

Anglophone students at McGill University had formed a hockey club in 1876. Three years later, they decided that the rubber ball they had been using was inadequate. They took the initiative of slicing the rubber ball to make it into a disc—and the puck was born. The puck would become an object of contention, of desire. An object of worship.

In contrast, the first French-Canadian student hockey club wasn't formed until 1899. Perhaps French Canadians had concerns other than hockey. In the city of Montreal, the income of a French Canadian was only a quarter that of his anglophone neighbour. French-Canadian workers, who had little education, found jobs in the port of Montreal, where strong men became longshoremen, in the mills, in the leather and tobacco industries, in construction and roadwork. Families lived below the threshold of poverty. The work-day was ten to twelve hours long, six days a week, fifty-two weeks of the year. Families lived in crowded tenements, often without hot water or toilets, and it was not uncommon for two or three families to be crammed inside one of them.

At work, conditions were unhealthy, with rotting garbage, inadequate ventilation, stifling heat in summer and unbearable cold in winter, flies, poor lighting and foul odours. Women earned half the salary men did. Often, parents would falsify the ages of their children so they could have access to jobs, where absent-mindedness or clumsiness could lead to beatings. Sometimes the workers would be locked up in the cells that some companies kept for rebellious employees.

Yes, French Canadians came to hockey slowly. In 1904, we sent two teams into battle, the Montagnard and the National. Their mission: "To prove to the world that if they'll only take the trouble, French Canadians can excel at anything." Despite nationalist mur-murs, both teams were weak. But defeat would only be a step along the way. Regardless of their setbacks, we supported our two teams. In *La Patrie* we read: "French Canadians who care about the future of our institutions will have excellent opportunities to demonstrate their patriotism." We must persevere. We'll win tomorrow! This small people does not want to vanish! In 1906, the National won several victories.

At the same time, the Société du Parler Français au Canada, an organization that promoted the use of the French language, was concerned about the threat of anglicization that weighed on French Canadians because of hockey. Among themselves, players used the game's English vocabulary. The Société published a hockey glossary in which English words were replaced by French equivalents, in order to defend French "against any corruption."

In 1907, the Montagnard carried off the championship of the Federal Hockey League. "This is a victory not just for the Montagnard but for all French Canadians," one newspaper proclaimed.

Throughout all these crises, hockey was making progress. Teams multiplied. Entrepreneurs found that hockey offered splendid opportunities for making profits. Ambrose O'Brien, a millionaire from Cobalt, Ontario, was the first to understand the advantages of owning an entirely French-Canadian team. As team manager he hired a legendary figure, Jack Laviolette, a hockey player who also played lacrosse, raced automobiles and drove motorcycles. Laviolette recruited star players such as Didier Pitre, who over nineteen seasons with the Canadiens played in 181 games, scoring 240 goals, and Newsy Lalonde, who would lead the league in scoring five times.

Laval, Montreal's French-language university, was accepted in the university league in 1907. Already the league had teams from Queen's University in Kingston, Montreal's McGill and the University of Toronto. The proud French-Canadian students lost their first game to Toronto, 19–1. For several years the team lost to anglophone teams. Does that help explain the delight of fans when Maurice Richard rushed at the Toronto net? He was the Avenger. The one who wipes away humiliation. The one who avenges the honour of his race. In 1907 the Rocket hadn't been born. His father was a kid playing street hockey. The Rocket's life begins long before the Rocket.

The year is 1914: World War I is devastating hockey. Several players enlist, weakening their teams. Their play is less interesting. When peace returns, a group of businessmen and professionals join forces to form the Club Athlétique Canadien. Of the thirty shareholders, only seven have English names. The French Canadians are businessmen, lawyers, doctors, MPs and the managers of the three most influential French-Canadian newspapers, *La Patrie*, *Le Devoir* and *La Presse*.

We came to hockey slowly. The great writer Stendhal once observed that the novel is a mirror along one's way. The same could be said of hockey. And on this long road did anyone see the Rocket coming?

1946. World War II has just ended. During the summer in my village, some of my friends don't have shoes; in the winter, everyone has skates. In the mid-forties, the winters are generous with snow and cold. The automobiles of the leading citizens, stored away till the snow melts, wait patiently for spring. During the winter, horses rule. Dignity is restored to the animals. They have the road to themselves. And they have all the time they need. The farmers, languidly holding the reins, take the time to enjoy a pipeful of tobacco with no fear of cars coming along to scare their animals. They doze and let their horses lead them.

Only a group of children playing hockey in the street can make them stop. The horses are used to it. They're serene. They observe with the great, wise eyes of connoisseurs and wait for the goal. They wouldn't dare to disturb hockey players.

Sometimes a horse will leave us a bouquet of turds. Using the tips of our sticks we put some aside. The cold is biting; they'll soon be hard. We don't have a puck. A horse turd will do the trick. Even if a goal is scored with a horse turd, it's still a goal.

And so, as we play hockey on the main street, we're its masters. The horses wait patiently. The only ones who dare to disturb our game are the bent and shrivelled old ladies going up the hill to the church. They're not as patient as the horses. In a little voice that trembles like her hands, the grandmother issues orders:

"Make way for Granny, all you little Maurice Richards."

We're concentrating hard as we play. How could we hear the quavery voice of a little old lady who wants to go by just as Maurice Richard is about to skate around Bob Davidson of the Toronto Maple Leafs?

"Holy Mother! I'm sure your Maurice Richard isn't a wicked little boy like the lot of you."

We let her pass, then it's back to our little war. We have our injuries too: a bloody nose, a scraped leg, a goalie hit on the forehead by a frozen turd. We also have the defector who goes away in tears to report an injustice to his mother. Sometimes we have to skedaddle: some mothers won't tolerate injustice.

Most of the time, nothing disturbs us. Aficionados stand and watch. Now and then we'll hear a prediction:

"That one, in the red tuque. Take a good look—he's a little Maurice Richard. It's no lie, I'm telling you."

Or the house painter goes by with his ladder over his shoulder, paint bucket in his hand, singing a song:

> *"Je suis loin de toi, mignonne,*
> *Loin de toi et du pays . . ."*

The painter falls silent, watches Maurice Richard's dazzling rush to the net. The future of hockey is ensured. Our village team will grow even stronger. The neighbouring villages will have to respect us. We'll travel through those foreign villages with our heads high. Satisfied, the painter picks up his ladder, crosses the territory of our game and continues along to his customer:

> *"Je suis loin en Angleterre . . ."*

The horse, that peaceful animal with his big dazed eyes, must be wondering, Why are these little two-legged creatures struggling so hard to drive my frozen turd between two school bags sitting on the snow?

The steeple of the church at the top of the hill touches a sky heavy with snow that soon will come pelting down. The school is a little farther away, on the other side of the hill. We're not afraid. We're playing hockey, we're champions.

We know that on the other side of the hills is the St. Lawrence River and then the sea and then, on the other side, Europe and the

France of our ancestors, where war was raging a year ago. We know that people were dying: many were soldiers but there were other people, too, who weren't soldiers; there were even women. We know that children went without food for a week inside their devastated houses. We know that people had to run away at night, with their children, sometimes with babies, to hide in the forest, even in the winter. We know that bombs rained down on cities that burned like logs.

"Hey, you little Maurice Richards, let Granny pass."

This one is another grandmother, who's come from the previous century. She watches us. She's prepared to wait till the next century so as not to disturb our game.

We sons of French Canadians who drifted onto an ungrateful land all the way to the nearby hills of the state of Maine, sons of a small people uneasy about its future, in this world torn apart by World War II, on the main street of our village, wearing felt boots if we're sons of small families, or rubber boots if our family is a big one—our name is Maurice Richard. We're strong, we're fast, we're brave.

We are eight, nine, ten years old. The priest and the nuns assure us that each of us has an invisible guardian angel who protects us. Do we need the protection of angels? Maurice Richard is with us. He's the one who is handling our hockey sticks. He's the one who, with our eyes, levels a devastating gaze at our opponents. He's the one who, with our legs, makes breakaways towards the net. He's the one who, at the speed of a shooting star, slams a frozen horse turd between two school bags.

That's our life as champions!

We don't yet know that a hundred years before us, in 1845, so many Irish children played "hurling" in the streets of Quebec City that a municipal bylaw prohibited the sport so that the good burghers could walk around in peace.

Already, night is spreading over the village. Windows glow with a yellowish light. We haven't noticed that the day is over. The match goes on. Shouts of triumph, insults, the clatter of sticks as they meet. The click of the blades of our sticks against the turd. Our mothers, shivering in their open doorways, call us to come in and do our homework. It's pointless. When we're playing hockey we don't hear our mothers.

Maurice Richard also played hockey on the street in Bordeaux, his neighbourhood in northeast Montreal. He too didn't hear his mother calling.

A Childhood on Skates

1921. During the first years of the twentieth century there are a great many poor people in the province of Quebec. Those who are less submissive, more enterprising, leave the misery of the countryside for Quebec City, Montreal or, in many cases, for towns in the United States. Having left the misery of the countryside, they're transplanted into urban misery. Like so many others the parents of Maurice Richard leave their native Gaspé Peninsula on the shores of the St. Lawrence, which at that spot resembles the sea. The Gaspé is a land of rocky soil, fishing boats, rough seas, salt cod and endless winters that make the wood creak in poor houses crammed with pale children.

In the towns, factories are offering jobs: sixty hours, six days a week. Apparently it is possible to escape from misery. These people are used to hard work. But when Onésime Richard packs his bag and takes the train to Montreal, he doesn't dare to dream too much. A modest labourer doesn't get rich.

Gaspesians in Montreal are homesick. They have family get-togethers at Dominion Park on Notre-Dame Street. Onésime comes from the Matapédia Valley, in the centre of the Gaspé Peninsula; he's a man of the land, the forest. Fate is waiting for him in the park. He meets Alice, who's just arrived from the Gaspé, from

the headland on the Gulf of St. Lawrence. In 1534, that was where
Jacques Cartier planted his cross when he took possession of
the land of Canada in the name of France. A lot of English people
have come there since. The main occupation is fishing for cod
and salmon.

For some time now the pulp-and-paper plants have been unable
to meet the demand. Dams are being built for the new hydroelectric
industry. The Jacques Cartier Bridge, which will link Montreal to
the south shore of the St. Lawrence River, is under construction. In
the port of Montreal, close to two thousand boats dock every year;
muscular arms are needed to load and unload them. French Canadians who have come from farms or forest find in this work an
avenue towards the future.

With the surrounding prosperity, a regular salary and all the
new conveniences they'll be able to afford one day, life is better here
for Alice and Onésime than it was in the Gaspé. When they write to
their relatives who've stayed behind, they have to choose their
words carefully so they won't sound like upstarts.

It is in this atmosphere of mingled hope and concerns that
Onésime and Alice get married and take up lodgings in the east
end of Montreal, not far from Parc Lafontaine, in a modest little
house with a greystone front. Onésime is a carpenter. Shortly after
the birth of their first son, Maurice, the Richard family moves to the
Nouveau-Bordeaux neighbourhood in the northeastern part of
the city where small houses can be had for reasonable prices.
Everyone is French-Canadian. And the Rivière-des-Prairies is
practically at the end of the street. It may not be the St. Lawrence
or the Gaspé sea, but it is water.

This relative prosperity doesn't bring security. There are still
worries. While there's plenty of work there are still many jobless. In
the wintertime the unemployment rate climbs as the temperature
drops. In the winter of 1921, the year of Maurice Richard's birth,
Montreal's jobless rate is more than 26 percent. There's a lot of misery in the city.

One morning near the end of winter, Onésime is happier than he's ever been. He's less severe. His voice is different. The Canadiens have won the Stanley Cup. The Canadiens are world champions. Young Maurice knows what hockey is: it's the game the big boys play in the street, with sticks and skates. Now that the Canadiens have won the Stanley Cup, there's reason to celebrate. Even though he prefers baseball, Onésime enjoys hockey. When he was younger he was a fairly powerful player who hated not to win. He looks at his son. Next winter, the boy will have a pair of skates. His "little man" will play hockey. Maurice watches, listens: winning the Stanley Cup must be something very important. The Canadiens have won! His father has won! Maurice is proud.

The 1924 Stanley Cup was a victory for Joe Malone and Howie Morenz, as well as for manager Léo Dandurand, coach Édouard Dufour, Billy Boucher, Billy Coutu, Sylvio Mantha, Aurèle Joliat and Georges Vézina, who demonstrated once again that French Canadians can be successful. That's what was being said in the pool halls, restaurants, taverns and—on Sunday—on the church steps.

Young Maurice goes to the grocery store with his father. The men are gabbing the way men gab in the country. French Canadian: what does that mean? He doesn't know. But he does know that he is one. He's one of those who won the Stanley Cup.

On his father's knees, through the smoke of Onésime's cigarette, Maurice looks at the hockey players in *La Presse*. His father reads their names. He repeats them. Some of the names are difficult. He can't pronounce them. One whole page is taken up by a player in a red uniform leaning on his stick. His name is easy: Pit Lépine. Maurice repeats it. He can't of course read the words of Pit Lépine: "After a game or a practice there's nothing like a Buckingham, the only cigarette that's easy on the throat." Lépine isn't the only one who promotes the use of tobacco. Among those taking part in this advertising campaign are two other French-Canadian celebrities: Alfred Laliberté, "Canada's greatest sculptor," and Charles Marchand, "Canada's greatest singer of folksongs." People smoke a lot in the province of Quebec: 3.6 pounds of tobacco per capita every year. They drink a lot of beer, too. The priests see the souls and bodies of their flocks drowning in alcohol; they preach sermons. Onésime Richard doesn't drink. "The bottle diverts the puck," the parish priest has confirmed. He hopes that Maurice will play hockey. Or baseball.

At four, he's too small to understand all these things the adults talk about but he's big enough to stand up on his first skates.

There aren't many cars on Montreal streets in 1925. When they drive by on their big balloon tires, people take the time to count them. The people who sit in these carriages are very lucky. How have they got to be so rich? Sometimes a policeman will go by on a motorcycle. It backfires. Maurice plugs his ears. The policeman is hunting for bandits. What Maurice would like is to get a look at the eight-wheeled bus that some people have seen.

On the side streets in winter, the snow is allowed to accumulate. It hardens under the feet of pedestrians and is polished by the sleighs that transport things. Often it turns to ice. On his skates, young Maurice darts, glides, falls among the big boys with their sticks who are fighting over a "road apple" left there by a horse. They're as serious as if they were doing battle for the gold of Peru.

The men who watch them play are talking politics. In 1927, the federal government adopts a law that will ensure a pension for those who are embarking on old age. The government of the province of Quebec sees this as an intrusion into its jurisdiction. The adults debate, Maurice skates. He's strangely fast. Like a ravenous little dog running after his bone. The adults enjoy watching him. He insists on staying with the bigger boys, even though he's smaller. So he doesn't always get his share. He's unhappy. His mother advises him: "Play with children your own age." He perseveres.

For the Richard family, thinking about their parents who stayed behind in Gaspé, a pension for old people who have slaved away all their lives seems like a well-earned reward. On the other hand, this pension will cost something. Will the government take the money for it from their pockets? Don't they already pay more taxes than they can afford? They work and work and there's nothing left. For the time being, Onésime has work.

There are those who think that something unpleasant is looming. The local notary, who is well informed, says that the value of distillery stocks increased by 420 percent from January to November 1928. When the economy goes crazy it strikes the poor.

Without listening, Maurice hears this old tune about the problems in life. Running in the fields, climbing trees to the highest branch, playing ball and, in winter, playing hockey in the street; pushing and shoving to get the puck, and forcing it into the net: that's what is fun. His parents always feel threatened by some impending bad thing. They're always small in the face of something big. They're never the strongest. At hockey, though, they can win. In that game Maurice has a power that his parents don't have in life. Does he understand that? The game is teaching him that through his efforts he can build his own destiny.

On an ice-covered street in a modest working-class neighbourhood, something amazing is happening: the birth of a passion, the one that consumed Balzac, Shakespeare, Picasso, Leonardo. Like those other geniuses, Maurice Richard will be devoured by his art. And like all geniuses, he will devour his art.

Maurice Richard never takes off his skates. He learns how to fall on the ice without crying. He learns how to follow the bigger boys, how to skate as fast as they do. The bigger boys look down on him. He persists. He hits back. He barges into their matches, he clings to the game. In the backyard snow behind the house, Onésime makes him a rink, flooding it with buckets of water. Other children show up. They play, they wear themselves out, they quarrel. When the night is too dark or when the mothers shout very loudly to call their children, they go home. The time has come when they have to write in their school notebooks.

Soon it's time to leave the family rink; the one at school is smoother and, more important, it's bigger. And there's the little lake not far away, in the field. Young Maurice is growing. He always wants to go further; the Rivière-des-Prairies is the biggest rink there can be. Maurice doesn't take off his skates to go to where boys are playing hockey. He doesn't take off his skates to wolf down his meal at the table. The future Rocket is forming the muscles in his legs. Young Maurice doesn't know that. He plays. And plays. And plays.

In 1927, the grown-ups are talking about some very complicated political question. The English in England have taken away a piece of the province of Quebec called Labrador from the French Canadians. What does it mean? Sometimes, in his part of town, neighbours putting up a fence will try to gain a few inches on the surveyor's line. Because of it, the parents squabble. The mothers shout insults. There are impassioned protests by the labourers in Bordeaux when the Privy Council in London gives Labrador to Newfoundland. That island isn't even part of Canada.

Young Maurice sticks out his chest and goes off to play. He won't let anyone take what is his. He scowls: no one's going to steal the puck from him.

His father reads in the newspaper words that he doesn't understand very well but that he agrees with. A professor at the university swears that transferring Labrador to Newfoundland "compromises our security, compromises our free economic expansion and cuts off our access to the Atlantic via the northwest."

On a Saturday in May 1928, the mothers are feverish with excitement. Maurice and his friends are playing with a rubber ball and a stick in the street. On their balconies, the women are talking about the Eaton's store on St. Catherine Street. Eaton's is inviting women to come and see the new summer dresses. The dresses at Eaton's are very expensive. And the women feel more at home at Dupuis Frères. The people there talk French like we do. Yes, but the dresses are nicer at Eaton's, in the west end of town. The west is far away. It's like another country. One day Maurice will go to see that other country. The mothers are also talking about an airplane. "Life is getting to be so fast." It's the first time since the creation of the world that dresses have arrived at Eaton's so quickly. Three hours earlier, the dresses were still on the sewing machines in the factory in Toronto. They were folded into boxes and the boxes were piled onto trucks that sped to the airport. An airplane transported them from Toronto to Montreal, a distance of 480 kilometres. It took only two hours and thirty-seven seconds. And a few moments later, the summer dresses could be seen in Eaton's windows, before a crowd of incredulous women. This fashion is too new. The airplane is too fast. In the Bordeaux neighbourhood, the mothers chatter away. The world is changing. The world is moving quickly. The world is going to move more and more quickly. Strange things are happening in the world now. And it's all so complicated . . .

Maurice loves things that go fast: his bicycle, cars that travel at a hundred kilometres an hour, the train on the bridge over the Rivière-des-Prairies, airplanes—and his skates.

＝＝＝

1929. A tidal wave of misery is about to devastate Montreal, home to 818,577 of the 2,874,255 inhabitants of the province of Quebec. During the 1930 Christmas season, 22.8 percent of the population is jobless. By 1932, that portion has risen to 31 percent.

Businesses are failing. Companies are collapsing. Factory windows are boarded over, the gates in the fences that protect them are chained and padlocked. Even churches are affected: the priests are losing the parish funds that they've invested on the stock market. The Université de Montréal no longer has money to pay professors. Some are condemned to beg. During the good years work was started on buildings to house the young people who would invent the province's future; lacking the means, the university stops construction. In 1932, more than two hundred schools are forced to close. In Montreal and smaller towns alike, children, like little white crows, rummage through garbage dumps in search of a piece of bread. Tenants who can't pay their rent are evicted. They can be seen waiting—for what?—in the street, sitting on boxes, surrounded by their piled-up furniture. Some evictions nearly set off riots. One ejected tenant is killed by a policeman's bullet.

In spite of this misery, the rural poor are still leaving behind their gardens filled with vegetables, their chicken coops with clucking hens, their stables with lowing cattle and bleating lambs, to come to the city. What dream is attracting them? In Montreal, no one is dreaming now.

Many of those with nothing to do are condemned to roam the streets. Others, better off, have shelter. They share rooms where they can go when their turn comes. By day, by night, the bed is occupied by four jobless men who lie across a bare mattress to sleep. Another two or three are on the floor.

Maurice's father loses his job. He is a father responsible for eight children. Despite a regular job with the CPR, he's never been able to amass savings. The family lived from one payday to the next. Now there's no more payday. Maurice is the eldest of the boys. Even though he's only nine years old, he must do his share. He has to find a few cents, come up with places where he can do some small jobs, discover something that can be sold or traded. Now he's a caddy at a golf course. He lugs the players' bags. He's not lazy. He brings home a few cents.

Gaunt, unshaven men in threadbare clothes, men who are idle, penniless, disappointed, wild-eyed, stand in the icy cold waiting to take their turn in a shelter where they can warm up and drink some hot soup. In the summer, these unfortunates gather in the parks. That's where socialist, even Communist, missionaries explain that they are victims of capitalism. Only the Revolution can restore justice. Political and religious authorities are worried. Such pernicious ideas could inflame these uneducated minds stirred up by misery. The desperate must not deny their Catholic faith. And so the church opens more shelters to get the unemployed out of the parks where they might be contaminated by dangerous ideas.

Those who still enjoy the privilege of working dare not complain about their shrinking salaries. The unemployed regard them with jealousy. Forty-five thousand women still have jobs. These women are stealing jobs from fathers of families. The unemployed men also envy immigrants. Giving jobs to these imports means stealing work from real Canadians. Right across Canada, in fact, resentment towards these newcomers is so intense that the government has to shut the door to immigration. In 1929 the country took in 169,000 immigrants. In 1935 the number is down to 12,000. As well, during that same period more than 30,000 landed immigrants are expelled from Canada because they are sick or jobless.

Jews persecuted by the Nazis, who risk losing not just their property but their lives as well, beg Canada to take them in. But the impoverished Canadian people are selfish and don't want to share the misery of these people. Eventually they tolerate the government's acceptance of four thousand of these tragic individuals. During the same period the United States takes in 240,000, Great Britain, 85,000, Argentina, 25,000.

It is urgent that this misery and widespread demoralization be fought. Municipalities think up projects to create jobs for their unemployed. Montreal mayor Camillien Houde starts up projects in the parks. He creates new playgrounds, builds public baths, renovates public markets. He improves traffic signs, and in various parts of the city he erects shelters, which the people will christen *camilliennes*, where passersby and the poor can relieve themselves and, in wintertime, warm up for a moment. In 1932, work gets under way to dig the Wellington tunnel in the southeast part of Montreal. These few thousand small jobs have little impact on unemployment or hunger.

The federal government also starts large-scale public works: renovating the railway, constructing highways and country roads. In the middle of winter, on the heavy snow that covers the province of Quebec, unemployed men charged with repairing the road spread gravel though they're not sure that the road beneath is where they think it is.

Quebec premier Louis-Alexandre Taschereau asks the federal government for more generous financial aid. Why does Quebec receive less than the other provinces? That's a question that was asked by the newspapers of the day. That's a question that is turned over and over during political discussions and repeated time and again. Discussions that are heard by the young Maurice Richard. It's all so complicated.

Yet jobless men learn that help for needy families is in store. It's what is called "Secours Direct," or direct assistance. With a set of coupons, destitute families will be able to get food. For months when Maurice's father is out of work, these coupons will allow the family to eat. Your appetite is big when you're a growing boy who spends days at a time on his skates chasing after a puck.

Onésime has his pride. He's incapable of going to the corner store and paying with the coupons of the poor. Onésime would work if there was work to be had. He's a man with a trade, a father who doesn't drink, a responsible man. Why is he reduced to taking charity? He would rather go hungry than accept it; that's what he says to Alice. Maurice hears. Maurice is also capable of going without food. You have to eat, his mother tells him. Onésime doesn't want to be seen buying food with those charity coupons. Alice asks Maurice to go to the store.

Maurice is proud too. He doesn't want his friends to see him at the grocery store with poor people's coupons. His mother insists; he's a big boy, he has to show how he can be useful. On his skates he glides to the grocery store. He doesn't want to pay with coupons. When he presents them, everyone will know that the Richard family is poor. They'll ask him if his father is looking for work. And he's afraid of not having enough coupons. What will he say if he doesn't have enough for everything he's supposed to buy? He steps up to the counter. The grocer spots the coupons in his mitten. A customer arrives who has real money in her purse. "You with the coupons, hang on there a minute." Along comes another customer. And another. They have money and Maurice only has poor people's coupons. He must wait his turn. The poor people's turn. Finally, he's

served. Last. Why last? Why is he poor? Why did his father lose his
job? Why doesn't his father want to show his face at the grocery
store? Maurice goes home with his bag of food. On skates, he's never
the last. He arrives at the goal before all the others. There, no one
asks him if he has money or coupons. He delivers the puck to the net
more often than those people with real money. On his skates, he
doesn't wait, he goes first. At the grocery store everyone else went
before him. Because he has poor people's coupons. He feels like crying. A man doesn't cry. Hugging his bag of food he skates quickly
down the street as if he had the puck, as if he had real money to pay
the grocer. When he's a man like his father, nobody's going to push
him to the end of the line; he won't be ashamed to go to the grocery
store. He won't pay with poor people's coupons.

When he gets back to the house his mother remarks:

"You're all sweaty. In cold weather like this . . . You'll come
down with consumption."

For its part, the Société Saint-Vincent-de-Paul distributes
meat, bread, milk to starving families; during the winter, volunteers
who aren't afraid to blacken their faces transform themselves into
coalmen to bring these families bags of coal. At the coldest point in
the winter of 1931, the Minister of National Defence deems the situation to be so grave that he takes the underwear being kept in
reserve for his soldiers and gives it to those who are cold.

Does the ten-year-old Maurice, skating down his street over
the hardened snow, comprehend the dire straits of the inhabitants
of Montreal? Like any child, he thinks that the world and himself
began at the same time. The world in which he is starting to make
his way is a harsh one. He already knows how hard the pushing and
shoving on the ice can be. In the great game of life, the pushing
and shoving are even more unrelenting. People and families struck
down by poverty don't get back on their feet. Onésime, miserable
because he can't give his family what a man ought to give, withdraws into his humiliation. His anger. His own suffering he keeps to
himself. Maurice wishes he weren't a useless little boy. He tries
to earn a few cents. He who loathes begging asks around the

neighbourhood whether anyone needs him to run errands. People know that this little boy is honest and strong and not afraid of work. And like his father, he's a boy of few words.

On the rink where he plays as seriously as a person who's doing something more important than playing, Maurice is swept into a world very different from that of the Depression. Here, the rules are clear, and simpler than the rules of misery. On the ice, no one is automatically condemned to lose. Anyone who tries hard, who works, who is fast and clever, can win. Every time he gets hold of the puck, Maurice starts a new life. The one he was given is of no importance. He grabs the puck and invents his life. Manoeuvring the puck he traces a movement that depends only on his heartbeats, on the strength in his legs and the agility of his arms. No obstacle is impossible. That's what Maurice learns when, with frozen feet, he strives to become a little man on the ice.

The world is a place where you're alone. Even if there are others around you, you're alone when you face up to your chal- lenges. If you're beaten, you are even more alone. The moral of the story: become strong, fight, win. In victory you're not so alone.

The government? The people around Maurice think that it's useless. Can it get rid of poverty? No. Can it give food to starving families? No. Can it restore life to the crippled machines that are rusting away in silence? No. The government lets the little people die while it offers favours to the big ones. The adults often say that, with passion. He doesn't understand these things but he hears them. Moreover, the government is rotten. In 1936, when Maurice is fifteen years old, businessmen, senior officials, even Premier Taschereau's brother, pile up substantial profits through embezzlement.

Doesn't the economic crisis prove that the priests of the Catholic church are right? For a long time, in both country churches and city cathedrals, they've been preaching that the city is a place of perdition, eaten away by poverty and vice. The only salvation pos- sible is to return to the land where all the virtues reside. In a joint project, church and state set up a program of internal settlement. The time has come to flee the cities, those "killers of people" where, according to both preachers and recruiters, the powers of the race "become sterile."

In 1930 and 1931, the Canadiens win the Stanley Cup. These victories undoubtedly bring comfort, but from 1931 to 1932 more than thirty-seven hundred families leave town, steered towards the Saguenay or Abitibi. Often the soil is rocky, the bush dense, the mosquitoes murderous and the winters endless. The priests believe that their flock will be safer there than in the cities where they were exposed to materialism, Protestantism and English.

THE WAR IS COMING

1937. Why have the people been plunged into this Depression where they are stagnating and which they don't understand? Henri Bourassa, editor of the newspaper *Le Devoir* and a speaker with a bombastic little voice, blames the big industries. Their inordinate appetite for profit, he charges, has caused the Depression. He recalls that Catholic teaching is opposed to the excessive search for worldly goods.

Then another voice rises. In 1936, Maurice Duplessis has defeated Taschereau, friend of corporations, friend of English capitalists, friend of profiteers—and enemy of agriculture. Duplessis is convinced that the Depression has been caused by collusion among American, British and English-Canadian capitalists, with government complicity.

Other voices still, more discreet, know of just one way to heave oneself out of poverty: let the people be inspired by the Great Revolution in Russia! Let the people rise up against those who are exploiting them. Let the people impose justice. Duplessis is quick to impose silence on these Communists: in 1937 he passes the Padlock Law, which gives him the power to shut down and padlock any establishment that disseminates Communist doctrine. Who is a Communist? The law does not define one. Some policemen consider that anything written by a Russian is Communist: Dostoevsky, for example. The Catholic church applauds Duplessis. "Proselytism through error" must be opposed by "proselytism through light," the bishops preach. Duplessis appears to them in 1937 as "the proud soldier of the sole Catholic truth."

Dismay. Poverty. Unemployment. Despair. The sense of being too small in a world that is too big. The sense of being victims. The conviction that one is suffering because of a fundamental injustice. Tremendous repressed pride. French Canadians have survived foreign occupation, they've resisted policies of assimilation, they have persisted in the face of their own ignorance. Now they're coming up against doors that are closed to the future. What this small people needs is hope.

In this world, though, it isn't the season for hope. Civil war has broken out in Spain, a conflict that heralds a much broader one: the most obvious sign is the extreme militarization of Germany. Neighbouring countries are already aware of the threat. Though far away, Canada is stepping up its defence budget considerably. Prime Minister Mackenzie King declares that if freedom is threatened, Canada will defend it. During a visit to Germany he repeats this message to Hitler.

In the province of Quebec there is a certain sympathy for heads of state like Salazar in Portugal and Franco in Spain. These men aren't afraid to use their power to defend the Catholic religion. To obey the teaching of the Gospels, they feed the hungry by employing them on major public works. Unlike so many governments weakened by corruption, they're not afraid of barring the way to the atheistic Communists who are moving to conquer the world.

It's not Hitler we should be wary of, according to the elite of the province of Quebec. It's Communism. Let us erect a wall against Communism. On October 25, 1936, one hundred thousand people gather at the Champ-de-Mars in Montreal to proclaim their refusal of Communism and to acclaim the kingship of Christ. The president of the trade union council issues a vibrant *cri de coeur*: "Let us respond proudly to Communism that we recognize Christ as our Saviour, our Redeemer and our King."

At the same time, in the city of Quebec, fifteen thousand of the faithful have turned out to hear Cardinal Villeneuve denounce the pernicious ideas of Communism. He thanks God for giving us Duplessis who has stood up like a true Christian to say to Communism: "Satan, you shall not pass!"

Is it surprising that this small people, unsure of itself, of its future, should feel inspired by strong leaders who have united their people to guide them in the right direction? These dictators in Portugal, Spain and Germany drove out the sirens of Communist propaganda. Is it surprising that some should see in them a bulwark against godless Communism? And the priests aren't alone in professing sympathy towards dictators. Mackenzie King notes in his diary for March 27, 1938, that Hitler may be someone like Joan of Arc: the liberator of his people and perhaps the liberator of Europe.

Maurice is sixteen years old, seventeen. In his east-end Montreal neighbourhood it seems that French Canadians would have a better life if a strong leader were running the affairs of the province of Quebec and getting some respect. We don't trust our governments any more.

No, the world doesn't offer much hope to French Canadians. It is on the verge of giving birth to a storm. You can feel it coming, the way that in the countryside in July you can feel the heavy sky before it bursts open. We value our religion. We value our French language, the most beautiful language in the world. Faithfully, we still speak it the way our ancestors in the old countries spoke it: the language that the English masters tried to make us forget, the language that proclaims to America and to the whole world that French Canadians are "a race that knows not how to die."

On the evening of June 29, 1937, rain is falling on the city of Quebec. Thousands of people have braved the weather and come to the Colisée to listen to speakers on the occasion of the second Congrès de la Langue Française.

Lined up on the stage are Cardinal Villeneuve in his purple cape, several political dignitaries, some important judges, a row of bishops wearing black soutanes trimmed with purple, canons who are a little plumper and not quite so decorated, and some ordinary members of the clergy all in black. At the microphone, speech follows speech. Laments over the wounds of the past that can't be healed. Sombre words about present-day suffering. Already it's nearly ten o'clock. The next speaker is announced. The crowd jumps to its feet. Thunder roars and lightning lashes above the city of Quebec. The clamour of the crowd drowns the rumbling from on high. In the face of the immense ovation a frail little man in a simple black soutane stands at the microphone, waiting for silence. He is the Abbé Lionel Groulx, the historian. For several minutes, he waits. Ill at ease. From behind his little round glasses he rereads his speech. Finally the ovation runs out of steam.

He launches into his speech. His thinking is abstract; he doesn't try to please the people with the demagogic behaviour of some politicians. His thinking is precise, though his sentences are pompous, long and solemn. Now and then a declaration sets off an ovation as intense as the one that greeted him at the microphone. Certain bishops feel a little uncomfortable. This triumphant priest in his black soutane is talking not about religion but—quite boldly—about politics. Others are reassured. Did God not give His church responsibility for directing the faithful in the affairs of heaven and earth? They exchange worried, approving, impassive looks. All at once the little historian declares: "We will have our French state. And we will have a French country, a country that will carry its soul on its face."

At these words, which the radio carries to every region of the province of Quebec, the crowd in the Colisée dances, applauds, shouts, chants: has the Messiah returned? Some bishops, uncomfortable, wish the ovation would stop. Has Abbé Groulx considered the consequences of his speech? "A French country": does that mean that he advocates the separation of the province of Quebec from Canada? Among the worried listeners on the stage is Maurice Duplessis. He's not prepared to set out on the road proposed by the historian's daring speech, but in light of the crowd's approval he must be cautious. Tonight he cannot contradict the popular feelings of the flock.

At an official banquet the next day, Duplessis has had time to prepare the necessary words. During his toast to the province of Quebec he declares: "If there is anyone who wants to preach isolation . . ." The audience know he's about to attack. His eyes turn in the direction of little Abbé Groulx. Wagging his forefinger at the priest, he makes his grand declaration: "If anyone wants to preach isolation, I would say to him: You want to shrink the French soul, you want to restrict a power that is too beautiful and too great. But we are not willing to impose any limits on the French spirit in America." The tone is restrained. The audience has understood. Rather than separate from Canada, French Canadians could conquer America. What a dream! This conquered little people could conquer America.

At sixteen, Maurice Richard has no interest in these political speeches. They're discussed around the dinner table. At school, some teachers know them by heart; they explain them in class. All these words are like wind. The future is far away. He'd like to work in a factory, make parts for machines. Evenings and weekends he'd have time to play hockey.

Within him seethes a boundless energy that he has to burn. Long bicycle races. No matter how hard he pushes the pedals, he wants to push even harder; the more energy he expends, the more he has. His legs never grow heavy. His muscles demand more and more effort. Dives from the railroad bridge into the Rivière-des-Prairies. Maurice puts off as long as possible the moment when he'll resurface. Then he climbs back on the bridge, nine metres above the river, and dives again. Long swims in the tumultuous current. Sessions of boxing with friends. Games of baseball. And in winter, all those hockey games.

Of the brew of words that is politics all he hears is a distant murmur. The real world is the ground he plays on. The strength that interests him is the strength that bats the ball out of the field, that delivers a punch to make his opponent stagger, that makes a puck invisible to the goalie's eyes. What does a person know at the age of sixteen? That he won't get old like his parents. Play is more fun than work. Goalies can't resist the sensational intelligence of his shots. In his neighbourhood he's already famous. Has Maurice, busy as he is with his games, heard the shrill voice of Abbé Groulx, the little white mouse in a black soutane?

Throughout the province of Quebec a deep disappointment prevails. The truths learned in the countryside are put to the test in the cities. Life isn't like the teachings of the church. In spite of everything, French Canadians are standing tall in their history. Fate has reserved a great future for them. In school chapels, students sing in chorus a hymn that sets their young hearts on fire: "Look lovingly at a great River's shores, at a still young people quivering as it grows. More than once You have saved them from their foes . . ." The province of Quebec believes in the Messiah. It also believes in miracles. God will not abandon his French Canadians, isolated on the American continent.

A basilica is being constructed on the mountain to honour St. Joseph, the adoptive father of Jesus. Because of the Depression, sources of financing have dried up. Work has been stopped. The walls are up, but the building has no roof. Will St. Joseph sleep under the stars? What's to be done? A basilica can't be left unfinished. The humble Frère André is consulted; it was his simple piety that inspired the flood of piety towards St. Joseph. The humble brother suggests placing the statue of the saint inside the walls, under the absent roof. There will be rain. And cold. And snow. St. Joseph will decide whether or not he wants a roof. Some months later the people know that he wants one. It's a miracle! A miracle! Somewhere in paradise, the carpenter saint has worked the levers that opened the floodgates. Money comes streaming into the oratory.

Is this not as fine a miracle as making the puck appear in the opponent's net? With his black eyes and his thick hair, Maurice looks so serious that he doesn't seem to be enjoying himself. He knows the names of former hockey players like Howie Morenz, the Canadiens' top scorer from 1925 to 1932. His father talks passionately about Aurèle Joliat, who led the team in scoring—and penalties—from 1932 to 1936. He knows the names of today's players, which he reads in the paper and hears on the radio. The one he most admires is Toe Blake. Instead of listening to games on the radio, Maurice would rather see the Canadiens in the flesh, on the ice at the Forum. "Toe Blake is at the blue line . . . He skirts the defenceman, he's at the goal line . . . Toe Blake is alone at the goal line . . . He shoots—he scores!" He would like to hear their skates rip up the ice, their shots rebound off the boards. He'd like to hear the crowd's shouts roar like thunder. He'd like to see Toe Blake put the puck in the net. He'd like to watch with his own eyes the players whom he imitates on the ice of parish rinks. Leave his neighbourhood and go to the west end of town where the Forum is . . . It's not a trip to be made on the spur of the moment. You need to have a good reason for crossing the boundary line of St. Lawrence Boulevard, which divides the city in two. And then you have to pay for the streetcar ticket and the ticket for the game.

By the end of ninth grade, Maurice has climbed the steps: peewee, midget, bantam. Along with his regular matches, he often enjoys his favourite game, "hog." The rules are very simple. The person who seizes the puck tries to keep it as long as possible while the other players try to get it away from him. To hold onto it he feints, he defends it, he charges into a forest of sticks and races away with the precious disc, pursued by the pack. With this game he develops his speed, loosens his movements, strengthens his balance, improves his endurance, sharpens his reflexes, refines his tactics. Does he know?

Maurice is now too strong for his school league. His services are required by the Bordeaux, the toughest team in the parish. The players are older than he is, stronger too. He will toughen up, learn, match them, surpass them. His father gives him some advice. Maurice has already made a big decision about his trade: he'll be a machinist. It's a good trade. There are ads in the newspaper looking for machinists. With the cars, trucks, airplanes, tractors and all kinds of new machines that are doing the work of men, men are needed who know how to make parts for them. It pays better than carpentry, his father's trade. He enrolls in technical school. Maurice Richard will play on the school team, of course,

but he doesn't want to leave the Bordeaux. For two years he'll play
on both teams at once.

The owner of a team in the Parks League notices this player
whose determination makes him seem much older than his sixteen
years. He invites the young man to join his team, the P. E. Paquette,
named for his service station. In his first game, Maurice scores six
times. For three consecutive years he leads his team to the championship of the Parks League. During the 1938–39 season, P. E.
Paquette's total is 144 goals—133 scored by Maurice. In an average
game, he sends the puck into the net eight to ten times. The athlete
is being formed. His body is getting tougher; so is his will. Often he
plays two games in one night, four in a weekend. And on Sunday he
doesn't say no to the practice sessions suggested by Onésime.

After the Bordeaux games, the coach often invites the players
to his home. They devour sandwiches washed down with a Pepsi or
a Kik, talk about hockey, listen to the sports news on the radio or to
music on 78 rpm records. Sometimes they push back the furniture
and dance. Maurice isn't talkative. What's left to say when you've
scored seven goals during a game? That you'd have liked to score
ten? That you would have scored ten if you hadn't made those stu-
pid mistakes? Maurice hates dancing. He's seventeen years old.
Lucille, the coach's thirteen-year-old little sister, undertakes to
teach this big boy how to rumba. He's so shy. He's wearing a suit
that can't have cost very much. When he dances he tenses up as if
he were expecting to be hit by another player's shoulder. When he
talks he never says more than one sentence. Short. Like the other
boys, all he can talk about is hockey. He could dance the rumba if
he'd only try. He could dance it quite well. But he doesn't really
want to dance well. Lucille knows a lot about hockey. With her
mother's permission, she goes to see her brother's team play.
There's no doubt about it: Maurice is the best player in the league.

The sky weighs more and more heav-
ily over the countries of Europe. Those who knew World War I
maintain that this time seems like that time. In September the

leaders of the principal countries meet in Munich. Hitler says that
he's ready to set his war machine in motion. To prove it, he annexes
part of Czechoslovakia while France and England look on passively.
Peace is even more uncertain. Weapons will be needed. Paradoxi-
cally, the machines that are beginning to drone in the war factories
offer Canada's unemployed a little hope.

Preoccupied by Hitler's ambitions, Canada reinforces its
defence on the Atlantic coast. The RCMP, fearing sabotage, keeps an
eye on strategic factories. On April 26, 1939, Great Britain imposes
military service. It is predicted that before long Ottawa will follow
London. The federal capital is home to many devoted servants of the
British Empire. There is good reason for King George VI to come to
Canada a few days later. In Quebec City, His Majesty reviews the
Royal Twenty-second Regiment, the famous "Van Doos." Recruitment is beginning. If it's necessary to go and fight, Maurice will fight.

Many French Canadians are opposed to the idea of conscription, which would send their sons away to die in Europe. The Young
Patriots issue a pamphlet: "French-Canadian youth would rather
live freely in its old French Quebec than die in the service of an
anti-French Confederation that's more British than Canadian."
Can young people be criticized for preferring life to death? The
Young Patriots express their discontent at living in a country that is
so submissive to England. A few months later, on the Champ-de-
Mars in Montreal, Mayor Camillien Houde speaks to a crowd of students. After the suffering and humiliation they've been subjected to
by the English, he doesn't understand, he says, why French Canadians should go and die for England. And if France herself were to
join the war, what reason would French Canadians have to shed
their blood for her? France is no longer the same country as the
mother country of our ancestors: it's no longer a monarchy, no
longer Catholic. There is a ripple of emotional applause. No, young
French Canadians must not give their lives for France! By allying
itself with England, France is showing its approval of that country's
unjust policies towards French Canadians. The young crowd on the
Champ-de-Mars stamp their feet.

Events move quickly, with no one showing concern for our misgivings. On September 1, 1939, Hitler invades Poland. Two days later, Great Britain declares war on Germany. France immediately joins in. At once, police surround the German consulate in Montreal. Across Canada, German nationals are arrested. All trade with Germany is forbidden. At the Maisonneuve Market in the francophone east end of Montreal, citizens protest Canada's entry into the war that may soon be announced by the federal government, England's lackey. A nationalist politician named René Chalout harangues a crowd: "Ottawa cannot tie down the French-Canadian people." Maxime Raymond, another nationalist Member of Parliament, tables a petition signed by one hundred thousand French Canadians demanding that Canada not participate in foreign wars. *Curés* in their churches remind their flocks that French Canadians are a small people, threatened on all sides. To survive, it needs all its blood and all its youth. We must not shed our blood or waste our young people in foreign countries.

When Ernest Lapointe, Mackenzie King's influential minister of justice, advises him that his French-Canadian colleagues will resign if the government brings in conscription, the prime minister swears that he is "not insensitive" to the objections from the province of Quebec. Reassuringly, he declares that he does not believe it necessary to implement conscription for service overseas.

On Saturday, September 9, 1939, after a harrowing debate, the federal government, in a show of hands, expresses the wish that Canada ask the King to declare war on Germany in its name.

New income taxes are announced. New taxes even on electricity consumption. The population is asked to eat canned fish: fresh fish should go to feed the soldiers in Europe. Newspapers and radio stations are under surveillance. Politicians must have their declarations approved before they are published or broadcast. Duplessis refuses to submit; never will he have his speeches approved by Ottawa!

War expenditures will be phenomenal. The federal government issues a war bond. The federal government will use every opportunity to reduce the autonomy of the provinces, declares Duplessis.

This time, the excuse is the war, a war that the people of the province of Quebec don't want. Duplessis enjoins his electors to rise up against this war bond. Opposition leader Adélard Godbout even pledges to leave the Liberal Party if a single French Canadian is mobilized against his will. In Ottawa, ministers and MPs from the province of Quebec continue to oppose conscription.

Does Duplessis have Nazi sympathies? There are those who suggest that he does. One morning Montrealers find a strange leaflet in their mail, illustrated with photographs of Stalin and Hitler. If you fold the paper as suggested, Hitler and Stalin form a portrait of Duplessis. The leaflet doesn't circulate for long. The police seize it because it violates the Padlock Law. Since it displays the face of Stalin it is obviously an instrument of Communist propaganda.

Finally *Le Devoir*, newspaper of the intellectual elite, ends the debate: French Canadians won't vote for Stalin or Hitler or Chamberlain or Churchill. They must choose between "Ottawa as master in Quebec and Quebec City as master in Quebec."

Unlike the notary and his parish priest Maurice Richard doesn't read *Le Devoir*, but like all Montrealers he has seen soldiers parading in step in the streets, rifles on their shoulders, marching with conviction to the war. The enemy is across the ocean in countries as remote as the ancient lands the ancestors came from. If necessary, Maurice will go to the front. Firing a bullet must be like firing the puck into the net. But he won't wear a skirt like the soldiers he saw parading along elegant Sherbrooke Street the day before. They were members of the Royal Highland Regiment of the Black Watch, with their bagpipes.

On Sunday, people go to the port to see a warship that's moored there. Notices in the post office, grocery stores, restaurants and the plant all warn: the enemy's eyes and ears are everywhere. Be discreet! The army is now surveying the entrance to the Lachine Canal to prevent enemy infiltration. Soldiers train in the parks. In gymnasiums, students practise handling bayonets. It's said that eight thousand Canadian volunteers have secretly set sail for Great Britain.

Maurice hears nothing but complications and contradictions. It seems to him that life is one big quarrel. He doesn't run away from a squabble as long as it's not one that is fought with words. It seems to him that life is more than words. He doesn't like talking. He doesn't like people who talk too much. Everybody seems to talk too much. He feels helpless in a world where people talk too much, where everything can be contradicted, where rules are ephemeral. To this world that's too big he prefers solid ice, with well-defined limits and clear laws. He feels at home on the rink, on the baseball field. There you can accomplish something that can't be disputed: score a goal. Win.

People are soaking up ideas like eggs in vinegar. People argue, complain, worry. French Canadians are treated unfairly, they are threatened with ruin. They feel inferior, like outcasts; in their discomfort there's a visceral pride at having survived so many misfortunes, and there's also an atavistic anger. More than a century and a half of submission has held them back, but one day that force will explode.

In the fall of 1939, young men in Maurice's neighbourhood are signing up. Some work on airplane maintenance and repair. Maurice would like that kind of job but he's going to play for the Verdun Juniors, a farm team of the Canadiens. Maurice ends the season among the top scorers. And Verdun wins the provincial championship. The strength of the Verdun players is their desire to play for the Canadiens. At the same time Maurice, a day student at the École Technique, is still on the P. E. Paquette team. His goals are noted under the name Maurice Rochon.

During the summer holidays he works for Crane, a company that manufactures plumbing supplies. The factory is several kilometres from home and he goes there by bicycle. It's a way to train his legs. He's encouraged to take boxing lessons. He signs up at the school of the renowned Harry Hurst. Some fans think they've discovered a future champion. He is preparing for the Golden Gloves tournament when an unfortunate punch in the nose by his coach prevents him from taking part. His energy is boundless. A number of teams would like to lure this young player who is so well prepared. Will he have any time for school?

Plants have gone into production again. A poster shows a machinist like Maurice concentrating on his lathe as he applies himself to making a part. Behind the worker an Allied aircraft is bringing down an enemy plane. Thanks to the worker's labour, our armies will be victorious. Maurice applies himself to his own lathe. His father has taught him that if a job is worth doing, it's worth doing well. Above all, he has within him an obsessive instinct that makes him start over again and again until the part is perfect.

Politics is raging. What support are Canadians prepared to deploy to help Great Britain in the war against Germany? In September 1939, the Duplessis government is defeated. During the federal election campaign in 1940, candidates in the province of Quebec, Conservative and Liberal alike, swear that they're opposed to conscription. Can they be believed? French Canadians remember World War I, when the government imposed conscription even though a vast majority had rejected it.

In 1914, the clergy feared that if young French Canadians were forced to fight in Europe they would have "deleterious" experiences in those not very Catholic countries and when they came home from the front, their damaged souls would be incapable of virtue. For generations the clergy had encouraged large families to counteract the threat of anglophone immigration. If Canada wanted a reasonable proportion of Catholic French Canadians, they would have to produce lots of children: the revenge of the cradle. These fine young people shouldn't go off to be massacred in a foreign war, they should stay in Canada and bring up families with many children. Nationalists upheld the same argument: French-Canadian blood must not be wasted on foreign soil. French Canadians should fight but they should fight in Canada, for the survival of their people. In Ontario, in New Brunswick, in Manitoba, French Canadians couldn't exercise their right to live in the sacred language of their ancestors, the true founders of Canada. It was in Canada that they must fight for their future instead of going to lose their lives for England. That was how the priests and the nationalists spoke in 1914. Now, they are saying the same thing in 1940. Mackenzie King hears the French Canadians, and he pledges that he will not impose conscription. On March 26, 1940, he is brought back to power with very strong support from the province of Quebec.

After invading Denmark and Norway on April 9, Hitler extends his hold over Belgium, Holland and Luxembourg in the weeks that follow. In Montreal, a fifth column of fascists prepares to become Hitler's first patrol once he has conquered Canada. During a spectacular raid, the RCMP surrounds them: its members are German- and Italian-born, French Canadians and English Canadians. The group's leader, Adrien Arcand, is put in jail along with ten accomplices. To the threat of Nazi expansion has been added the threat from within; some Canadian provinces demand conscription.

The Nazis enter Paris on June 14, 1940. This humiliation is one that French Canadians understand; it resembles the one they suffered in 1759 on the Plains of Abraham. The mother country is defeated. Church and school have celebrated the glory of France so much that French Canadians have thought it invincible, "eternal" as the speeches put it. Now France has been crushed under the Nazi boot. We feel the war coming closer.

Immediately, Mackenzie King takes advantage of the situation to announce compulsory military service on Canadian soil. Anglophone MPs applaud enthusiastically while those from the province of Quebec feel betrayed: King pledged that he would never impose conscription.

In the Quebec Parliament, nationalist member René Chalout wants the house to declare its opposition to compulsory military service. The new Liberal premier, Adélard Godbout, retorts that the federal government is doing its duty when it asks young Canadians to defend their country, which is in danger. Chalout's motion is rejected. Duplessis, the leader of the opposition, votes in its favour.

And so they must go into battle; but the army is an English institution. People remember World War I. That army was not the army of the French Canadians. It was the army of those who don't recognize the rights of French Canadians, of those who don't respect the autonomy of the province of Quebec, of those who don't respect the rights of French Canadians in New Brunswick, Ontario, Manitoba. At home, people are saying that the Canadian army wants French Canadians because it needs cannon fodder, just like in 1914–18. In July 1940, at Canadian army headquarters, only four officers out of eighty-eight are French-Canadian.

Unmarried men and childless widowers are called up for compulsory service. Preferring the dangers of marriage to those of war, young people move quickly to persuade a friend or an acquaintance to rush off to church with them. Marriage ceremonies are speeding up at the same rate as the war factories. People get married at every hour of the day, in series, in groups. Priests and ministers are exhausted.

Mackenzie King agrees to take charge of some Germans who have been taken prisoner by Great Britain. On July 6, hundreds of Montrealers go to the train station to watch as, under the surveillance of armed soldiers, these enemies parade two by two to the train that will take them to detention camp.

Montreal mayor Camillien Houde accuses King of lying to the French Canadians. On August 5, he is arrested by the RCMP and taken to a camp in Petawawa, Ontario, where spies, fascists, and nationals of enemy countries have been interned. His responsibility is to cut wood to heat the camp that winter.

The war doesn't stop the flowers from growing, it doesn't stop the leaves from falling. In September, Maurice Richard is seething with impatience. He's determined to burst through the opponent's net. He feels strong. He's young. Let them come to the rink.

You'll Be a Canadien, My Son

1940. Following his performance with the junior Verdun team, Maurice Richard is invited to the Senior Canadiens training camp. The machinist is nineteen years old. In his first game he gives of himself as if he and he alone were responsible for winning the war. Two goals! Quite an exploit for a rookie. But not enough for Maurice. He grabs the puck, he zigzags down the ice, he's checked, he breaks away, he charges, he outsmarts the other player, he's checked again, he gets the puck back and then, driven by spectacular determination, he heads straight for the goal. An opponent charges, he staggers, loses his balance, gets the puck back, spins under the impact, collapses, skids onto his stomach, feet first. The human meteor is stopped by the boards. Maurice hears a dry crack. Like breaking ice. His ankle. The blade of his skate has got caught in the chink between two boards.

The season is over for the fantastic new recruit. Some maintain that Maurice's future stops here. After this accident, they're convinced, his leg will never regain its strength. What a waste of an exceptional talent! Leaning on his crutch throughout the fall and winter, the young machinist sometimes shares their conviction. But if his hockey career is over, why is his desire to play so intense? When he still has to get around on one leg, why is he so drawn to the rink? And why does he feel the strength returning to his damaged leg? He will play again: he's determined to play.

If he's not working, he's bored. If he can't get drunk on sports, he is forced to pay attention to what's going on. People can feel the weight of the war. Several of his friends have signed up. The nationalists are sounding off against conscription. The church, which had been at their side, seems to be changing its opinion. Cardinal Villeneuve asks the entire people of the province of Quebec to get down on their knees and ask God for the victory of our armies over those of Hitler, who is threatening Christianity. Laying his crutches on the pew of his parish church, Maurice Richard kneels, despite the pain. He prays, but it seems to him that a good flat-out fight with the Germans would be more effective than a prayer. He's not afraid of a Nazi. But how can he fight? With an injured leg he can't even play hockey.

On February 9, 1941, nearly ten thousand persons gather at the Notre Dame Basilica. The choir of the church is aglow with the hundreds of candles that surround Premier Adélard Godbout and some cabinet ministers, archbishops and bishops. At the microphone, federal justice minister Ernest Lapointe reads a special prayer for peace as if it were a political speech. The bishops grant fifty days of indulgence to those who will repeat it. That means fifty fewer days of suffering in purgatory after they die. After Mass, the congregation takes part in a military procession.

In Quebec City, prayer is transformed into a brawl. Four hundred soldiers of the Highland Light Infantry from Brantford, Ontario, decide to protest the arrest of two of their colleagues, whom police have caught in a brothel. What were the police doing in a brothel? When the anglophone soldiers start shouting insults at the bystanders, the Quebeckers rediscover the army the way they know it: an anglophone institution that has no respect for them. This time, they won't be humiliated! They will fight! They will resume the hostilities begun on the Plains of Abraham where they were left off in 1759.

Others would have stayed in their armchairs, but in March 1941 Maurice Richard goes back to the Senior Canadiens for the playoffs. In his opinion, he doesn't do anything spectacular. The playoffs aren't enough for him. He can also be seen in the ranks of his old team, the P. E. Paquette. Maurice Rochon contributes to fifteen of the team's seventeen goals.

On the evening of June 9, Montreal disappears into darkness. At 10:30 P.M., as if enemy submarines were sailing up the St. Lawrence, windows go black, the streets become dark, automobiles come to a standstill, their lights off. They'll have to start again. The rehearsal wasn't perfect. Some incredulous citizens wouldn't douse their lights. Enemies could have spotted the city. Bombed it. Next time, discipline will be stricter.

Maurice is called to the recruitment centre in Longueuil, across the Jacques Cartier Bridge. He pictures himself in the uniform of the Royal Aviation, but he comes home empty-handed. He is deemed unfit for service because of his broken ankle.

The federal government issues its war savings bond. The propaganda department has rechristened it a Victory Bond. To underline the event, the citizens of Montreal are invited to a neighbourhood party in Parc Lafontaine. The people of our peaceful province need to be educated. Accordingly, they're shown a scene of war. The crowd is struck with horror as they watch the replica of a convent collapse under a bombardment, with terrifying effects of flames and explosion. When the wind drives the smoke away one can read in luminous letters above the disaster: "Buy Victory Bonds!"

On June 22, Hitler attacks Russia. Housewives are asked to cut down on their use of vegetable fats. Like all mothers and without really knowing why, Maurice's mother, Alice, salvages animal fat and bones after meals. In September, women are invited to join the army as auxiliaries. Already twenty-five thousand women are working nights in weapons factories. In his parish church, Maurice hears the priest explain that a woman's place is at home: everyone must do his part for the war, but women shouldn't be exposed to the moral dangers of being with men at night. A woman must be at home to teach Christian values to her children. That's why God created her.

═══

1941. That fall, Maurice Richard is back with the Senior Canadiens. His ankle is fully healed. His speed is back. His skating is powerful, precise, incisive: he's at the peak of his form. He won't tolerate any obstacle. He seems to suffocate if he doesn't score goals.

Watch this breakaway. He withstands the impact of the defencemen. He approaches the goalie. How can he take him by surprise? Instead of letting loose a powerful shot, Maurice turns right, goes behind the net and, before the dazed defencemen can catch up with him, lets loose with a backhand. Finally a defenceman arrives. He brings his stick down on Maurice's leg as if he were wielding an axe. His skate skids. He loses his balance. He spreads his arm as he falls. His wrist, out of his leather glove, hits the goalpost. Iron. Maurice hears the sound of breaking bone. Experts decide that a cracked wrist after a broken ankle spells the end. What terrible luck. Immobilized once again, Maurice is bored. He leafs through *La Presse*. Sees a full-page colour illustration of a handsome soldier in a khaki uniform standing at attention; his sweetheart is gazing at him as if he were the Great Pyramid of Egypt. "Love and pride," declares the caption. "She works in a factory, he's in the army." A dream couple. The young lady has an elegant hairdo and is wearing a stylish dress buttoned up to the neck. Thanks to her factory job she can afford to get her hair done, buy stylish clothes, even an understated necklace of imitation pearls! The war is a fine thing. Maurice turns the page.

On December 7, the Japanese attack Pearl Harbor. Once again, *La Presse* wants to make its readers dream with another illustration. New Year's Day. A large family is gathered around a table well laden with tourtières and pies. The door opens. It's the son, a conscript who is coming home after completing his four months of training camp. He's an impressive sight with his long khaki overcoat, grey gaiters, gleaming boots and kit-bag. His white-haired mama kisses him. A young sister offers him a platter of doughnuts.

Sitting at his kitchen table, Maurice Richard daydreams. War is not
about coming home; it's about fighting, about guns spitting fire. He
wishes he could fight the Nazis. Last year, he was rejected because
of his cracked ankle. And now his wrist is broken. Still idle, he's
irritable. Ready to explode. He restrains himself. He doesn't understand the confusing war news reported on the radio. He prefers
songs, especially country and western.

At the beginning of this year, 1942, the federal government
announces that a national plebiscite will be held: Mackenzie King
has vowed that he will not implement compulsory military service
overseas; now he's asking the people to free him from that electoral
promise. Adélard Godbout, premier of the province of Quebec, tells
him: our mother countries now at war need ammunition, weapons,
food; the best way for Canada to help Europe would be through its
agricultural and industrial resources. Sending our young people to
war would be a "crime," *Le Devoir* announces: Canada, which has
no responsibility in this war, has no right to undermine its own
security.

At the Marché Saint-Jacques in east-end Montreal, ten thousand people declare a resounding NO to compulsory military service.
One speaker maintains that while French Canadians are ready to
give their lives to defend their own small homeland, "leur petite
patrie," they refuse to die for "the other homeland," that of the
Toronto Two Hundred who run the country, that of international
profiteers, of merchants in rubber, petroleum, cotton and opium.
These words rush through the crowd like a tidal wave of fervour.
The turnout is so big that there's not enough room inside for everyone. Thousands have gathered outside the hall to listen to the voices
over loudspeakers. It's hard to hear. Streetcars rumble by fre-
quently; this artery joins the east end of the city to the west end. The
crowd becomes impatient. Those streetcars go by too often. They're
too noisy. The crowd is going to stop the traffic. Some streetcars
push their way through the crowd. The crowd gets angry, tries to
overturn one. The passengers inside are terrified. The vehicle is too

heavy; it stays on the rails. The frustrated crowd attacks its windows. They bombard the streetcar with hunks of ice. Passengers disembark. Insults. Threats. Blows. They defend themselves.

There are anglophone servicemen present. One of them complains that he can't understand a word: "This is an English country. Those French Canadians ought to speak English." The suggestion isn't welcome here at the corner of Amherst and Ontario streets in east-end Montreal. French-language patriots attack. The brawl turns into a little war that spreads through the crowd. Because they don't like being whacked on their cute little faces, some students decide that it would be more fun to go to a local brothel and evict the clients without giving them time to put their pants on. Police on motorcycles charge. Those who can, board streetcars. Police on horseback plough into the crowd. Bleeding noses. Broken teeth. Bloody heads. Nineteen are jailed. Thus ends a demonstration in favour of peace.

It's obvious that French Canadians don't understand that the Nazi danger is imminent. The government steps up its propaganda. Tanks lumber by to lend their weighty support to the second issue of Victory Bonds. An advertising campaign extols the efficiency of Canadian factories: they turn out a motorized vehicle for the Allied Forces every three minutes. Machinist Maurice Richard can't not feel proud. If they were placed end to end, these Canadian-manufactured war vehicles would form a procession 960 kilometres long. The walls are covered with posters. One shows weary warriors; the horizon is streaked with explosions. All around them, desolation: charred tree trunks, overturned tanks, barbed wire, the ground ripped open by shells. Doesn't the soldier deserve our help? Another poster shows a rosy-cheeked female worker holding a shell in her arms the way a mother would hold her baby: "I make bombs and I buy Victory bonds." What more could she do?

At the beginning of January 1942, the government rations sugar. Maurice's mother, Alice, is upset. Her family likes sugar. How can she get along without it? This war is complicating a mother's work. The children need sugar to grow. And Maurice is as thin as a nail. He exerts himself too much in his sports. He needs sugar. If only this war would end!

In April, the government brings in gasoline rationing. The new law forbids driving over forty miles per hour. It will take down a peg or two those drivers who think they've got the right to knock over anyone who doesn't have a car. Tires and inner tubes are rationed as well. The government needs rubber for war vehicles.

Adélard Godbout, who once opposed conscription, proclaims his admiration for the soldiers: "If Prime Minister King asked me to go to Europe and clean the soldiers' boots, I'd go," he declares in one of those bursts of frankness that politicians display when they're contradicting something they used to think. He prophesies: "In one month, the enemy could be here." Conscription, he implies, is necessary.

Shortly afterwards, twenty thousand people hurry to the Atwater Market in west-end Montreal to cheer nationalist speakers. Mackenzie King promised not to send their children to the war; let him respect his promise. In the plebiscite on April 27, 1942, voters in the province of Quebec refuse to release him from it. Over 71 percent vote No; in some regions, the figure is 90 percent. In the other provinces, the vote is 80 percent in favour. Canada is divided.

During this troubled period, the Senior Hockey League playoffs are taking place. Maurice knows the enemy: five players and their goalie on the other side of the blue line. In hockey, he knows where he has to go: to the net. He doesn't feel useless as he does when people talk about the war. He knows how to defeat the adversary. This battlefield isn't on a foreign continent. The other side of the ocean is so far away. His ancestors left that country and never returned. The rink is a clearly delimited battlefield. At the end of this 1941–42 season, the playoffs are more real to him than World War II. Only weeks after breaking his wrist, Maurice, healed, is back in the game, jumping onto the ice as if he were going to bring the war to an end. In four games he drives the puck into the net four times.

On May 11, incredulous Montrealers learn that a Canadian merchant marine ship has been torpedoed by a German submarine in the Gulf of St. Lawrence. That's hundreds of miles from the street where the Richard family lives, but the St. Lawrence is a river in the province of Quebec. The event took place in the Gaspé, where Maurice's mother and father come from. They still have relatives there. In June, newspapers report that in the area around St. John's, Newfoundland, another three ships have been sunk. A hundred or so survivors escape drowning. Horrified, they describe their adventure to the villagers. The government can no longer stand there with its arms folded, doing nothing.

During the summer, Maurice works in a war factory. The hours are long but they don't absorb all his energy. He practises swimming, he plays baseball and he spends time with his girlfriend, Lucille. He went back to reintroduce himself to the aviation recruiters, but he was turned down because of his broken wrist. Last year, it was his ankle. He wishes he could sign up like his friends. See the country. Repair airplanes. Learn to speak English, like them.

The government in Ottawa finally gives itself the power to call up all those who are able to fight. His mother doesn't like this law: they could come and take away her older sons. Maurice reassures her: he's not afraid of Nazis. Onésime is silent: the Richards are peaceful people.

The summer passes amid a serenity that isn't troubled by the distant war. On August 20, 1942, however, Canadians lift their eyes to the sky, in the direction where they think Europe is. More than a thousand Canadian soldiers have been massacred in an attempted landing at Dieppe, in Normandy. The Allies thought they would surprise the enemy. The Germans were waiting at the top of the cliff. More than a thousand more Canadians have apparently been taken prisoner. Have friends of Maurice's been killed? If the military authorities hadn't rejected his candidacy, could he have been sent to Dieppe? Would he have been luckier on the Normandy beach than on the ice where he's been injured so often? Would he still be alive? This is a sad day. But he's alive. Death didn't want him; that's why he was judged unfit for military service. God looks after us. The good Lord wanted to keep him alive. To do what? During the days that follow, Maurice thinks about the massacre in Normandy. Never before has he thought about the fact that he could be dead. The soldiers landed on the pebble beach. There they found themselves offered up to enemy fire. The sea turned red with blood. Maybe he'd have been able to scale the cliff. The soldiers who reached the summit played like good hockey players.

The season will be starting soon. Before attacking, he will think about those soldiers who, in spite of bullets and grenades, climbed the cliff and advanced into enemy territory. So many young men dead in eleven hours of combat . . . A rumour is going around that there are women in the Bordeaux neighbourhood carrying children who'll never know their fathers, who died at Dieppe.

In the tightly knit Gaspesian community in Montreal the adventure of two fishermen is being recounted. A father and his son were bringing in their nets when suddenly the sea rose up as if they were on the back of some huge animal. Their boat was nearly overturned. The water was torn apart before their eyes and they saw something like an enormous cod: a submarine. Two fair-haired Germans stuck their heads out. They did not speak French. The fishermen realized that they wanted their fish. The fair-haired men took their whole catch. They paid for it. With American money. So people say.

Maurice listens. Should he believe it? He does his push-ups. The hockey season will start soon. He's preparing himself. He rides his bike to work. The factory is several kilometres away.

German submarines have come as far as the St. Lawrence River. On September 8, villagers in the Gaspé hamlet of Saint-Yvon discover a torpedo "as big as a man" on the shore of the river. A few days later, Gaspesians on the shore watch incredulously a battle between a German submarine and a Canadian navy patrol boat.

At the factory, Maurice perseveres. Maybe one day the army will need him. His broken ankle and his cracked wrist are healed now. Smiling, he thinks: "If I can play hockey, maybe I can go to war." Last year, the Senior Canadiens played an exhibition game against the army. The next day a reporter wrote: "Richard beats the army at the Forum." But the army flunked him.

On October 8, a four-thousand-tonne merchant ship sinks near Matane. Outside Sydney at nearly the same moment, the *Caribou*, which shuttles between Nova Scotia and Newfoundland, is torpedoed: 137 lose their lives. A poll shows that 90 percent of French Canadians are opposed to conscription, yet in the midst of this peaceful population, behind thick walls, in secret laboratories hidden in the universities, British, American and Canadian scientists are working on bombs that will kill huge numbers of people.

Even as the citizens detect the smell of war, the Canadiens are getting ready for the next season. Far from abolishing the sport, the government is encouraging it. Hockey is a healthy distraction. Eighty-odd NHL players have volunteered to go to war. As a result, there are few players, their number reduced to fourteen per team. The League has done away with overtime in the event of a tie; because of wartime restrictions, trains can no longer wait in the station till the match is over before they set off with the travelling team.

Ever since they first met, Lucille has followed every match Maurice has played, most often outside, under the stars, chilled by Montreal's intense damp cold. The wind goes right through her cloth coat with the fur collar pulled up around her neck to protect her cold-reddened cheeks. She rubs the tip of her frostbitten nose against the fur. To cover her ears, she ties a scarf knitted by her grandmother under her chin. The cold drives needles into her toes through her little fur-trimmed boots.

She's seventeen years old. Maurice is twenty-one. The machinist no longer worries about the future. He earns at least twenty dollars a week. With the war, there's plenty of work. The hours are long, the work painstaking: the parts will be used in the war.

More players leave for the army, including most recently Syl Apps of the Leafs and soon Ken Reardon of the Canadiens. The shortage of players might make it easier for Maurice to join the

Canadiens. Some people think his bones are too delicate for the NHL. In Boston, the Bruins don't hesitate to take on a sixteen-year-old rookie, Armand "Bep" Guidolin, the youngest player ever to join the League. The Detroit Red Wings are defended by seventeen-year-old goalie Harry Lumley. Even referees are scarce. Former players like Aurèle Joliat and Bill Chadwick are begged to take on the job. This year, Red Horner is asked to become a referee. For eight years, the former Leafs captain, a defenceman, held the League record for penalties.

The Canadiens want Maurice to play for them: the genuine Canadiens! The team of Toe Blake! Of Howie Morenz! Of Aurèle Joliat! He doesn't need to be asked twice to turn up at training camp. A few days afterwards, on September 12, he marries his sweetheart, Lucille Norchet. Maurice is going to play for the Canadiens. People in the Bordeaux neighbourhood can't believe the news. But at the same time they do believe it because they know Maurice: "I'm lucky. A lot of the men have gone to war. There aren't many players left. That's why they're letting me have a turn."

Manager Tommy Gorman and coach Dick Irvin are familiar with Maurice's feats. They also know that his bones break easily. The impetuous rookie is endowed with an insatiable desire to score goals. He's half wild horse, half well-disciplined soldier. Manager and coach decide to bet on this glorious animal, even if he is delicate. His young bone structure will firm up. They offer him a two-year contract.

The Canadiens haven't won the Stanley Cup since 1931, eleven years ago. Last year they finished sixth; the year before that, seventh out of six, as we used to say in school. In Montreal, the crowds at the Forum demand victories. Fans want the Christians to devour the lions. Since the Canadiens have stopped winning, the team often plays to empty seats.

Thin, with a hard, muscular body, with a face as rough as a stone in a Gaspé field and the piercing eyes of someone who has the gift of seeing things invisible to others, Maurice Richard joins the Canadiens. He arrives as silent as if his soul were inhabited by a

rage that's about to break loose and with a will that resembles an
obsessive stubbornness. He thinks about his father, Onésime, who
left home with a few pieces of clothing in his bag and settled in
the big city, Montreal. He has often recounted his expedition. When
Maurice arrives at the Forum with his equipment bag, he too feels
like an immigrant. This part of the city is foreign to him. He hears a
language being spoken that's not his language. A language he was
taught not to like because it's the language of the masters. He looks
at the walls, which vibrated with the cries of the crowd when Joliat,
Malone, Morenz or Blake scored a goal. He approaches the ice. It's
no longer the time of Joliat, or Morenz. Now it's his time. The time
of Maurice Richard. It's his turn to go to the net, to show that no
one can stop a French Canadian. That spark in his eyes is hunger.
Like his father, like all French Canadians who leave their villages to
seek a better life in Montreal, he has a blazing hunger for life. He is
on his skates, on ice that shines like a mirror, on this rink where so
many others dream of playing. He's like the schoolboy before his
open workbook, like the poet before his blank page.

Maurice Richard is joining an organization that is English, as
are all the companies that have jobs. Maurice knows very little English. He comes here with the conviction that those of his race have
been dominated, humiliated. That's what the teachers, politicians
and priests have taught him. Here on this rink, Maurice won't be
able to blame anyone but himself. He won't let himself be mis-
treated. He'll meet every blow he receives with another blow. He
looks at the empty net at the end of the ice. He's going to put the
puck there. He's not afraid of working hard, he's not afraid of being
hit, he's not afraid of taking risks. He's not afraid of pain. He's not
afraid of his dream.

Maurice plays his first match against the Bruins with Elmer
Lach at centre and at left wing Tony Demers, who'll soon be going
off to join the army. Twice, Demers scores. The young rookie provides an assist. The Canadiens win.

Maurice Richard didn't score but his will to win impressed the
linesman, Aurèle Joliat, who in the early 1930s was the Canadiens'

top scorer and the most penalized player in the NHL. Hockey is also a big family. At a friend's urging, Joliat has been following young Maurice's development ever since his exploits with the P. E. Paquette team. Maurice doesn't spend a lot of time reliving the past. It's the present that obsesses him. And the future is no further away than the opponents' net.

For the next match, the Canadiens travel to New York. It's no longer so easy to cross the border between Canada and the United States; there's a war on. Spies and other dangerous enemies like Butch Bouchard, Ken Reardon and Maurice Richard could infiltrate. Three are turned back. The Canadiens lose 4–3.

Maurice hates being intercepted when he wants to go somewhere. Since childhood he has trained himself to get around obstacles or to knock them down. The Canadiens have been beaten by the customs officers. He didn't find a way to get through the American defencemen who were blocking their border. Maurice can't speak English. But Reardon can and so can Butch. They should have been able to get across. Maurice takes responsibility for the defeat. For this young man, the world is very unfair. He is counting the hours till the Rangers come back.

The following day, November 8, they arrive at the Forum. Maurice is convinced that he'll be granted a moment of revenge. It will be up to him to strike. He grabs the puck from an assailant who has got close to the Canadiens' net. He heads for centre ice. The opponents rush at him. He swerves like a motorcycle, dodging them. His gaze sweeps the ice. He has analyzed the opponents' positions, he knows what their next move will be; in one brief moment he mentally traces the path that he must follow through the obstacles. Head down, eyes on the net, he speeds ahead with the puck; his blades etch zigzags on the ice like lightning bolts. His opponents impede him with their sticks, but it's no use. Maurice arrives in front of goalie Steve Buzinski, alone. Maurice shoots him a look that's like a punch. The upper corner of the net is open. With a backhand, "Maurice Richard shoots—he scores!" The young player has avenged the American injustice.

This is Maurice Richard's first goal in the NHL. The sparse crowd at the Forum is on its feet. They have recognized the Messiah they've been hoping for. They howl their pleasure. In seats at the rear, old fans with white hair under their flat caps remember Howie Morenz, the greatest hockey player of all time. The old champion is at the Forum. He saw this goal. Morenz has heard the clamour. He remembers. He knows that the crowd doesn't make mistakes.

Those who did not witness the new Canadien's exploit are incredulous. They want to see this young Richard. He doesn't disappoint those who come back to the Forum. November 22: three goals! His first hat trick in the NHL.

Off the ice, this amazing number fifteen is self-effacing. No one would notice him if it weren't for his black eyes which pierce whatever they focus on. Before a match, he withdraws into himself. After a match, he is silent if he's lost. If his team wins, he's also silent.

And then, like many of the fans who come to see him play, he doesn't speak English. In the locker room, the Canadiens speak English. Not understanding frustrates him. He only knows a few words. If he tried to speak he'd be ridiculous. He'd rather be proud and silent. If he has something to say, he'll say it with the puck! With deftness, cunning and the power of his shots. Maurice retaliates for his discomfort at not speaking the language that's spoken around him.

It's not that he refuses to learn English. What he hates is not knowing. He feels as awkward as if he didn't know how to skate. At school, the study of English wasn't encouraged; French Canadians had to be protected from English. If he listens, he will learn. He'll speak later. What matters now is to drive the puck into the net. And to withstand fatigue. Like Maurice, a number of Canadiens players also work in weapons plants. The team has to hold practice sessions outside work hours. Sometimes, they play a game between two full days spent over their machines. It's not uncommon to go to the plant on the train where they've spent the night after a match.

With Tony Demers off fighting the war, Dick Irvin puts Maurice on the offence with Buddy O'Connor and former Leaf player Gordon

Drillon. After fifteen matches or so, young Richard has five goals and six assists to his credit. Were people too hasty when they compared him with Howie Morenz? They discuss it like theologians. And unlike theologians, they agree: Maurice's statistics are just slightly above average but the way he scores goals is absolutely mind-boggling.

Two days after Christmas the Bruins are at the Forum. Maurice has outsmarted the goalie once and he's earned two assists. The final period begins. On the ice for three minutes, he calls on all the resources of his passion. Sweating, he's trying to get his wind back. The Bruins have rallied. They've decided not to leave without a victory, despite the damage they sustained at the beginning. They fight powerfully. The puck is swept into Canadiens territory. Maurice grabs it. He's out of breath. For a moment, he takes shelter behind the net. With his black gaze he analyzes the positions of his opponents and teammates, then lowers his head like a bull about to charge. With the first thrust of his skate the crowd is on its feet. It follows him, watches him move around obstacles, smash them. The fans begin to applaud the inevitable goal.

He still has to outsmart Jack Crawford, a defenceman with shoulders "as wide as that." He's wearing his famous leather helmet. Here comes Maurice. The defenceman is getting closer, massive as a tank. The crowd holds its breath. Collision! The thud as two bodies collide. Maurice falls to the ice. And the heavy Crawford comes crashing down on him. Maurice lands on his own bent leg. When Crawford collapses on him he hears the familiar sound of breaking bone: his ankle. He grimaces. This young French Canadian will never be another Howie Morenz.

More than once, Dick Irvin has advised him to look up when he charges. With his head down he's more vulnerable to being checked. Maurice listened to his coach's advice but continued to skate in his own way. Dick Irvin wouldn't want him to lose speed. He's a stubborn man, this Richard. Maurice is proud, even when he's leaning on a crutch.

Gorman and Irvin consider getting rid of their young star rookie whose bones are like china. They offer him to the Red Wings, then to the Rangers. Both teams would rather have powerful players than delicate artists.

The future is uncertain. He wants to play hockey but it seems that hockey is rejecting him just as the sea in the Gaspé rejects flotsam, as his mother used to say. Maybe his body wasn't built for this sport. His father saw him more as a baseball player. Are all these injuries signs that he should take up another sport? He's responsible for a pregnant wife now. If he breaks a limb, if he becomes crippled, it will have consequences. Why does he attract so much bad luck? It can't be a punishment from heaven because he does nothing against religion: he doesn't steal, he doesn't get drunk, doesn't curse, he's got just one woman in his life and that's Lucille. Should Maurice be content with his machinist's job? As they say, the wages are good. It's a good trade. And it doesn't look as if the war will be over soon.

On April 24, 1943, a full page in *La Presse* draws his attention; it shows a huge hand plunking a heavy Nazi helmet onto a church in a typical Quebec village. That's the danger! That's what French Canadians must defend themselves against. You need more than money to win. Our soldiers need meat. Canada is a big producer of beef and pork. Canadian meat will go first of all to the Allied troops and our own troops. Now it too has to be rationed. That means problems for Lucille. After a match, Maurice could eat an ox. He won't be satisfied with codfish. It's true that he's not playing— because of the crutch. The sight of rationing coupons reminds Maurice of the "Secours Direct" coupons during the Depression. That's something he'd rather not think about. The factories are in production, the workers are slogging away. Every week Canada produces six warships, eighty airplanes, thirty-five hundred motorized vehicles, 336 armoured vehicles, nine hundred cannons, 525,000 shells. And Maurice is hopping around on a crutch.

The months of convalescence are difficult. His soul is a torrent streaming with life, but once again he is paralyzed. Newspapers have written about the young star's extreme fragility. Some have condemned him to never play again. Number fifteen swallows these words as if they were mud. One day he'll be healed. And then . . . Instead of playing hockey, he should join the army like so many others.

As soon as he gets rid of his crutches, he goes back to the army recruiting centre. The corporal recognizes the famous Canadiens player and explains to him that to be accepted by the army, you can't be brittle: the army needs sturdy men. War is not a game.

WHEN A MAN
BECOMES A ROCKET

1943. Maurice is plagued by doubt when he returns to training camp. Is he really fit to play in the NHL? To elude his concerns he throws himself into the fray. Competition is fierce. A number of rookies want to play for the Canadiens. Maurice goes all out. Jostled, he resists. He's fast. He's determined. It's hard to believe that he has fractured both ankles and broken his wrist. This young man is different from the others. His self-confidence is back. Elmer Lach, who has been playing with the Canadiens for three years, is amazed at the wiles this raging young rookie can call on to thwart his opponents.

When the season opens, NHL players have to adjust to an important change. A new red line divides the rink down its middle. Until now a player in his own zone couldn't pass to a teammate on the other side of the blue line. Now, that player will be able to pass to his teammate as long as he's not past the red line. This will make the game livelier, management believes. Imaginative passes will open up the game, make it more spectacular. Drawing a red line on the ice may seem like a small thing to do when the greatest human tragedy in history is taking place on the battlefields and in the camps, but for Maurice, this red line is a serious source of concern. He thinks about possible moves, he invents combinations. How can he use this line to speed up his attack? How can he, from his own zone, confuse his adversaries and make an unpredictable attack?

Canadiens goalie Paul Bibeault has been called up for military service and Bill Durnan of the Montreal Royals has been brought in to replace him. Durnan is a goaltender who rarely lets the puck get away. He sees it coming; it lands in his glove. Ambidextrous, he's had special gloves made that allow him to hold the stick in either hand, to confuse enemy players.

Dick Irvin has observed his players carefully. He decides to combine on the same forward line, in the same test tube, three ingredients that through a chemical reaction ought to produce the equivalent of one of those secret bombs. Maurice Richard, Elmer Lach and Toe Blake will form the Canadiens' principal line of attack.

Maurice is on the same team as Toe Blake—now he'll be playing with him. Toe Blake! Toe Blake, the hero of the games he used to listen to on the radio: "Toe Blake is at the blue line . . . He's moving up to the net . . . Toe Blake shoots—he scores!" Toe Blake, the hero he used to imitate on the parish rinks. Maurice never imagined that this would happen to him. He passes Blake the puck for a shot on goal. Toe shoots it back to him. The opponent is confused. "Maurice Richard shoots—he scores!" Toe Blake outdoes himself so he won't be outdone by this energetic young man.

On October 23, Lucille gives birth to a little girl, Huguette. The father, as proud as if he'd just won the Stanley Cup, shy and tense and hard as wood, goes to see Dick Irvin. He fires a few words at him, like pucks aimed at the net. The coach is amazed when Maurice says that from now on, he'd like to wear number nine on the back of his sweater. He'd like that, he explains, because his little girl weighs nine pounds. Somewhat surprised by this sentimental outburst, Dick Irvin agrees.

Number nine: a new life. This simple symbol lies deep inside Maurice's soul, expressing his love for the child and for the mother, his generosity, his paternal instinct, his devotion. This number nine says what he can't say with words. Because of its emotional charge, number nine will give him an extra burst of strength for bombarding the net. Starting now, Maurice will be playing for this little nine-pound girl—to astonish her, to make her proud, to protect her. When a battered boxer goes back to his corner wishing the battle would end, drained of energy, his will to defend himself gone, his face swollen and bleeding, to bring him back to life, to revive him, his coach will tell him: "Think about your child. He wants you to win. You want to win for him."

With the number nine on his back, Maurice will be given a push by his chubby little daughter. She doesn't know yet how dangerous is the place where her father plays out his life. Hockey is a violent jungle. Using his stick like a machete, Maurice clears a path for the little girl who follows him, all nine pounds of her. To celebrate her birth, he promises to score two goals: one for the mother, one for the daughter. The Canadiens defeat the Bruins, three to two. Maurice has scored twice. And that is how, urged on by a little nine-pound girl, the Punch Line takes off.

In the war, a number of French Canadians have sacrificed their lives in Italy, the pope's country. A platoon of the Van Doos was responsible for cleaning out the Casa Berardi, on a hill that was infested with Nazi snipers. As they went into the attack, soldiers fell beneath enemy bullets. Their names were Bernier, Chapdelaine, Beauchamp, Fugère, Lalumière. In spite of the volleys of shots, they persisted, they prayed like French Canadians, they swore the way people swear in the Beauce, in Portneuf County, in the Gaspé. The commanding officer saw twenty-six of his twenty-eight soldiers fall. The two survivors finally reached the top of the hill. They took over Casa Berardi. Wounded in the legs, the commanding officer couldn't walk. Dragging himself along, revolver in hand, he took a prisoner. Threatening him with his weapon, he had the man transport him on his back to a rescue station behind the lines. Maurice Richard would have liked to be there.

Despite his successes, Maurice is troubled by a conviction that bad luck is pursuing him like some evil influence. This athlete who bestows on his opponents a gaze as piercing as the drill bits that pierce holes in metal at his plant is suddenly afraid of bad luck. Can he play hockey? Is he with the Canadiens because the real warriors are fighting the war? When he got injured last season should he have quit? The angel of doom is lying in wait for him; he can feel it. And now he's responsible for a wife and a little girl.

Can he really believe that he's unlucky when a hungry little girl has just been born? Nine pounds. Huguette is robust and hearty, with all her limbs, as Maurice's mother says, thanking the good Lord. Can a man truly believe he's unlucky when he has a wife like Lucille? When he has played with Toe Blake? When he's wearing a new number on his back because of a little girl who will think that her papa is the strongest, the fastest man in the world? Maurice can't shake off his fear of the angel of doom. Is he strong enough for the NHL? Is his body tough enough for violent body-checks? Maybe he really is delicate as some journalists have been quick to write.

Is it possible that the doubt gripping him is the doubt of the small people from whom he springs? Maurice is skating towards a future greater than his dreams and he's petrified. He thought that he didn't have a future. Having been wounded in the past, the French Canadian feels condemned to be wounded in the future too. Is it worth taking the risk of walking with a limp? Is it worth being injured in a game when there's a war on? He doesn't want to hesitate. As a member of the famous Canadiens he must give himself to hockey as if his whole life lasted only as long as a thrust of a skate, as a sharp turn before the opponent, as a pass to a teammate, a shot on the net. By day, he works in a factory. The night isn't always peaceful. In the bedroom of the little apartment, the baby demands to be nursed. The young father realizes that his daughter is as stubborn as he is. If he's thinking about his bad luck it may be because he's a little tired.

A bodycheck sends him into the boards. Dammit! His shoulder is dislocated. This time his career is finished. The experts are sure of it. A week later he's back on the ice. He has missed only two matches. Two matches! He has to make up the time that he's lost.

Since young Richard has been playing regularly, the spectators are coming back to the Forum. His shoulder has been fixed up but the pain is still there. Still, he applies himself to the game.

Blake at left wing; Richard, though he shoots left, at right wing; and Elmer Lach at centre. Dick Irvin is proud of himself. His Punch Line is a beautiful sight. His players' generosity will work miracles.

The newspapers are talking about the devastating V1 and V2 rockets with which the Nazis are spraying London. During a practice at the Forum, the Punch Line has let loose a volley of shots. This time, Maurice Richard is handling the puck. A player shouts: "Watch out, here comes the Rocket!" A reporter hears him. What a fantastic image! He puts it in his article. Immediately Maurice, now the Rocket, is propelled into history at electrifying speed.

He is plagued by the pain in his shoulder. It slows him down when he contracts his muscles. The Rocket can't bear any constraints. He persists. He won't accept being a slow rocket. He steps up his efforts. With this constant pain, he's continuing to have doubts about himself. Is he too delicate for the NHL? But he's determined and he won't give in to pain. He wants to remain in flight. Up until December, troubled by pain and doubt, he participates in twenty-eight matches. Only eight times does he deliver the puck into the net.

His team is doing well, though. The Canadiens have won twenty-two of their twenty-five games, the other three ending in ties. Bill Durnan is invincible. Whether he holds his stick in his left hand or his right, he's faster than the puck.

On the last day of December, against Detroit, the Rocket scores a hat trick. After weeks of agony and the doubt that it caused him, the pain in his shoulder has vanished. And at this sad time the fans are rediscovering a young player who's like fire on the ice. He plays as if hockey were more important than the war. In twenty-two games, he scores twenty-three goals. On February 17, 1944, in the third period, against the Red Wings again, he executes another hat trick—in the space of two minutes and thirty-three seconds.

Goal after goal, the Canadiens now occupy first place in the NHL. They haven't been there since 1925, nearly twenty years ago.

Last year, the Canadiens only made it to fourth. What has changed? First of all, goalie Bill Durnan has let in on average only 2.18 goals per match. Then, the chemistry of the Punch Line creates chain reactions; it meshes with the Canadiens' impetus. Finally, the spectacular Rocket is also the painstaking author of some surprising initiatives.

In March 1944, the Canadiens are in the semifinals against the Maple Leafs. They lose the first game. On the twenty-third they make a comeback. The Rocket exhausts himself on the job: Bob Davidson, a rugged defenceman, is covering him, clinging to him, barring his way. The Rocket is powerless. He's tried every way to shake him off. Nothing works. Now, though, Davidson is getting winded. He's slowing down while the Rocket is skating faster. Davidson can no longer follow him, can no longer cover him. The Rocket, free, breaks away and scores a goal that surprises the fans as much as the goalie. No sooner is the puck out of the net than he slams it back in. Two goals! Nothing can stop him. In the words of a failed-poet-turned-sportswriter, his energy is "volcanic." At the Forum no one has ever seen him move so fast. Now the third period begins. A third goal for the Rocket! And there's more! The Canadiens win 5–0. The Rocket scores all five goals. Is the Forum's steel framework strong enough to keep it from collapsing under the dancing fans?

On April 4, the Canadiens go into the first game of the finals against the Chicago Black Hawks. They win 3–1. The Rocket is responsible for all three goals.

Soon the Canadiens have a three-game advantage over the Hawks. On April 13, the fourth match is played at the Forum. Montreal fans have little respect for the other team: the Black Hawks don't come up to the ankles of their Canadiens. This game will be the last in the series. And the fans heading for the Forum are already celebrating the victory. Those Hawks are nothing but hens . . .

And yet, in the third period the Black Hawks have a 4–1 lead. The Canadiens seem helpless. They're awkward. The Black Hawks are mocking them. They've been anaesthetized. The fans don't understand the team's collapse. What magic has allowed those miserable Black Hawks to subdue the Canadiens? What pill has transformed some mediocre players into a team that's outplaying the Punch Line? These players have been crushed by the Canadiens three times in a row. Why are they so successful tonight?

It has been thirteen years since fans at the Forum have seen the Stanley Cup. The last time was in 1931, during the Depression. Some of them were children at the time. Tonight, the fans want to celebrate their Stanley Cup! Do the Canadiens want it too? The fans won't let their players stay behind. Spectators stamp their feet, lambaste their team, demand the Cup which the Black Hawks seem to be confiscating. The Canadiens are indifferent, sloppy. Even the Punch Line has lost steam. The puck waltzes, it never goes where it should. The Canadiens are heading for an inevitable defeat. Yet all the conditions for a victory were there. They could practically touch the Stanley Cup. Now their ship is adrift. The Cup is moving away.

The Stanley Cup has been made ready for the official ceremony that was supposed to follow the winning game. Manager Tommy Gorman sends it back to his office, the door carefully locked, along with the champagne, the beer, the pastries and sandwiches.

Feeling let down, some fans understand what's going on. The Canadiens are superior to the Black Hawks; of that there is no doubt. If they don't win tonight it's simply because they don't want to win. This verdict travels quickly from seat to seat, like a spark along the wick of a stick of dynamite. It's all becoming clear. The Canadiens are playing at losing tonight to extend the series. The longer the series, the more the team earns. And the players receive a bonus. The Canadiens know they're going to win the Stanley Cup. Why not stretch out the job? The cry of a spectator rings out:

"Fake!"

"Fake!"

The word is taken up again.

"Fake!"

The cry spreads through the angry spectators.

"Fake!"

Soon the whole crowd is roaring:

"Fake! Fake! Fake!"

The Punch Line won't accept this accusation. When they come onto the ice the fans see warriors, not fugitives. With a few strokes of their skates, a few stinging passes, they subjugate their opponents. They move with disciplined anger. The Black Hawks are worried. In the Forum there is only silence from the crowd, the swish of skates slashing the ice and the music of the puck as it slams against the blades of sticks or thuds into the boards. The crowd was dreaming of victory. Then that dream was destroyed. And now their dream is reborn. The Canadiens have set off again to conquer the Stanley Cup. Chicago is leading 4–1. Mission impossible?

Winning is not impossible because the crowd is demanding the Stanley Cup. It's not impossible because the Canadiens are the best players in the world. It's not impossible because the Punch Line works miracles. The crowd no longer doubts. The score is now 4–2 thanks to a fantastic shot by Elmer Lach. Goalie Mike Karakas was lucky: the puck could have lopped off his head.

A few minutes of play remain; the road to victory is impossibly long. The Punch Line is determined to go all the way. The Rocket is battling like a soldier attacking a hill where the enemy awaits with its machine guns. With a backhand, he catapults a projectile. Karakas feels a breeze: 4–3. The minutes are flying . . .

Can they move any faster? Toe Blake sets out on a tumultuous ascent, but he's stuck behind the Chicago net and can't shoot. The Rocket appears so quickly that the defencemen can't step in. Under attack by the Black Hawks, Toe Blake sends the puck between their legs to the Rocket, who catches it and delivers a slapshot. Karakas's hand wasn't fast enough: 4–4. The Rocket has tied the game. Now nobody is shouting "Fake."

The fans howl, cry, sing, pray. Tonight they're going to have the Stanley Cup! Maurice Richard, the little French Canadian, plays hockey the way Jesus worked miracles. Tommy Gorman asks to have the Stanley Cup brought back out, along with the champagne, the beer, the pastries and the sandwiches.

The Canadiens come back for the overtime period as vigorous as a prisoner on death row who has been told: "If you score a goal

your life will be saved, you'll get a truck full of gold and a night with
Greta Garbo." There is such determination in their attack that they
can't not win. The powerful Black Hawks resist. For nine minutes,
the Canadiens launch attack after attack, without let-up. They're as
fresh as if they've just come onto the ice. From the blue line, Butch
Bouchard passes the puck to Blake, who is already close to the
enemy zone. "Toe Blake shoots—he scores!" The Canadiens win the
Stanley Cup.

A tremendous hum of joy rises into a sky that is also filled with
the cries of the war raging across the ocean. No one in Montreal is
thinking about that. Now the end of a small war is being marked.
We've won! Let's celebrate! The Cup hasn't been seen in Montreal
for thirteen years. Overshoes, hats, newspapers, scarves, gloves
rain down on the ice. There is shouting. The celebration overflows
into the street. A banquet is given for the players at the Queen's
Hotel, then they go back to their factories and plants. They've won
the Stanley Cup but they haven't won the war. Maurice goes back to
his munitions plant.

Toe Blake has been playing with the Canadiens since 1935
and this is the first time he has touched the Stanley Cup. The veteran is trembling with emotion; he's holding back tears. He has
won this cup that he holds at arm's length as he skates around the
rink. Then he passes it to Maurice Richard. Toe Blake wouldn't
have won the Stanley Cup without the Rocket's two goals which
tied the game.

In this Canada that their ancestors discovered, the French
Canadians are the servants, the hewers of wood and drawers of
water. The language of their ancestors, their language, is looked
down on. Winning the Stanley Cup is a proud revenge. The newspapers serve up laudatory headlines: "Richard and Blake, Authors
of the Canadiens Victory!" They refer to the glory days of Joliat,
Lalonde, Vézina, Lépine, Leduc, Mantha. The Montreal crowd celebrates the return of the Stanley Cup as if it had won the war.

But it's not over. The great debate on conscription for overseas service isn't finished. Since the beginning of the war, French

Canadians have been pushed into a conflict that doesn't concern them. They've been deceived by the federal government, which promised not to send their sons into battle. On the one hand, French Canadians must resist the federal government, which is imposing its will, contrary to their desires. On the other hand, thousands of French Canadians have a father or a son fighting overseas, or a daughter working in the support services. Could their sacrifices, their bravery be contrary to the interests of our future? The French-Canadian people is plagued by contradictions. Their province is being torn apart by the debate over conscription, divided by language, culture, economic disparities.

Around the ice in the Forum, however, the crowd has found a world in which they are not powerless. Perhaps the puck is another form of the Host before which French Canadians prostrate themselves every Sunday. Workers and bosses, English and French, Jews and Gentiles, sons of ancestors and sons of immigrants: with one voice, the population of the province of Quebec cheers the French Canadian whom already their children are imitating in their games. With his muscles strained as taut as bowstrings, Maurice Richard lays claim to the territory of hockey. He occupies it with authority. And through this ritual, French Canadians are regaining confidence in themselves, in their future. Each of them feels a little less defeated, a little less humiliated, a little more strong. The Mass at which the Communion wafer is made of rubber is teaching us how to win.

On June 6, 1944, 250,000 Allied soldiers, including many Canadians and French Canadians, set foot on the soil of Normandy, in France.

———

To become a man in my village, you have to go to the slaughterhouse. One winter morning my father announces:

"Today, I'm taking you . . ."

Since I've started school, my father hasn't been talking to me very much. Before, he was proud to take me everywhere: to the general store, the town council, the blacksmith shop, to his customers, the pool hall. I was curious and he liked my curiosity. I liked to follow him; I felt like a little man.

But after I started school, things weren't the same. My father wasn't at ease with books, dictations, spelling, arithmetic, catechism, sacred history. For him, that's my mother's domain. She was a schoolteacher before her marriage. School is something women talk about, like babies and dresses.

A father who wants to make a man of his son establishes a gruff silence where you understand each other without talking. Where you don't understand each other too. Fathers and sons don't talk to each other. That silence makes a son strong.

And so there had to be a good reason for my father to break our silence. The slaughterhouse. The time has come for me to learn how animals are killed. Exactly where you have to hit the forehead of a bull with a sledgehammer to put it to sleep. How you use hoists to lift the animal's body to eviscerate it. How to listen without getting a lump in your throat to the plaintive lowing of the animal when life is struggling to remain in a breath that is dying away. How to look without getting disgusted at the belly swollen with undigested hay. How not to close your eyes at the sight of a heart that's still beating in a bowl and a tongue in one corner that flickers as if it were still licking the block of salt. How to tolerate the crying of a lamb that doesn't want to die.

The butcher shows me the point on the shivering breast of a hog where you must plunge the blade of the knife to slice the artery. He makes me touch to see how warm the blood is that's collected in a saucepan to make blood sausage. I learn how animals die. Like a man, I look at the spurting blood, the tangled viscera, the twisted guts, I look directly into the eyes of the pig's head on a shelf and at the head of an ox that's hanging from a hook on the wall. I walk around in this bloody debris like a man.

The war is raging in the old countries, killing women and children, tearing them to shreds.

"Is the war like this?"

"It's a lot worse," says one of the old men who smokes a pipe.

Another man, who is not old and who has several children, says: "Us, here, we know why we kill animals. It's so the women can turn them into tourtières, *cretons*, sausages or roasts. But can anybody tell me what their reason is for killing people in the war?"

Silence fills the slaughterhouse. The only sound is that of the blade which is cutting off a pig's knuckle. The men observe and suck on their pipes. There's a lot of smoke. The place stinks: of strong tobacco, of blood, of the animals' urine, of their viscera. As soon as the hog has been bled, boiling water is poured over him to make it easier to get rid of the bristles. They explain to me that those bristles will be used to stuff a horse collar. I'm happy to be enriched with the knowledge of these men.

In front of the cut-up animals, the men talk about war. It's far from our village but gas, sugar and meat are rationed here. No one wants to go to war. Here in our parish we don't have enough arms to do what has to be done. We don't have time to go and get killed "over there," on the other side of the ocean. We children can't understand all these adult matters but we know that the adults are preoccupied. They listen to the news, ears pressed against the radio. Because of the words they've never heard before, they don't always understand and sometimes our fathers and mothers squabble. We don't like this war. In June 1942, our town council voted against it. We told the government what we thought. In spite of it, several sons of the village have gone to fight. Others who didn't want to enlist arranged to disappear. We're not supposed to even talk about them. At least two soldiers from the village have been killed by the Germans. In the newspapers there are a lot of articles about the war. I look at the photographs: there are buildings that have been destroyed, people walking with suitcases, soldiers with their hands flung up like bandits who've been caught.

My father, who travels in the nearby countryside, gathers up everything that's made of metal: toothpaste tubes, battered old saucepans, tin cans; all that scrap metal will be used for making guns. I admire my father. He will make guns for beating the Germans.

One of the men breaks the silence:

"We won again, Saturday night."

And he lets out a long trail of smoke that he's been holding in for quite a while.

"Maurice punched another hole in the Toronto goalie."

We won the game. The men have no more worries. We've won. And we'll win again.

"Nobody can stay in his path. His passes are like rockets."

"That's where he got the name Rocket."

"They ought to give him a French name."

"There's not one anglo would remember it."

I listen to these experienced men. I'm learning things. I can't wait to be a man, to have a beard and know things like the war and politics: all those things that men understand so well. I'm only a child and they have faces that bear the marks of life.

"There's some that say, never since the creation of the world has there been a man that skated as fast as Maurice Richard."

"His weakness is, he's delicate."

"Delicate? About as delicate as a thunderstorm."

"You didn't know Morenz, the rest of you, Howie Morenz," says the horse trader.

Everyone falls silent. No one ventures to say a word. With the horse trader, you never know if he's serious or if he's about to tell a joke. You could become the laughingstock.

"He was as fast as a bullet, Morenz. At the beginning of the thirties there was nothing faster. Morenz was so fast on his skates he didn't even bother to dodge the defencemen. Often the two bulls would land on their asses and they didn't even see who'd charged them. Morenz: no hesitation, no precautions; he'd connect like a phone call. With him there were no little tricks, no special effects: it was zzzip right into the net. A player like that we won't see again in our lifetime."

A moment of silence as the heads take some time to collect their thoughts. I know the names of all the Canadiens, including the coach, Dick Irvin. My grandfather often talks about Morenz.

"Now Morenz was fast," says the horse trader. "Nobody on the other team could catch him. Did you ever see Morenz play, the rest of you?"

"Did *you*?" asks the town secretary.

"No," replies the horse trader.

He smokes his cigar. He's an important man; he organizes our MP's elections. Unshakable despite the town secretary's question, the horse trader describes Howie Morenz's funeral as if he'd been there. In 1937, during a game against the Black Hawks, an opponent checked him into the boards. He broke his leg. He never recovered. His life withdrew from him. He could no longer run away. Death caught up with him on March 8, 1937.

"Two months before I was born!" I exclaim.

"The funeral service was held where he'd lived, on the ice. The Forum was too small to hold the crowd that came to pay tribute to him. Morenz was a real champion . . . He sped like lightning. And lightning's a lot faster than any little rocket."

The horse trader is attacking Maurice Richard. I have to intervene.

"Maurice Richard skates faster than Morenz because Morenz is dead."

I feel proud.

"Yeah, sure, but Maurice is delicate."

The town secretary agrees. Professionally, he lists his injuries.

"Maurice is very delicate," the horse trader insists.

"Too bad his bones aren't as hard as his head," suggests one of the old men.

My father gets up. I do too. It's been a fine morning at the abattoir with these bearded, bald, toothless, wrinkled men.

"If you ask me," says my father, "there's nothing in this world that's as beautiful as a goal by Maurice Richard."

One of the men is still very concerned.

"I've got one of my boys, he doesn't give a hoot about hockey. I wonder if we'll ever make a man out of him . . ."

That fall, Mackenzie King fears the breakup of Canada: English Canadians hope that increased aid will be provided to the Allied Forces; French Canadians of the province of Quebec don't want to shed their blood in a European conflict. Once again King postpones a decision, though it's inevitable. His cabinet minister responsible for the Armed Forces resigns.

The Allies need men. During a meeting on November 22, King's principal military advisors finally persuade him to establish compulsory overseas service. The French-Canadian ministers resign from the cabinet.

Demonstrations to denounce conscription multiply. In Montreal on November 29, at a rally organized by the Bloc Populaire, André Laurendeau, a journalist with the newspaper *Le Devoir*, asks Canada to declare itself independent from England to avoid servitude to the mother country. Quebec opposition leader Adélard Godbout declares that all Quebec Liberals are opposed to conscription. Duplessis, who was returned to power on August 8, has a ministerial order adopted that accuses the government in Ottawa of violating the "sacred promises made to the people."

The hockey season has started. Maurice Richard scores goals. Days afterwards, in the towns and in the countryside, people describe them again, in inventive language. In places where men get together to smoke, where children come to listen in on the grown-ups, wherever men get together to drink beer, wherever families get together for a meal, wherever schoolchildren take their time before they obey the bell, wherever children go to a rink, the Rocket's goals are recounted like the exploits of long-ago heroes.

Already fans are speculating on the chances of holding on to the Stanley Cup. Bill Durnan is the best goalie in the NHL. New players like Ken Mosdell have just been released from the army. Dick Irvin is keeping the Punch Line. And the Canadiens can call on another two excellent forward lines. They'll win!

Last year, Maurice was made to pay dearly for the name "Rocket." He came in for more than his share of blows. No injury, though, stopped him from playing. He regained confidence in his own agility. Now as he moves he no longer feels the weighty fear that his bones might break. Maurice Richard steps onto the ice impetuous as a thoroughbred. Conn Smythe, owner of the Toronto Maple Leafs, is back from the war. When he first notices young Richard he offers $25,000 for his contract. Maurice won't go to Toronto, swear Gorman and Irvin.

From now on he can scale the steep cliff of ice whose summit is dominated by the opponents' net. He is no longer liable to the fear that an avalanche of opponents will break his limbs, dislocate his joints. Maurice no longer hears the angel of doom breathing at his back. Instead, he sprouts wings, becomes Icarus. He can rise up, up towards the opponents' net. The wax of his wings doesn't melt. He won't go crashing into the ground. On his skates he's as sturdy as a peasant whose boots sink into his native soil. Or maybe he's that other Greek god, Hermes, who had wings at his heels. The thrust of his skate that whips the ice and burns it, that thrust of his skate, the burst of raw strength that goes straight to the target, is also endowed with the delicacy of the brush stroke of an old monk tracing an illumination.

At the beginning of January 1945, the first conscripts set sail for Europe. Nearly 15,000 young Canadians have been called up. Many refuse to go away to die. A number of them don't show up. By April, 4,000 deserters have not been traced. Of that number, 2,500 are from the province of Quebec. There is concern for the boats loaded with soldiers that are leaving to cross the Atlantic, which is infested with German submarines. People talk about how the deserters have fooled the military police. And they're amazed at Maurice Richard's latest exploit.

The old folks compare him with the legendary Victor Delamarre, "The King of Strength." His most famous accomplishments: harnessing a 455-kilogram horse to his back like a knapsack and climbing up a post with the animal. He also ascended to the top rung of a six-metre ladder with a 1,027-kilogram automobile attached to him. He even lifted with his back a 1,027-kilogram bridge with a 1,364-kilogram car parked on it that had six hefty passengers inside. Every French Canadian knows about these prodigies. We're proud to be part of that small people among whom God caused the strongest man in the world to be born.

The Rocket is worthy of Victor Delamarre. He moves away from his partners, he advances alone towards the blue line. He's going to charge the Red Wings' barricade. The very brawny, very tough Earl Seibert is waiting for him. The Rocket speeds up his waltz with the puck. He lowers his head. Will he outsmart the Detroit player? Will he topple him? There's no doubt about it: he'll go to the goal. But Seibert moves towards the attacker. Instead of slowing down, the Rocket skates faster. A muffled shock as the bodies of two athletes collide. They both wobble. They don't fall. They regain their balance. The Rocket has held on to the puck.

To stay on his feet, Seibert holds on to him. The Rocket shakes his shoulders to get rid of him. The defenceman doesn't let go. The Rocket squirms. Seibert tightens his embrace. Weighed down by this unexpected burden, the Rocket persists. He wants to get to the net. He resumes his ascent. Weighed down by the two players, his skates tear into the ice with every glide. The crowd can hear the sound of grooves being cut in the ice. In three strokes, despite the burden of Seibert on his back, the Rocket has recovered his speed. Seibert drags his skates across the ice in an effort to slow down the attacker. The Rocket plants his blades in the ice as if they were grappling irons, he advances as if he were racing up the icy face of a vertiginous mountain. With his right hand he controls the puck at the end of his stick, he traces embroidery that confuses his opponents, who have rushed up one after another to reconstruct their unassailable wall; with his left hand the Rocket checks Seibert, trying to shake off the well-secured burden that refuses to let go. Despite the cumbersome defenceman on his back, he travels the twenty metres between himself and the net. Still weighed down, he arrives at the goalie, Harry Lumley. "Maurice Rocket Richard shoots—he scores!"

Thus are legends born.

"That's unbelievable, outsmarting a goalie with a man on your back."

"Victor Delamarre had a horse on his."

"Delamarre wasn't on skates."

"With a horse on his back he went up to the top of a church steeple."

"Wouldn't make sense for Maurice to climb a steeple—there's no goalie up there!"

Our small people with its unhappy past, its repressed present, is unable to sketch its dream for the future. All at once this young athlete has appeared who won't let anyone dominate him. The faithful and uncertain people is fired with enthusiasm for this son who refuses to be submissive.

At the end of February, the government relaxes its rationing laws. Good news! Now Maurice will be able to tuck into a thick steak before his match as he used to. He's rather embarrassed by the attention he's receiving. He's just one player on the team; he's only doing his job. Why all this fuss? Despite his exploits, he never misses a practice. Afterwards, most of the players go to the locker room but he stays on the ice to work on his skating, to fine-tune his movements, improve his shot. That puck has to hit the target, it has to obey him as if it were his very thoughts. He'll need all his strength and all his speed. The opposing teams have found the best tactic to curb the Canadiens: curbing the Rocket. They must surround this player who at least once per game puts the goalie on the spot. They must scatter obstacles along the Rocket's way.

Each team designates a player whose mission is to slow down the Rocket. Every means is acceptable. Harass him, insult him, trip him! They have to block his move towards the blue line. For the Leafs, Bob Davidson is charged with covering the Rocket. Kenny Smith has the same responsibility for the Boston Bruins, Ted Lindsay for the New York Rangers. These players apply to the Rocket the subtle techniques that nightclub bouncers on St. Lawrence Boulevard use on undesirable customers. The Rocket has endurance. They use every means to expel him from the ice. Legal tactics, illegal ones. They harpoon him with a stick. They crowd him, nudge him, smash him into the boards. They pound him with elbows, with knees. Several players at once are sent to attack him. They mock him because he's French-Canadian; they jeer him because he doesn't speak English well. These poisoned darts creep inside his carapace and slowly anger him. It's been noticed that beneath his anger there is violence. Now he is determined not to drive the puck into the net but to demolish those who insult him. And the referee hands down a penalty.

Maurice Richard can drive the puck into the net faster than anyone. He's a champion. And yet when he tries to speak English he doesn't have the necessary words. This champion who stirs up crowds stammers English like a child. It enrages him that he can't speak like a man.

He will learn English, the language of the factory bosses, the language of Wolfe's soldiers on the Plains of Abraham in 1759, the language written on the façades of Montreal buildings, the language of the banks, the language of the United States, the language of songs on the radio, the language of movies, the language that threatens the French language, the English language which is that of the army—as if a soldier who speaks French weren't as brave as an English-speaking soldier; he will learn the English language that French Canadians have refused because they wanted to hold on to their French language, he will learn the language of the Protestant religion; he will learn the language of the National Hockey League, the language of the Canadiens team. The Rocket will learn.

In the locker room, his pride forbids him to speak incorrectly and feel ridiculous. Scowling in silence, he sometimes pretends he's not listening. Now and then he understands a little. Now and then, on the rink, he thinks that he's understood the words an opponent flings at him as he skates by. But he doesn't have the words to reply.

Game by game he learns the meaning of the insults that sting his ears. Unable to answer insult with insult, he responds with his stick or his fist. Or a goal. Attacks on the Rocket are so relentless that Tommy Gorman, fearing that his star will be demolished, demands that the referees protect his player. Maurice Richard is no saint either. He's very good at mowing down an opponent with his left hand while with his right he's stickhandling the puck out of reach.

In New York on December 17, the Rangers' defenceman whose mission it is to irritate the Rocket is called Bob "Killer" Dill. This tough nut also practises the noble art of boxing, which he learned from his uncles, Tom and Mike Gibbons, who were famous boxers. In the first period the Rocket dodges his brutality, but Toe Blake and Elmer Lach are shaken by his crude manoeuvres. It's inevitable that the Rocket and the Killer find themselves face to face. It's written in big letters, like a newspaper headline. The crowd is already delighting in the explosion that's looming. On the ice, the tension is tangible. The players can feel the gathering storm. They struggle warily. Nerves make them move hesitantly. In the stands, people bet on the outcome of the Rocket-Killer fight. At the beginning of the second period, the two players trade punches behind the New York net. Other players from both teams join the fray, threatening and slugging. The crowd relishes it. But the referee imposes peace. The truce will be short-lived. It's not just that Dill is laying down the law by intimidating the Punch Line. The Rocket doesn't accept the Killer's law. This is what he wants to yell at him, staring him straight in the eyes, but he doesn't dare to speak; his English isn't good enough. He's spitting fire. Killer Dill knows his handicap. He knows his pride.

"Goddamn Canuck!"

This insult is one that the athlete from francophone Bordeaux understands. The Rocket may not have the vocabulary to answer back but his right fist sinks into the Killer's face. The boxer lands on the ice. The referee sentences the two pugilists. In the penalty box, there's no dividing wall between the adversaries. They sit side by side. After a few moments of dizziness, Killer Dill comes back to himself and wants to resume the brawl where it was broken off. After a few insults, he tries his fists. The Rocket dodges, controls himself. But he controls himself like a bomb that's about to go off. Suddenly, he explodes. Struck on the eye, Killer goes back to the land of dreams.

Fans from the province of Quebec feel tremendous pride. Once again, with dazzling clarity, Maurice Richard has demonstrated that a little French Canadian does not retreat before an opponent who's bigger than he is. Even if he doesn't speak English he can still make his way. With pride and his fists . . . With pride and his fists, the French language is not inferior to the English language. A French Canadian doesn't fear anyone who speaks English. When Maurice Richard rushes forward as if this stroke of his skates were the only one he'll be allowed to make during his time on earth, when he shoots the puck as if it were the only shot that he's allowed to fire during his time on earth, the Rocket expresses our will not to lose all the time but to win one day.

Killer Dill, two knockouts. Along with his boxing victory, Maurice has also scored a masterful goal and the Canadiens have won, 4–1. Going back to the Belvedere Hotel on 49th Street, he spots Killer Dill at the door. Is he lying in wait for another round with the Rocket? The Rocket looks furious. He clenches his hard fist in his overcoat pocket. Against all expectations, Dill is smiling. Without loosening his fist, the Rocket wonders if he ought to smile too. He never smiles without a good reason. Quite simply, in his halting English, the Rocket offers to treat his opponent to supper. Touching his jaw, Dill mumbles a few words. The Killer can't chew.

Three days after Christmas, icy snow covers the outside staircases of the houses in Bordeaux. Today, Maurice and his family are moving. They're leaving the third-floor apartment on Papineau Street. Maurice can offer Lucille the small luxury of one fewer set of stairs to climb. If things go badly with the Canadiens, he'll still have his machinist's trade. Maurice and his brother go up the stairs, down the stairs and up the stairs again; they finish the move late that afternoon. Tonight, the Canadiens play the Red Wings. Detroit goalie Harry Lumley is the best in the League after

Durnan. To relax, Maurice visits his barber and arrives at the Forum locker room saying he's tired, with "a bit of a sore back." His teammates are surprised to hear him complain. He's not in the habit of discussing his little aches and pains. He stretches out on the massage table and asks to have his muscles put back in place.

When his skate touches the ice, sparks shoot up! The afternoon mover is as light as a ballet dancer. He scores a goal, pirouetting on one skate. He plays the clown and scores another, after falling and sliding on his stomach. He's as fast as a meteor. As sturdy as a great warrior. The other side follows him, but to no avail. He's crackling with tricks. He deceives them at will. He outsmarts two, three, four players who are blocking him; he slips away. They can't bring him down. He bounces back like a rubber ball. His ecstatic fans, chanting "Maurice! Maurice!" are dancing in the stands. The Rocket scores a goal whenever he wants to. There's hysteria at the Forum. The Rocket: five goals, three assists. He has driven home two goals in eight seconds. The Canadiens win 9–1.

The fans stay behind where the miracles occurred. Crammed into the corridors, pressed one on top of another, they push and shove, wanting to get close to Maurice, to catch a glimpse of him, get his autograph. At his typewriter the failed-poet-turned-sports-writer wonders, in a burst of inspiration: "Is the Rocket mortal?" The athlete is twenty-four years old.

A game against Toronto is never an ordinary game. The two cities, one French, the other English, are rivals in terms of their development and their influence. These matches are a metaphor for daily life. On the ice, Montreal fans see on a human scale the challenge laid down by Toronto. Tonight, February 25, 1946, will the Rocket overpower Toronto? He has scored his forty-fourth goal of the season. He's the first player to achieve that summit since Joe Malone in 1918.

As for the Leafs, they don't want the Rocket to surpass Malone's record against Toronto. History would remember such a weakness. The Leafs have to handcuff him. Two excellent defencemen, Bob Davidson and Nick Metz, work on it. Maurice is hooked, insulted, blocked. It's considered more important to surround the

Rocket than to keep an eye on the other Canadiens. Blake, O'Connor, Bouchard and Lach take advantage of that decision and score. The Rocket weaves his way through, he's caught, he's clutched, he's flattened into the boards. He gets away. Toronto players pursue him. He's so fast. He wants to score this goal. Now. The crowd is fired with enthusiasm: "Go, Maurice!" The Rocket is at the blue line. The Leafs are losing momentum. The crowd is gasping for breath. Now he's alone in front of the net. He shoots. The crowd will have its goal! Frank McCool grabs the puck. The fans get back in their seats with a rumbling of disappointment. Play resumes. There's not enough air in the Forum. At any moment, the fans get to their feet and lash the Rocket's back with their cries. It seems to them that he's not working as hard as they know he can. The tension is palpable. Everything is about to combust! Skirmishes break out here and there. Three times the players erupt in all-out brawls. The fans heap invective on the Leafs, they urge on the Canadiens. The players flail, tear off uniforms, slash with their sticks, roll onto the ice, strangle one another. Then calm returns. The crowd get back in their seats as they wait for Maurice's forty-fifth goal. It's tonight, at the Forum, before his fans and against the Leafs, that the Rocket has decided to score the goal that will be a world record. Tonight! He's desperate. He feels like a beast that's fallen into a ditch. He's worked up. He tries to dig his way out. The more he's paralyzed, the more agitated he is.

The hand on the clock shows the fifteen-minute mark in the third period. Is it too late? Another five minutes of play. For Maurice, it's never too late. Four minutes. The Rocket only needs a few seconds. The Rocket will score that goal. "Give 'em hell, Maurice, you can do it!" The fans are on their feet, ready for the triumph. They're demanding that goal. With loud cries. Despite his exhausting efforts, he seems as fresh as when the game began. He goes towards the opposing side as if he were following a trail. Toe Blake passes him the puck. The Rocket's in front of the net. A frenzy of encouragement. He makes an abrupt turn. Three minutes. The goalie can never gauge where the shot will come from. Maurice chooses a difficult angle. His shot will have to be inordinately precise. The projectile whistles by. McCool feels him pass. He didn't see him. "Richard shoots—he scores!" His forty-fifth goal. A world record.

Fourteen thousand fans go into a trance. In a storm of adulation, objects fly onto the ice. The delirium goes on for eleven minutes. The security officers are worried. Will the Forum hold up?

But the excitement dies down. The fans need to rest. From their seats they've played this match along with the Canadiens; they've skated in Maurice's skates. Now they're worn out. The muscles in their arms contracted with every one of the Rocket's shots on goal. They've just scored their forty-fifth. The match was violent: the referee handed out eighteen penalties. No one is thinking about the other violent game that's being played in Europe, the one in which projectiles that arrive at their goal bring death.

A frail, white-haired man advances onto the ice. Just a short time ago, it seems to him, he was zigzagging across it like the young Rocket. He remembers the cries of the crowd when his shot struck down the goalie. The loudspeakers announce his name: Joe Malone! In 1918, he established the record that tonight the Rocket has beaten. The crowd greets him as if he were still the champion.

And an unbearable emotion is reborn like a fire on the forest floor. Hearts beat wildly. Lumps in throats. Tears. The hands that applaud are like birds dancing around Joe Malone and Maurice Richard. The old champion hands the young champion the puck that has beaten his record. This is life. A champion surpasses a champion so another can surpass him. Malone seems very small.

Because it has given birth to sons like the Rocket, this small people knows that its destiny is great. Tears are blotted. The former champion and the new one leave the ice together. Fifty years from now, people will still talk about this moment. The French Canadians are no longer condemned to be hewers of wood and drawers of water, to be servants, employees. We're the champions of the world!

What is Maurice thinking about? He's pleased, but his fiftieth goal is still far away. Forty-five goals: not bad, but he wants to score fifty. To the reporter on the radio he says merely, "This record honours all French Canadians."

A few days later, he is playing his last match of the regular season, before his fans. He has forty-nine goals behind him. He wants to give them his fiftieth. The Black Hawks have decided to keep him from moving. Any move is justifiable: that's the order. They have to dig a trench in front of the net that can't be crossed. The fans know that Maurice is going to score his fiftieth goal here. So why doesn't he send the puck into the net? They're growing impatient. He's missed another shot. Never have they seen him shoot so well beside the net. The puck is getting away from him. The fans are becoming agitated. The Rocket multiplies himself, invents stratagems, tricks. His will is strained in the extreme. Too strained. He's nervous. Too nervous. He fails again. The crowd demands the goal. He'll give it to them. Electrified by his will, he'll burst through the defence. Take the puck into the net. He's so determined; his natural instinct has left him. The supreme animal makes calculations. His genius is no longer guiding him.

Maurice Richard goes into the third period. Desperate. Perplexed. Disappointed. Determined. He'll knock down whatever is in his way. He's driven by a mad energy. The muscles in his legs are powerful springs. The opponents aren't fast enough to step in. The Rocket is about to score his fiftieth goal. He can feel it. The crowd can feel it. The fans are going to get the record they're demanding with loud cries. The Rocket charges. The goalie knows he's condemned. The fans raise their arms for the triumph. Coming along as fast as he can, Wilf Field crashes into the Rocket, who loses his footing and is laid out on the ice. The offence is obvious. The official gives the Rocket a penalty shot. This time, it will be his fiftieth goal! The fans are dancing.

Tense before this crowd that's asking for the impossible, he fires a shot. Struck on his pad, Doug Stevenson is driven back into the net. The puck lands in front of him. Maurice Rocket Richard doesn't score his fiftieth goal at the Forum. The fans leave as if something has been stolen from them.

It's in Boston, a few days later, that the Rocket scores his fiftieth goal.

Now, the playoffs. The sea is dangerous. One must get to the island where the Stanley Cup is waiting to be embraced by the champions. The Canadiens feel invincible. But the Stanley Cup is coveted by pirates, the Maple Leafs. Their coach, Hap Day, has drawn up his plan of attack and they all understand it. Essentially, they have to break up the Punch Line by isolating the Rocket. Any means will be acceptable. Maybe they'll get a few penalties. The consequences will be less disastrous than if they allow the Rocket to rule. Bob Davidson is rather proud that he's been picked again to exasperate Maurice.

In the first game, Maurice comes up against Davidson at every turn. His persistence is cumbersome, oppressive. The Rocket can't accomplish anything. This afternoon, when he was trying unsuccessfully to take a nap, he was mentally playing tonight's game in advance. As he lay awake he could see the slowness of the defence. He felt ready. But because of Davidson, Maurice is powerless. Lowering his head, he'll charge at the goalie like a bull at the torero's red cape. Davidson won't let him get away. He can't grab the puck. If it lands on his stick he can't pass it. Maurice is caught like a cod in his mother's Gaspé. Twenty-two seconds before the end of the third period, Ted Kennedy scores. Toronto shuts out Montreal, 1–0. Hap Day had warned his players: if their underwear wasn't soaked in sweat at the end of the game, they'd be kicked off the team.

In the next game, the Leafs apply the same treatment to Maurice Richard, who thunders, agonizes—and accomplishes nothing. The playing is tough. The Leafs injure Reardon, O'Connor, Lach and Bouchard. The Rocket is no more productive than if he'd been injured too. But he doesn't lose heart. The more they try to hold him back, the harder he struggles. Like Shakespeare when he ran out of inspiration. Like an earthquake that will shake up everything. But this time, his magic wand doesn't work wonders. At the Forum, the Leafs humiliate the Canadiens, 4–1.

After so much disappointment the Canadiens finally win the third contest. But the Rocket doesn't gloat. When he can't get to sleep he replays the game in his head. He's not very pleased with himself.

Fourth game. Weighed down with frustration, the Rocket skates. Davidson is waiting for him. Hap Day's tactic hasn't changed: isolate the big cat to keep him from hunting. Suddenly, just as he has so often prepared to do during sleepless nights, Maurice Richard takes flight. And the puck, like a bolt from the blue, hits the back of Frank McCool's net. This cannonball, which he has tried repeatedly to fire, was propelled by the conviction that an unsuccessful shot is a moment of life that's stolen from him. Every defeat is a death.

Goalie Frank McCool suffers from unbearable ulcers brought on by the tense anticipation of the shots to be fired at him. The pain is sometimes so severe that he can't stand up on his skates. After the shot inflicted on him by Maurice Richard, he rubs his stomach with both hands to alleviate the pain.

French Canadians have been following the slightest move of their hero. And they've received a message from him: persevere! Persevere! It's what their priests and political leaders preach. Persevere.

The next match, the fifth in the series. Just as the St. Lawrence River long held in the grip of winter breaks free of its ice, the Rocket explodes for a tremendous celebration: four goals. The Canadiens triumph 10–3. The Leafs have been carried away by the waves. Canadiens fans are hopeful once again. Maurice hasn't lost his magical power. The Stanley Cup will come back to Montreal!

On March 31, the last game in the semifinals is played. Once again held captive by Davidson and the others, the Rocket can't score. The Punch Line is reeling. The entire team is struck with inertia. And the Canadiens are eliminated. Ted Kennedy, Bob Davidson and Mel Hill have imposed their law. The Maple Leafs take back the Stanley Cup from the Canadiens. For the Rocket, this defeat is unacceptable. The top scorer of all time, he has lost the Stanley Cup. He stabs the door of the locker room with his skates.

Maurice is inconsolable. On April 13, Lucille gives him a son, whom he takes in his arms, unable to hold back his tears. Tears come more easily than words. He takes this child, who is too light for an athlete's arms, and holds him up at arm's length as if he were the Stanley Cup that the Canadiens couldn't win. He'll have the same name as his father. Then he'll have someone to imitate, to outdistance. It's to him that Maurice would have liked to dedicate his fiftieth goal. So that this child will learn determination, so that he too will be lit up by the urge to fight, to push the limits, to demolish obstacles, the Rocket will conquer other records. Little boy, watch your father dash towards his one-hundredth goal, his two-hundredth . . . But the arrival of this son does not console him for the loss of the Stanley Cup. He spends sleepless nights thinking about the Canadiens' failure. Console yourself, Maurice! Already your son, Maurice Junior, is being nicknamed "the little Rocket."

Elsewhere on planet Earth, the ravages of the war have spread. Germany has been greatly weakened by the defeat of its armies at Stalingrad. Two hundred thousand soldiers have lost their lives; more than ninety thousand have been taken prisoner by the Russians, who won back their city house by house, neighbourhood by neighbourhood, while in North Africa the Allies are making gains. The French army, breaking away from the Vichy collaborators, regains its unity. The Free French forces join the Allies. Now Germany has no choice and on May 8, 1945, it capitulates.

Peace! Now people can think about the future. To prepare for a prosperous future, Canada's population must be increased. The challenge: first of all, to increase the birth rate. Wouldn't it be better to step up immigration? And the argument begins. If the birth rate is bolstered by issuing a family allowance, won't that be tantamount to turning French Canadians, who already have too many children, into rabbits?

A family allowance? The province of Quebec doesn't like this new intrusion into a provincial jurisdiction by the government in Ottawa. And Ottawa won't pay the allowance to children under sixteen who are not attending school. The honest farmers, the honest workers of the province of Quebec need the help of their children. Will the family allowance law change the Quebec law that lets children leave school at fourteen? And the family allowance will decrease after the sixth child. That's another hypocritical manoeuvre by the Protestant English who, as everyone knows, don't like having a lot of children; it's an assault against our people's future. Distinguished ladies denounce the family allowance as a covert means of bringing back home women who have jobs in factories . . .

Wouldn't it be better to speed up immigration? But immigration holds its own threat. After the uprising of the Patriotes against the government of Lower Canada in 1837, Lord Durham came from London to study the situation of the French Canadians under British domination. This official saw just one solution: to augment anglophone, Protestant immigration and turn this French Catholic group into a minority that could be controlled. To resist the recommended drowning, the Catholic clergy launched a campaign to increase the birth rate: the revenge of the cradle. Since then, there have been fears in French Canada that immigration is a way to drown our people. And they won't accept drowning. French Canadians are no longer afraid to stand tall.

The family allowance law comes into effect. On July 1, 1945, Lucille and Maurice Richard receive a cheque from the government because they are the parents of two children. But that doesn't replace the Stanley Cup, either.

POLITICS IS HIDING
INSIDE SPORT

Hockey is only a game. A simple
game: you shoot a round rubber disc into a net while your opponents try to stop you. Of course those padded athletes are ridiculous
compared with the soldiers who've had their chests blasted open as
they advanced under enemy fire. Men fighting over a piece of rubber aren't serious. While people were enjoying the game, thousands
of men, women and children are being killed. Is it not disquieting
that the crowds gathered around rinks for the little war that is
hockey scream and shout but are silent when emaciated prisoners
are driven towards showers from which they won't return?

In Montreal the war was far away. People felt safe. They had
work. They were earning salaries. Yet deep in their souls was a
gnawing little concern. Could this war spread to Canada? Radio and
newspapers reported bombardments and the destruction of cities.
Why does the good Lord allow so much evil to exist? Why does He
allow men to destroy his creation? There were those who knew
nothing because they hadn't had the opportunity to learn anything.
There were those who had too much work and didn't have time to
think about the war. There were young girls who could buy pretty
dresses now because they were earning a salary by stuffing powder
into the shells that were going to kill people. There were those who

believed that all the young people in the province of Quebec should have been in uniform to fight the Nazis. There were those who declared that young Quebeckers should have stayed in the province of Quebec so that the life of this small people, which is also under threat, could go on. All these individuals came together around the ice at the Forum. The circumvolutions of the ridiculous disc that Maurice Richard manipulated—twisting, turning, oscillating with the blade of his stick—united the population.

The Rocket and his puck: the movements may be absurd, but in Shakespeare's time weren't the words that he set down absurd in the face of the plague in London, religious persecution in Ireland and Scotland, plots to accede to the throne, the execution of Mary Stuart, the war with Spain, the destruction of the Invincible Armada and the expansion of maritime and industrial activities in the time of Elizabeth I?

Gradually the fighters are coming back from Europe. The ones who are alive. Six hundred thousand Canadians fought in Europe. Ten thousand French Canadians have given their lives. On July 30, 1945, a first military ship enters the port of Quebec with forty-five hundred aviators and soldiers on board. I'm eight years old and along with my parents I linger over the photo of the big boat on the front page of the newspaper. Smiling, the soldiers in uniform have gathered against the guardrail. On the wharf, parents, friends, brothers, sisters wave at them. A few days later, the federal government abolishes restrictions on the sale of alcoholic beverages.

On August 8, 1945, an atomic bomb wipes out Hiroshima. The war is over. It will not be reborn from its flames.

The starving populations in destroyed areas of Europe have to be fed. The government of Canada reestablishes the rationing of meat. In Montreal, the butchers maintain that meat rationing is no longer necessary. The war is over. People want to eat meat. Why is their business being punished? The government lets other businesses sell their products freely. On September 24, the butchers declare a strike. Some other merchants close their shops as well, in sympathy. A few butchers, not so fervent, stay open. Altercations, threats with knives, with axes, smashed windows, stalls knocked over, broken teeth, assaults with eggs, with tomatoes: the police intervene.

It is with peace and calm, however, that the soldiers of the Van Doos are greeted when they come home from the front. They've shown how brave French Canadians can be. Although throughout the war there was opposition to military service in Europe, now those who are coming home from it are given a triumphant welcome!

With peace restored, Prime Minister Mackenzie King sets out to rebuild the unity of Canada that was divided by the quarrel over conscription. Immediately, Duplessis sends King a reply that stings like a shot by Maurice Richard: "Confederation presupposes cooperation and cooperation cannot be reconciled with centralization."

Several NHL teams are strengthened by the warriors' return. Players trained to kill resume their places on their teams. For the Bruins: Milt Schmidt, Bob Bauer, Woody Dumart. Chuck Rayner rejoins the Rangers. Ken Reardon, always ready for a fight, as bold in war as in hockey, returns to the Canadiens after receiving a mention for bravery from Field Marshal Montgomery. Conn Smythe of the Maple Leafs is a hero who escaped death: his body was riddled with shrapnel. Some of them continued to play on makeshift rinks in their camps. All have been matured, toughened by their experience of danger. They've learned discipline, teamwork. After confronting the Nazis they are confident as they set out on this new campaign in the National Hockey League.

During this time Maurice Richard has fought his battles only on the ice. He has not had to face death. Players who have held a machine gun play differently now. Hockey won't be the same. The Rocket is preparing himself.

It looks like an exciting season. The fans too are convinced that the quality of play will be higher, but the Punch Line is more experienced now, more cohesive. It will be spurred on by the new challenge. As for the opponents, they're wondering how to send the Rocket into a stupor. The Bruins revive their Kraut Line (the name refers to the players' Germanic names), which was the best offensive line in the NHL before the war. Chicago presents its Pony Line, made up of brothers Doug and Max Bentley and Bill Mosienko. As for the Leafs, they've put together a hard-hitting line made up of strapping young players. Instead of being on the ice, these players ought to be bouncers in the nightclubs on St. Lawrence Boulevard. That opinion is shared by a number of Canadiens fans. Dick Irvin is confident. Only an atomic bomb could slow down his Punch Line, he says confidently.

Early October, opening game: the Punch Line muzzles the Pony Line and the Canadiens beat the Black Hawks, 8–4. Second game: the Toronto bruisers don't shake the Canadiens, who win 4–2. In the third game, the Canadiens defeat the Red Wings 3–1. The Canadiens have power; for them, the war isn't over. The Punch Line galvanizes the jubilant fans. They suffer their first defeat one month after the season opens, at the Boston Garden on November 4. Swiftly, the Canadiens pull themselves together and a week later, against the Bruins, they bring the situation back to normal with a 5–3 victory.

The match on February 5, 1946, resembles an episode in the war. A ruthless charge by the dangerous Kraut Line. Bill Durnan follows the puck. His eyes analyze the slightest ripple. How will the shot be fired? Schmidt and his acolytes arrive. He prepares his shot. In front of the net. He forgets to put the brakes on. A staggering collision. Durnan collapses like a blasted tower. His hand is fractured. Schmidt has to be held up: an intolerable pain tears through his hip.

Honour demands revenge: someone has to pay for these injuries. A fight ensues. Centre Bill Cowley falls to the ice, victim of Elmer Lach's shoulder. He gets up. His hand can't hold on to his stick. His wrist is broken. Ken Reardon charges at Bob Bauer. Dislocated shoulder. The debt gets bigger on both sides. Someone has to pay. The ancient law of blood applies. Pat Egan suffers a sprained knee. Murray Henderson injures his shoulder. In this chapter of the war on ice, the Canadiens are declared victorious, 4–2.

What's up with the Rocket? In every match he performs some astounding manoeuvre that makes the fans feel as if they too are stronger. Like champions. And it's as champions that they make love to their wives. For the past few games, though, Maurice hasn't been attaining his phenomenal speed. When did the people last see one of his exploits that send shivers up their spines? He no longer stands out from the other players. Is the Rocket on the ice? During his 134th game he scored his one-hundredth goal. Last year, he scored fifty goals in fifty games. This year, with more experience and even closer bonding among the members of the Punch Line, he ought to score more than fifty. If Maurice weakens, the Canadiens weaken and the entire French-Canadian people feels less strong.

The fans don't know that he is in pain. Every time he pushes his skate against the ice a severe burning sensation slices through his bones. Only the team trainer is in on the secret. Dick Irvin has noticed that he's moving more slowly. The Rocket insists on playing. But the hero isn't equal to his exploits.

Maurice reads the newspaper articles. Although he's tough when blows are struck, he is sensitive to words. The press gets more pleasure from trumpeting the hero's fall than they got from announcing his birth. The Rocket can't respond to those hitters of typewriter keys the way he defends himself against a man standing on his two skates. Before games, on the bench, in the locker room, he wraps himself in silence. Over long nights he doesn't sleep. The fiery knight can't forgive himself for having pulled some muscles in his knee, for having been slowed down, for suffering because of the injury. His anger is growing at the ordinary player he's become.

Bill Durnan has also been injured. Without his extraordinary protection and with a less productive Rocket, the Canadiens slip into third place. The Rocket is short-tempered. During a match against the Rangers, Muzz Patrick gives him a nasty shove. He pulls off his gloves and attacks the former Canadian heavyweight champion. Though he takes a few punches, he doesn't back off. Finally, after one round, the referee sends the boxers to do penance. For a moment, the Rocket had forgotten the pain in his knee. Some time afterwards, the Black Hawks' huge Reg Hamilton, with all the weight in his body, flattens the Rocket into the boards. Without weighing the advantages and disadvantages of taking on a giant, the Rocket has already hit him. A resounding counterattack. A tight dialogue of blows. The crowd enjoys this bare-fisted round so much that the referee doesn't dare to step in. Finally, the pugilists' exhaustion puts an end to the hostilities. The failed poet turned sportswriter observes, "If we were to bring together all the sticks that have hit the Rocket, we'd see a forest."

To survive, the Rocket has to be more than an artist at shooting a puck. He has to be a boxer. The repertory of wrestler's holds is equally indispensable: headlock, arm-lock, strangling . . . Maurice doesn't retreat before someone bigger.

The Punch Line's determination hasn't let up. The Canadiens have amazing reserves of power. They regain first place. At the end of a confrontation with the Rangers, Toe Blake scores his two-hundredth goal. Bill Durnan is back in the game. The Rocket regains his ardour. Don Grosso is assigned by his coach to curb him. The Houdini on skates escapes. The Black Hawks are humiliated 6–2. After this defeat, Grosso is replaced by John Mariucci at the blue line. His mission: to keep the Rocket from getting through. Two precautions are better than one. It's not enough to keep an eye on the Rocket at the blue line. Red Hamill will be responsible for clinging to him like a leech. Bothered by all this attention, the Rocket is champing at the bit like a penned animal.

Throughout the regular season he has suffered from these tactics. In the playoffs he lacks the patience to tolerate them. He won't put up with these two millstones around his neck. Mariucci is behaving like a bandit. In a brief lesson, Richard teaches him that human acts have consequences. The referee sends them both to the dungeon. His verdict: a five-minute major to Richard and a two-minute exile to Mariucci. Both men were in the same battle; the two fought with the same enthusiasm. So why two different sentences?

The Rocket's fans explain the injustice: the best hockey player of all time has the disadvantage of being a French Canadian. The referees are English, the NHL bosses are English, league president Red Dutton is English. The bosses are English and the workers are French-Canadian.

In the penalty box the Rocket is separated from Mariucci only by the presence of a linesman. He's chafing: a five-minute penalty while Mariucci got just two minutes. That's unfair. The punishment falls on the entire Canadiens team. So since there's no justice, why not merit the injustice? Over the linesman's head, he hammers at Mariucci's face with his fists, making his sparring partner pay for the injustice. His fans are relieved.

Maurice Richard gets an additional sentence: a ten-minute misconduct. He doesn't protest. This time the punishment is fair. Mariucci's face is swollen. The Canadiens, restored, seem to be using pneumatic drills as they demolish the Black Hawks 5–1.

The semifinals continue. The Rocket has a black eye and gashes above both eyebrows. He is constantly harassed, isolated. Implacably, the Hawks fly around him. Every goal he scores is a daring conquest of the territory, one stroke of the skate, one stroke of the stick, one feint after another.

After four games the Black Hawks lay down their arms. The last two encounters end with the humiliating scores of 8–2 and 7–2. The pitiful fate of the Black Hawks avenges the one they imposed on Maurice.

Exhilarated by the pleasure of crushing the Chicago team and convinced of the Punch Line's superiority over the Bruins' Kraut Line, fans at the Forum are already gloating over the final outcome. These fans won't tolerate weakness. Losing the first game would be a bad omen. The Rocket comes onto the ice. The crowd acclaims him as if he's already won the victory. The fans encourage their players the way their ancestors used to tell off their beasts of burden. But the Canadiens lose momentum. They've scored just two goals, the Bruins three. Fortunately, after some desperate attempts Murph Chamberlain evens the score 3–3. The fans celebrate the way the French did when Paris was liberated.

The fans who have a fundamental right to win are nervous. They've nearly lost this first contest. Up until the final minute of the final period this contest was slipping away from them. The fans demand a winning goal. They get to their feet, dead set against defeat. They will only accept victory! This isn't just hockey, it's their lives, their insecurity, their dreams: "Give 'em hell, Maurice!"

The Rocket hears. The score is tied 3–3. His heart swollen with the force of this wave that is rolling across the ice, he grabs the puck from an opponent who tries savagely to protect it; with no one able to intervene he goes through the defencemen as if these strapping players were just a breeze. He approaches goalie Frank Brimsek, black eyes flashing; then he fires a shot that lands as if the goal were empty. Victory! The score, 4–3. The Punch Line has torpedoed the Kraut Line. The Rocket has overturned fate. The fans are giants now. Children believe that they're Superman. When they get dressed the next morning, they are champions beginning a new day.

This first victory and the Rocket's exploit have profound reverberations. The Canadiens' will to win is even firmer. The Bruins have been struck in the zone of the unconscious where self-doubt lodges. The Canadiens take the finals in five games. The Stanley Cup comes home to Montreal.

And the fans celebrate enthusiastically. They've been avenged for the injustices committed against the Rocket, the injustices of their own daily lives. Because of the Stanley Cup, the province of Quebec is happier. We've won the Stanley Cup. We're going to survive!

The Rocket holds the Cup in his arms, presenting it to the crowd. When he was attending his neighbourhood school he was told the legend of the Holy Grail. For his small people who have no riches, who own nothing but their history, the Stanley Cup has magical power. He's forgotten the story of the Holy Grail. Brandishing the Stanley Cup above his head, the Rocket is all smiles, but the athlete is dissatisfied with himself. Very dissatisfied. Last year he scored fifty goals in fifty games. This season, he scored only twenty-seven, a little more than half of last year's total. He was only half as good as last year. His smile is strained. Just twenty-seven goals . . . For another player that would be an accomplishment. Yet he feels like a Gaspé fisherman who comes home at suppertime without enough fish to feed his family. During the entire season he had an unpleasant impression of being in chains. Now, after a brief blaze of success, he seems to be just another French Canadian doomed to a petty fate. Maybe when you're a French Canadian you suffer from vertigo as soon as you leave the floor of a barn, the floor of a factory, the floor of a fishing boat?

After a reception for the players at City Hall, where they're welcomed by Mayor Camillien Houde, the Stanley Cup is put on display at the Forum and the winners submit to a workout to prepare for a match against the best amateurs in the country. This will give fans who couldn't get tickets during the regular season a chance to see their Canadiens.

Is the party already over? Some newspapers explain that his frantic shots last year were possible only because the best players were away at the war, because the other teams were weaker. Now they're back. And the Rocket can't get through.

The Rocket is tormented. The fact that he scored so few goals torments him day and night. Yes, there was pain in his knee, but it should not have slowed him down. It was not severe pain. When Lucille sees him eaten away by his thoughts, she tries to comfort him: "Forget hockey, it's summer." She's right. He turns his attention to his little girl and tries to play with her. But a child's games don't soothe his soul. He is silent, all taken up with charging down his inner rink. How can he score more goals? He replays the last season's games in his head. He plays them as if he remembers having played them. He plays the way he should have played them. How could he have done better? He tries, as if the other player were in front of him, to outsmart this defenceman, to break away from that opponent. He goes over his shots time and again. As he did when he scored fifty goals. He tries over and over. He starts over and over. He has to understand what it was that upset him. The opposing teams of course would have liked to tie him to a post. But he has always torn himself away from his opponent, he always got the puck back when it was taken away from him, he always pulled himself up if he was knocked down. This year, something has trapped him. And he replays the matches in his head. What is it? Sometimes he felt that his skates were as slow as if the ice were soft. Sometimes the puck seemed heavy. Sometimes his stick didn't obey his grip. Little by little, he surmounts his anxiety. Little by little, he discovers how he'll play next season. His self-confidence is coming back. The year of his fifty-goal record, he had no doubts and he wore out the enemy defence. He scores a goal as he slips into sleep.

But he wakes up ready to leave for the showroom. He sells cars. A dealer wanted to outstrip the competition by offering customers the privilege of buying their car from Maurice Richard. This job kills a little of the endless time out that is summer. It also brings in some money. Customers come, look at him, often describe a moment during the season, ask for his autograph, kick a tire and ask a real salesman the mechanical questions. Then they go away happy. Seldom with a new car.

To relax he plays golf, but often when he's holding a golf club he thinks that he's holding a hockey stick. He sees himself in front of this defenceman, that goalie, and he fires a shot. The ball goes too high, too far. The rumour is going around that Lester Patrick of the Rangers has offered $100,000, a huge sum of money, to buy his contract. That doesn't ease his anxiety.

═══

June 29, 1998. My little sister is sentenced to death. I learn as she has learned that she has terminal cancer. The doctor has given her two or three months to live. Yesterday, she was with her pupils at the village school, visiting the big city of Quebec. She won't be there when classes begin in September. My little sister is a monument in the village. For thirty-five years she has been teaching the first grade. Every villager of forty-one or younger has learned to read from her. My little sister is as good as goodness itself. She's as generous as too much ice cream on an oversized slice of sugar pie. Her sense of humour is so tremendous that next to her, TV comics seem grim. Her capacity for love is as big as eternity. Her appetite is gargantuan. Besides that, she's a monarchist. No one knows more than she does about the princes and princesses of Europe. She has four video recorders for taping her favourite soaps. She looks at them all but she's falling behind. She'll never know how they end. My sister is doomed. What crime has she committed to be given such a punishment? Three months to live. Her husband, sobbing, repeats that she's going to die. Maybe I didn't understand properly.

I am incredulous. Astonished. Shattered. My little sister is going to die. She who is such a powerful whirlpool of life . . . I don't believe it. It isn't fair.

But I am alive! I stay alive. I jump into my in-line skates. I force myself to go as fast as I can. I tell myself again: my little sister is going to die. I simply can't believe it. My little sister has cancer. Will be devoured by cancer. I'm skating. I, her big brother, can do nothing. She has cancer. She has cancer like Maurice Richard. I skate. I want to wear myself out. I want to be exhausted so that I can sleep without being disturbed by my anger. By my grief. What can I do? In the face of this monstrous Grendel who devours humans, I am merely a powerless Beowulf on skates.

I skate. Fatigue finally muddles my thoughts. There's just one hope left: my little sister has to fight with the unflagging determination of Maurice Richard. He has beaten cancer. He drove it away the way he drove away opponents trying to stop him from going to the net.

1946. The war is over. The Canadiens have won the Stanley Cup. Premier Duplessis is watching over the province of Quebec. Everyone ought to be happy.

The Catholic clergy in their black soutanes rule over the French Canadians, who no longer seem to fear the devil. The threat of the devil no longer upsets them. The threat of hell no longer upsets them. Women no longer want to devote themselves to their duty as French Canadians and increase the Catholic population of this Protestant America. Wartime factory jobs have changed them. They smoke. They drink Pepsi. That can't be good for their children. Those soft drinks contain chemicals that are bad for the blood of French Canadians. Women are used to getting a salary and spending it frivolously in a way their mothers never did. They are insubordinate to the heads of the families. They're surrounded by all those modern things that debase morality. Movies, billboards, calendars humiliate woman by showing her undressed or naked. Movies sow dreams in people's heads that aren't very Catholic. The new songs encourage shameless loves. They're full of unclean insinuations. The magazines that women are devouring tell about scandalous lives. Comic strips have a pernicious effect on the children who ought to be forming their souls by reading the edifying lives of the saints. And Communist ideas are poisoning union leaders, who encourage the workers to revolt. All this is very troubling. The government seems to be blind. Immorality and immodesty are spreading like an epidemic.

Mackenzie King invites the provinces to a constitutional conference at the end of April. Duplessis is fighting against his centralizing policy. Duplessis is a hockey fan. He buys a season's ticket; he's had his box at the Forum since the late 1930s. He's an impassioned admirer of Maurice Richard. Like the Rocket, he works relentlessly. He accuses the federal government of having a "Hitlerian" attitude. Another shot: "The autonomy of the province of Quebec is the soul of the people." He struggles. A backhand shot: "This is not a battle between political parties, it is a battle for the homeland." Like Maurice Richard, he aims at the goal . . .

But is he a champion above reproach? He entrusts to the Hollinger North Shore Company, for the next ninety-nine years, the mining exploitation of a territory in Ungava four thousand kilometres square. Duplessis claims to be defending the autonomy of the province of Quebec; how then can he entrust the future of his province to a company whose only goal is to enrich its shareholders? He justifies his decision: Quebec doesn't have the $200 million necessary for developing the tremendous resources of this remote northern region. Opposition leader Adélard Godbout suggests taking out a loan against the guarantee of Ungava's wealth: uranium,

nickel, iron, copper and asbestos. Duplessis replies: the small people
will have to support the cost of the loan and pay even more taxes.
"This is the scandal of the century!" exclaims Adélard Godbout.

For the pope of Quebec autonomy, the transfer of Ungava is a
happy initiative. A good government must prepare for future generations. It has made a shrewd and sly investment. The people will see
the profits.

Companies come to his rescue. A brewery, a shoe manufacturer
publish messages in the newspapers to praise his keen vision. The
tide of unemployment has been rising since the end of the war.
The government is dangling the prospect of construction in that far-
off northland of towns near the mines: airports the workers will leave
from to visit with their families in the south, ports that will attract
hundreds of boats, railways, roads. Ungava today is a desolate region;
tomorrow there will be prosperity, everywhere and for everyone!
Duplessis understood this fact before anyone else: the modern world
needs Ungava, its iron, its titanium. French Canadians have to trust
him. Before all the others, he has seen the future. The development
of Ungava is a bold gamble by the new generation of progressive-
minded French Canadians. This message, illustrated with futurist
drawings, is well received. Workers who had jobs with the war
industry are wondering what their future will be in the industries
of peace. The war is over. Now what's going to be produced? Will the
industries of peace be able to absorb all the manpower of the war
industry? French Canadians fear the return of unemployment. Will
it regain its domination of the province? During the winter it was
worried fans who asked the Rocket to be a god.

Industry no longer needs so many workers. To avoid layoffs,
labour unions want a forty-hour workweek. For their part, companies are trying to bring down their production costs as low as possible. At the beginning of June 1946, the unions order a symbolic
strike. They want to make the bosses nervous. First, the textile
industry. Duplessis wastes no time making his opinion known: if
good French-Canadian family men are revolting against those who

put bread in their children's mouths, it's because they're victims of Communist propaganda. In July it's the turn of the lumber industry to be paralyzed. On August 13, in the textile town of Valleyfield, strikers wait for the strikebreakers, protected by the police, to leave the factory. They fight the way players brawl on the ice to avenge an insult. Duplessis gives police the order to lock up the union leaders: those Communists will have plenty of time to ponder the advantages of a free country.

In Ottawa, Mackenzie King contemplates the great country that he governs. Despite the divergence of the province of Quebec, he kept Canada from coming apart during the war years. Cracks are developing, though, in the country's unity. How can he rally all Canadians, regardless of their backgrounds and their ideas? A flag could become a rallying point for all the citizens. Unfortunately, this Prime Minister who dreams of uniting his country is unable to unite his own party. Some of his MPs call for the Red Ensign. Others wave the Union Jack. The French-Canadian MPs would respect a flag that was free of any sign of bondage, in other words of any British symbol.

Do French Canadians need a flag? They have the Rocket.

"The Knight against the Dragons"

February 1946. The soldiers have come home to my village. They seem to miss the war. Peace has returned but they're still wearing their army tunics. Why are they dressed up like soldiers? They stick together the way girls do when they have secrets to tell each other. It's as if they don't like talking to anyone who didn't go to war.

What they prefer to do is talk about it. The war is over, but they are on parade. There are four of them, in khaki uniforms. And there's an airman and a sailor. They form a single line at the top of the hill, in front of the church, and they go down the street marching in step. We observe them. Their soldiers' boots all strike the snow at the same time and are raised up at the same time. Whatever is in front of them has to get out of the way. The army is coming through!

They've learned bad manners in the war. They don't interrupt their parade for an old man or an old woman going up to the church to pray. If there's a girl nearby, they shout teasing remarks that make her blush. If there's a man nearby, they tell him he's afraid to fight. The war has hardened them. It's winter. The cold makes the nails pop in the walls of our houses, but the soldiers parade by barehanded and without wool scarves.

We children are eight years old, nine; we follow them, we spy on them. They've travelled by train, boat, airplane, they've crossed the sea, they've fought in tanks, in trenches, they've killed Germans. They have won the war. We can't wait to grow up. We'll go to war, like they did. We'll win the war, like they did. When we're back in the village we'll parade down the street and the girls will cluck. But this isn't wartime, it's school time.

As soon as school is out we play hockey. Usually I wrap Eaton's catalogues around my legs to protect them. They're quite heavy but elastics cut out of an old inner-tube from our father's car keep them in place.

Today I don't need my catalogues. One of my Christmas presents this year was some wonderful shin pads made of thick felt, trimmed with fine shiny leather and reinforced with wooden sticks. Shell-proof!

Our game has begun. We're winning, three to one. I've nearly scored a goal. And what do we see coming our way? An invasion. The soldiers are wearing skates. They take over the ice as if we weren't there. They commandeer the ice. They're wearing khaki tunics. Their hands are bare. They take the puck away from us. One of the teams has to leave the ice. Ours stays. We're going to play against the army.

From the way they skate we're sure that they've drunk too much beer. They seem to be skating for the first time. They're staggering as if the ice were covered with bumps. They lean on their sticks the way old people lean on their canes. Our parents say that the soldiers drink a lot of beer to forget the terrible things they've seen.

All at once I see Pouce Gagné. I know he's a sailor because the bottom of his pants is three times as wide as a normal man's. He's the biggest of the servicemen and his chin juts out like Superman's. He must be the one who killed the most Germans. He's the one I'm going to be like when I'm a soldier. Pouce Gagné approaches. Even if his legs are full of beer, he moves pretty quickly. I'm going to do like Maurice Richard: get the puck away from him. He's coming on like a bullet.

Did he guess my strategy? He stops abruptly. Hits the puck with a swing of his stick that sends it into orbit. It lands on my right leg at the speed of light. It arrives so fast that I shrink back three feet. The shock hurts. I must have a broken bone. I finally lose my balance. I spread out on the ice. It hurts so much my eyes are full of tears. I wipe my eyes. Maurice Richard doesn't cry. I'm playing hockey against the soldiers. This is no time to cry.

My felt shin pads aren't worth a fart; it's as if I'd put on a handkerchief to protect myself. To heck with felt pads with leather and sticks! Next time, I'll go back to Eaton's catalogues.

===

What does a president do? A new one has been named as head of the NHL. He's a Montreal lawyer. English, of course, and his name is Clarence Campbell. He looks like a real Englishman. Does he know hockey? He was an amateur player. He mustn't have had much talent because he became a lawyer. According to some people he was also, briefly, a referee in the NHL. He can't have been very good. French Canadians aren't eligible for those fine jobs which the English pass on to one another. The president can see all the games he wants for free. Clarence Campbell was in the war. He worked with papers, at a desk. He wasn't cannon fodder like the French Canadians. A Rhodes scholar, Clarence Campbell studied at Oxford. If the Canadiens fans knew that, they wouldn't be any more impressed. The man is aloof. They don't like his superior manner. He's certainly not the one who'll bring out fans to the Forum; the Punch Line and Maurice will do that.

The Canadiens get a new manager too, Frank Selke. He used to be with the Maple Leafs. People don't have a lot of confidence in someone who comes from Toronto. Leafs' manager Conn Smythe shipped him to Montreal as punishment for trading a player without his permission while he was away at the war. Smythe accused

Selke of trying to take his place as manager. Under Selke, the Maple
Leafs became formidable opponents and in 1944–45 they won the
Stanley Cup. The hostility between Smythe and Selke points to a
heated rivalry between Montreal and Toronto.

Selke's first observation: the renowned Flying Frenchmen are
fast but they're too light to take on his old team. He is familiar with
the philosophy of the Maple Leafs, he was the one who instilled it:
to win you have to stop your opponents from scoring goals. How to
do that? Simple: grab them, hold them, clutch them, crush them.
Frank Selke announces that he's going to hire a wrestler to add
some weight to the Canadiens. Conn Smythe retorts that he'll hire
Canadian wrestling champion Whipper Billy Watson to plaster the
wrestler's shoulders to the ice. Will fans get to see a battle between
this so-called champion they've never heard of and their idol, Yvon
Robert, the real champion, a French Canadian?

The season gets under way on October 16. Management wanted
to give the event a historic atmosphere. Today's success relies on
the successes of yesterday. The champions of the past prepare the
way for the champions of today. History nourishes the present. Jack
Laviolette, who drops the puck for the faceoff, was hired in 1909 by
Ambrose O'Brien, the Canadiens' owner at the time. This millionaire took on French-Canadian players to help the population of
Montreal identify with his team. The spectacular Jack Laviolette
also played lacrosse and raced motorcycles and automobiles. A racing accident in 1918 put an end to his hockey career. Another historic figure is with him: Joe Malone, who played for the Canadiens
from 1918 to 1921, the same Joe Malone whose staggering record
was broken by the Rocket. Elders remember that in the first match
played in the National Hockey League, in 1917, Joe Malone scored
five goals against the Ottawa Senators. In 1920, during a single
match he sank seven goals in the Toronto St. Patricks' net. The
future is the improvement of the past.

After this quasi-religious ceremony comes the real faceoff. The
two centres face one another: Elmer Lach against the Rangers' Phil
Watson. The puck barely touches the ice when hostilities get under

way. The war won't be over until one of the teams has carried off the Stanley Cup. Blake, Lach and the Rocket hypnotize the Rangers. They're magicians who make the puck disappear and appear. Their attacks are sly. Their tactics are inspired. The attacks are incontrovertible. Their energy is electric. Their determination is devastating. These players skate faster than the passage of time. Under assault the Canadiens prove to be as solid as Mount Royal. They scrap the way people box in Griffintown, a poor Montreal neighbourhood. Inflamed by the record of their predecessors, the Canadiens shut out New York 3–0. The Rocket scores two of the three goals.

The summer has been beneficial to him. Maurice is now reconciled with the ordinary player that he was last season. During the summer, Maurice rested, spent time with Lucille, enjoyed himself with the children, played golf and baseball, went fishing. He's in shape. Less taciturn. He doesn't ever want to be afraid of success again.

People think they're watching hockey, but it's war! There are shots. Blood. Wounds. No one wants peace. The Rocket outdoes himself. In mid-December he scores six goals in three games. In a match with the Rangers, he scores twice and provides two assists. Against Chicago on December 28, he racks up three goals. The Rocket won't be able to live with himself if he doesn't score fifty goals this year. Or more. He has to skate faster. Work out the moves of the opponent better. Pass faster. Move around the net faster. The more problems his opponents cause him, the better his breakaway, the sharper the thrusts of his skates, the more steam there is in the pistons of his legs. The Rocket is like a Catholic saint: the more he suffers, the better he becomes.

Suddenly, in the midst of his euphoria, the Rocket falls apart. Over five interminable matches, he's unable to fool a goalie. The Canadiens suffer five consecutive defeats. The fans are impatient. Journalists are alarmed. What is paralyzing the Rocket? Bad luck? Can bad luck paralyze you for five matches in a row? They remain optimistic. The Rocket will get back on the road to the opponents' nets.

Scandal! The federal government votes to increase the salaries of twenty-five senior civil servants. Our newspapers protest: only two are French Canadian, though we make up a quarter of the country's population. Discrimination: French Canadians supply manpower—hewers of wood, drawers of water—not civil servants. Our journalists investigate: of twenty-two deputy ministers, there's not one French Canadian. Zero. In Quebec City, the Legislative Assembly protests this injustice, fifty-eight votes to zero. The government of Canada is exactly like the army: an English business. Luckily, the people have hockey: "Give 'em hell, Maurice!"

Toronto has an English head. Montreal has a French heart. On the rinks of the two cities the passions of our political life are played out, larger than life. On February 6, 1947, the Punch Line centre, Elmer Lach, is violently checked by Don Metz. Was it a chance collision? A savage ambush? Lach doesn't get up. His head has struck the ice. Outraged, the Canadiens jump onto the ice to avenge Lach. Fencing with hockey sticks. Boxing. Wrestling. Of all the skirmishes between Toronto and Montreal, this is the most vehement. Lach does not move. The inconceivable brawl spreads. The stands become as animated as the ice. When the clash dies down, Don Metz is given just a minor penalty. Lach is still unconscious. A minor penalty? That's unfair. The still unconscious centre is carried away on a stretcher. The Canadiens have heavy hearts. A number of them saw Metz's sneaky attack on Lach. A two-minute penalty? Justice must be done. All hands on deck! They swoop onto the ice to attack the Leafs.

The Rocket provides a respectable contribution. He makes certain that he deals out more blows than he receives, that he hits out harder than he's hit. He is convinced that Metz gave Elmer a brutal shove. And the hypocrite got just a minor penalty—the Rocket would have been hit with a major. That's why there is so much anger in his fists. He distributes it wherever he sees an opponent's face. The League president won't correct the injustice. The Rocket doesn't like this Campbell at all. To hell with Campbell! The Rocket strikes. At age twenty-five, with his 181 pounds of taut muscle, he feels as powerful as Genghis Khan setting out to conquer China. Isn't he the NHL's top scorer?

Nine days later, the Maple Leafs and the Canadiens meet again. The swelling, the cuts, the bruises collected during the previous game may have healed, but not the Canadiens' wounded pride. What persists is a thirst for revenge. Both teams battle fiercely for the other's territory. Each team wants to eject the opponent. Three times the Rocket, inspired by perilous circumstances, manages to break through an impenetrable defence and the goalie for a hat trick. But Toronto is leading, 4–3. The match is drawing to an end. Desperate, his face swollen from the elbowing he's received, the Rocket is exhausted, but in his chest his breath is inexhaustible; as his fatigue intensifies, the connecting rods in his legs increase their thrust. The Canadiens score: 4–4!

The Rocket should be proud. As well as his hat trick he's credited with an assist on the goal that has saved his team from defeat. Reporters flock around him. A photographer asks for a smile. Why? "Rocket, you've scored a hat trick and an assist!" Why should he smile? The Canadiens didn't win.

When his team loses, the Rocket is bruised and gloom settles over the province of Quebec. Even if the Canadiens had won this time he'd still accuse himself of not playing as well as he should have. Such are the demands that he makes of himself.

During the rest of the season Elmer Lach is on the sidelines. Even deprived of his support and his passes, Maurice Richard is advancing towards his fifty-goal record. Any other player would be celebrating a tremendous success. The Rocket is dissatisfied. He hasn't scored enough goals. He's afraid that he'll miss his objective. He is a discontented volcano.

His passion for winning, however, doesn't spoil his rugged honesty: the honesty that makes you "walk straight," as his mother used to say. During a match in which the play is extremely brisk, the puck hits the back of the net. The Rocket was directly in front. The referee credits him with the goal. The shot was audacious. That's the Rocket's trademark. One more goal that brings him closer to the coveted record. But the goal doesn't belong to him. He goes to inform the referee of his error. The referee doesn't want to question his own judgment. The Rocket insists. The referee hesitates. Finally, he gives in. The goal will be given to his teammate Buddy O'Connor.

The Flying Frenchmen bring in the crowds. The amphitheatres of the NHL are packed when the Canadiens come to town. If the Rocket inflicts one of his goals on the local team, the crowd doesn't hesitate to applaud him. After less than five years with the Canadiens his scorecard shows more than 150 goals. The historic record belongs to Nelson "Old Poison" Stewart, who racked up 324 goals. In fifteen years.

━━

1947. The Rocket has speed, he has reserves of strength. His black eyes hold an intuitive sense of how the opposing side will try to dodge him. His intelligence is spontaneous, tactical. He can detect the enemy's weakness. His play is unpredictable. His determination is so convincing that it imposes on others a fatalistic attitude: his adversaries believe that if the Rocket tries to score, he will. Every one of his goals is a story with suspense and new plot twists: a story that will be told again and again, that will be listened to right to the end. Every goal is an event and different from the previous one. His stick, held in one hand, spirits the puck away. His opponents can no longer monopolize it. At top speed he guides it, slides it; he slips through a tight defence. His skates scar the ice. The blades hiss yet he seems to be just grazing the surface. He's the fastest skater in the NHL. Then, in a fraction of a second, he makes himself as motionless as a column. Before a stunned opponent, he has interrupted his trajectory and seems to be projecting himself in one direction when he's already moving in the opposite one. He has taken a shortcut towards the goal, leaving a perplexed opponent behind him. His backhand shot is as precise as a cobra's bite. Whatever obstruction the goalie puts in his way, his eyes spot the crack. His puck follows the imaginary line that his eyes have drawn to the back of the net.

On a rink surrounded by ten or twelve thousand spectators, this man, normally so reserved, is transformed into a spectacular artist. Quite unostentatiously he turns his slightest move into a spectacle. The generosity with which he deploys every movement stirs the crowds. He takes every risk. He follows through every action. Everything he does he does with emotion. Everything he does he does with contained excess. He skates faster. He fights harder. He shoots more powerfully. He does more than the others. Every moment is extraordinary. With every move he makes he is playing for his life. With every move he makes he gives himself as if it were his last move on earth. With every move he makes he gives himself as if it were the only moment in his life.

Like writers who venture to describe the Rocky Mountains, sportswriters search for the words to describe this athlete who brings crowds to their feet, who makes them roar, makes them shudder, makes them sing, makes them cry. In the words that emerge from their typewriters the Rocket becomes "fantastic," a "physical wonder," a "terrifying force," a "famished gull," a "bomb," a "monarch," a "meteor." In New York, he is "the Babe Ruth of hockey."

His knowledge of the English language has improved. He reads these compliments directed at him but he doesn't have much respect for these people who play hockey from their chairs, with typewriters. Their complicated words won't change the task he has set himself: this season he must score fifty goals! To do his best. The fans in the province of Quebec are clamouring for goals. He realizes that they're giving him the responsibility of representing the French-Canadian race on the ice. That race that wants to stop losing.

And now for the playoffs! The Rocket is ready. Inside his body that's marked with bruises, scrapes, cuts and scars there is a voracious appetite to win. The teams are displaying unbridled aggressiveness. Losing is a humiliation for which they wouldn't forgive themselves. Widespread brawling breaks out in Boston, Toronto and New York. The Rocket has never turned his back on a skirmish. How has he avoided being maimed? He's been lucky. On each team there's a bulldozer who is responsible for driving the Rocket out of his zone. For the Bruins, it's Kenny Smith or Woody "Porky" Dumart; for the Red Wings, Terrible Ted Lindsay plays the part with all too obvious pleasure. The Rangers count on Tony Leswick, while the Black Hawks have designated Doug Bentley or Alex Kaleta for this mission. These distinguished individuals don't don white gloves. Maurice has been elbowed, high-sticked, tripped, hooked, tackled, checked, assaulted, driven back, punched. He's been the victim of skates used like spurs. Players roll onto him like heavy trucks. He's been laid siege to like the tower of a city doomed to destruction. He's been struck as if he were a giant oak to be felled. The Rocket has come through every storm. The crowd has made him a hero. And heroes are supposed to be invincible.

Just before the end of the regular season, the Canadiens visit the Rangers. Ken Reardon is checked by Bryan Hextall. The Canadiens' defenceman wavers, is about to fall but gets his balance back. As he pulls up, Cal Gardner's stick lands on his teeth. Blood spurts. Reardon heads for the infirmary. Just as he's passing the Rangers' bench, a fan behind him shouts something rude. Across the boards, Reardon stretches out his arm between two rows of Rangers and sends his fist into the insulter's face. One of the Rangers is displeased. With striking honesty he returns the favour. Reardon isn't very popular with the Rangers. They're on him like the wolf on its prey. Dick Irvin doesn't need a motivation session to persuade his Canadiens to come to Reardon's defence. The horde rushes at the Rangers. Even goalie Bill Durnan has left his post. He's in the middle of the melee, brandishing his stick like a tomahawk. In the crowd, some boxing fans are impressed that certain players have mastered the techniques of the noble art. In this furious dance no one chooses his partner. They strike out at random. They strike out at whoever strikes out. They strike out at whoever is closest. Buddy O'Connor crashes to the ice after a blow from Bill Juzda's stick. The stick breaks; fists are used. When your fists are flayed, you move on to wrestling holds. When the enemy's on his feet, you bring him to his knees. When he's on his knees, you lay him out flat. When he's on the ground, you trample him. And if your arms are tired, you use your feet. Buddy O'Connor doesn't get up.

The Rocket has dived into the tussle the way that as a teenager he used to dive from the railroad bridge into the tumultuous waters of the Rivière-des-Prairies. Did he obey the instinct to defend a teammate being attacked? Did he obey the crowd that was asking him for some action? Improvising this violent ballet, the Rocket pursues three players who are fleeing his stick as it whirls, whistling, above their heads. All at once one of them brakes and whacks him on the face. The blow hits home. Maurice retorts. Stunned, the player slumps to the ice. Maurice peers at his victim with out-and-out contempt. As his black eyes, their pupils enlarged by fury, study the scene, he spots Juzda, who had knocked out O'Connor. It's Juzda who will pay the fine.

Meanwhile, Bryan Hextall is pursuing Butch Bouchard, trying to mow him down with his stick. Bouchard grabs the weapon, flings it. The two combatants move apart. Then, attracted by their anger, they light out at one another again like two rams locking horns. In the end, Bouchard lands an uppercut. Hextall topples. His skates fly into the air as his back crashes to the ice. Bill Moe, on his way to rescue him, breaks his stick over Bouchard's head. Concentrating on the task at hand, Bouchard hasn't noticed this latest move. What is the source of this blood that's coursing down his ear? The Canadiens' Murph Chamberlain spots Joe Cooper, who seems to be on vacation; leaning against the boards, he gazes out at the action. Chamberlain rushes at him and sends him toppling to the other side of the boards. Meanwhile, Kenny Mosdell is zipping back and forth across the ice, handing out as many punches as possible to the largest possible number of Rangers. Their coach, Frank Boucher, with a stick in either hand, threatens to hit anything that moves. Reardon, who had set fire to the powder keg, misses the party: he's in the infirmary, unconscious.

When peace is restored the two sides count their casualties. Reardon has suffered a fractured skull. Already bereft of the services of Elmer Lach, the Canadiens are also deprived of O'Connor, their other centre, who has a fractured cheekbone. It is with reduced manpower that the Canadiens set out to conquer the Stanley Cup.

Is this brawling hockey? In the stands, the crowd has been enthralled by the chaos. The spectators have risen up as if they too were under attack. They were going to defend themselves. Little by little the crowd came down from the stands and moved towards the ice. Some sketched a straight right, a left hook, as if they were on a team. Others applauded. Still others encouraged their favourite boxer as if they'd put money on him. Some, in the grip of anger, were silent. They were silent but their fists were trembling. A few women challenged a fighter. In general, they clung to their man, like women who don't want their man to go to war. But this isn't war. It's hockey. Just a game.

The players are fighting over a rubber disc. All at once that piece of rubber seems to have become a huge diamond. Through what magic? No sooner did players return from the European front than they were fighting the way they'd fought as soldiers against Hitler's troops. Others are struggling in the way they would hunt to feed their starving families. The French-Canadian players strike out as if they were fighting for their survival. All covet the puck as if it would save their lives. Speaking on the radio, without bravado, Dick Irvin can calmly guarantee that his Canadiens would be prepared to shed the last drop of their blood to win the Stanley Cup.

If humans invented art in order to explore and comprehend the mysteries of their lives, they also invented sports that let them wage war without killing. Hockey too is a depiction of life; along the way one encounters obstacles: the opponents. Hockey is a simple metaphor. It's governed by clear and simple laws. All the players know them, everyone understands them. All the players are bound to respect them. If the law is disobeyed, the guilty party is immediately punished. The punishment is known in advance. Hockey is like life, but simpler to comprehend. People aspire to more equity, more transparency, more simplicity. In hockey, every player is essential.

Instead of being dominated by the team, the individual contributes to its strength. Gathering around a rink, individuals are present at the show of their own lives and their own aspirations. This rubber disc whose course they follow, agitated by efforts, shrewdness, power, bad luck and good luck, represents above all their own lives.

Every move is delicate. The player who has the puck must exercise as many precautions as the Chinese man in the last century who transported the nitroglycerine to break up the rock in the tunnel under the Rockies.

It would be easy to say that the players can't tear themselves away from the manner of thinking of a war that's barely over. It would also be easy to say that confrontations on the ice give the players a chance to become instant heroes. It would be tempting to say that it's a treat for the crowd to watch these little wars on ice in which no one suffers and no one dies. Or could it be that these melees are reminders of our ancient tribal wars? Could they be instinctive rituals in which the players size each other up the way young animals do? Does this violence exist because words act more slowly than a punch?

The ice is clearly delimited, with a carefully measured playing surface. On it the player exercises his freedom with his power, his speed, his vigour, his cunning, his sense of invention. The only limits to his freedom are the limits of his own effort and the laws. Each individual is evaluated at the raw moment when the puck enters the net.

The fans who are watching a tough hockey game hope for a less complicated world where the individual would matter, where he wouldn't be ensnared in an inextricable net, where he could sometimes be right.

═══

At the end of the season, the Rocket is the NHL's top scorer with forty-five goals. That's not fifty. It's a dissatisfied Rocket who goes into the playoffs.

To take on the Canadiens in the semifinals, Boston Bruins coach Art Ross dissolves his Kraut Line; he wants to combine his forces more effectively. Woody Dumart is assigned to keep the

Rocket in line. Like all the others he immerses himself assiduously in the task. Despite their efforts, the Bruins are eliminated. Meanwhile, the Maple Leafs overwhelm the Red Wings. To the tremendous excitement of the fans, Montreal and Toronto will once again be competing in the finals.

In which city will the Stanley Cup shine? Hockey? This final series will be politics! Business! Theatre! It will be war! The coaches of both teams trade threats like enemy chiefs before they drop the bombs. They remember past offences. These finals will correct History, restore Justice.

Elmer Lach has suffered a fractured skull. Dick Irvin is convinced that Juzda's brutal attack was premeditated, deliberate. The Leafs dismiss the accusation. Hockey is a man's game; if you're too dainty you can get hurt. Dick Irvin takes God as his witness: the outcome of this series will be a sign of His judgment. God will follow the Stanley Cup finals from on high. If the attack on Lach was planned, "God will lead the Canadiens to the Stanley Cup," he says. Canadiens fans are convinced that Juzda attacked Lach in order to break up the Punch Line. In the same way, they're trying to get rid of the Rocket. God knows that. It's obvious: the Stanley Cup will go to the Canadiens!

In the first match God is playing along with the Rocket on the Punch Line. Dick Irvin has exhorted his players to avenge Elmer Lach, who is at home, out of the game. The Canadiens blank the Leafs 6–0. The Leafs have been punished by God.

The Maple Leafs will defend their honour. They didn't cripple Lach deliberately. It was an accident. If they don't win the second match Dick Irvin's accusation will prevail. His lie. Every move they make will reconstruct the truth. Every blow will be inflicted to defend the truth. Every shot will be fired as a reminder of the truth. Every breakaway will be an invitation to God to restore the truth.

At the start of the game you can sense the enmity between the two teams, as cold as a January night, on this April 10 spring evening. The play is extremely fast. Extremely impassioned. The Leafs take the advantage. The teams play as if they're being assaulted. There are no blows yet but the game resembles a brawl. The rules are respected but they're playing as if the rules didn't exist. The spectators follow the game, fascinated, as if they were gazing at the flame on the wick before the dynamite blows up. The Rocket is surrounded, controlled. All his shrewdness is useless: he can't tear himself away from the special surveillance that's assigned to him.

During the first period Bill Ezinicki, staying close to Maurice, doesn't let him get away. His stick serves as a hook to hold him back. As solid on his skates as a hydrant, he works relentlessly to shake the Rocket. Massive, he assaults repeatedly with his shoulders. The Rocket also receives the attention of Vic Lynn and Joe Klukay. The Rocket is slowed down; the whole team is slowed down. If they hold on to him long enough his anger will explode. That's what they are hoping for. He'll hit someone and be sent to the penalty box. So they reason. Accordingly, they lavish special attention on him: elbowing, high-sticking, slamming his ankles with their sticks, hooking, shouting racial jibes. And the Rocket rages. He's in shackles. He's seething. He wants to get away. A mountain is weighing on his back tonight but he's determined to move that mountain. He feels strong enough. He's surrounded. Skating in circles. Exhausted. He's unproductive. And the less successful he is, the more impassioned is his will. No one doubts that his impatience is exacerbated by the torture of his knee. He tore some ligaments again during a tremendous collision with Gus Mortson.

What was going to happen happens! At the six-minute mark in the second period, an attack forms towards the Canadiens' defence. The Rocket rushes to the aid of his sentries. Vic Lynn tries to slow him down with a hard shoulder. The Rocket staggers, regains his balance and, with his stick slashing the air like a sabre, goes hunting. At the sight of this flaming meteor coming his way, Vic Lynn raises his stick to warn the Rocket of the danger of coming any closer. Like a released catapult, the Rocket's stick comes down on Lynn's face. Blood spurts onto the ice where Lynn is lying, unconscious. Maurice Rocket Richard: a five-minute major penalty.

He deeply regrets the harm he's done to his team by picking up this penalty. When he's back in the game there is thunder in his stick. Even in the most remote stands, fans can see the lightning flashing in his black eyes. At this moment Toronto is flattening Montreal, 3–0.

Bill Ezinicki resumes his surveillance of the Rocket. Is it possible to keep a storm at bay? He clings to him. If the puck comes towards Maurice, Ezinicki deflects the pass. This constant assault is unbearable. And the pain in his knee is sharper. The Rocket can't tolerate what's being done to him. After another drive, he shows his teeth. Ezinicki brings his stick up to show him what's in store if he attacks. At the sight of the menacing stick, the Rocket is afraid that Ezinicki will offer him the same act of kindness he himself bestowed on Lynn. Before Ezinicki can strike, Maurice stuns him. A little blood. And the two gentlemen give a demonstration of barnyard fencing. Referee Bill Chadwick tries to get between them. The crowd, on its feet, demands that the Rocket turn Ezinicki into meatloaf. The belligerents, tired now, calm down. The fans go back to their seats. It's peaceful just now, but the storm isn't over. In the same way that lightning strikes, the Rocket delivers another blow to Ezinicki's head, over the referee.

In the jubilant crowd, a man is shouting insults at the Rocket: he's Conn Smythe, the Leafs' manager. Next to him a woman retorts, "If you is not happy, stay in Toronto, you!" The woman knows who she's talking to. Someone whispers to Smythe that she is Maurice Richard's wife, Lucille. Smythe, suddenly all refinement, tips his hat, apologizes and holds out his hand, which she refuses. Could she convince her husband to join the Maple Leafs? He'd give her a present if she did. "What a horse trader!"

The Rocket goes back to jail. The two gladiators were evenly matched: each got twelve stitches. The Leafs shut out the Canadiens 3–0. Dick Irvin is worried: with this victory to the Leafs, is God testifying on behalf of Juzda?

The third game is played in Toronto. The newspapers wonder, Will the Rocket be on the ice? President Clarence Campbell is busy analyzing the Ezinicki–Richard affair. Late that morning the NHL president renders his verdict: a $250 fine to the Rocket. And because of his bad behaviour he gives him a game misconduct. He won't be on the ice tonight.

Without the Rocket the weakened Canadiens are demoralized. Usually, Bill Durnan is as solid as a brick wall in front of his net, but tonight he's more like an open door. Everyone is welcome. The Canadiens are drifting towards an inevitable defeat. Afterwards Durnan doesn't even try to hide his tears. He played badly. Has he seen too many pucks in his life? Has his body got used to being bombarded? His muscles aren't reacting. Durnan feels that he's finished. The Leafs should have lost this game because they're a bad team. They've won again. Dick Irvin is so unhappy, he can't even find the strength to bawl out his players. He regrets having called upon divine judgment in the Lach-Juzda affair. God, who doesn't like to have His name taken in vain, has given the victory to Toronto.

In the fourth game, people are waiting for the Rocket. Fans are familiar with his temperament. He'll be wanting to make up for lost time. To make the Leafs pay for his penalty. The Canadiens are in an awkward position. The tougher the challenge, the more exhilarating for him. For him, an obstacle is a magic potion. The riskier the situation the more relentless he becomes. Beginning that morning tickets are being sold on the black market. Maple Leaf Gardens isn't big enough to hold all those who want to see their Leafs and the Canadiens settle their current affairs. The Rocket will be working hard. Like his coach, he believes in God. He does not, however, expect the hand of God to drive the puck into the net. That's his responsibility.

The Leafs, reassured by two consecutive victories, are skating confidently. The breath of God is swelling their sails. The coach has defined the objective: to maintain their advantage in the series. Their tactic: keep the Rocket from doing any damage, in other words, tie him up. It won't be easy. Furious with the referee, with Clarence Campbell and with himself (he knows what harm his misconduct has caused), he hopes that excess zeal will win him forgiveness.

This match is no gentler than the previous one. A skate slices open Butch Bouchard's leg. The Leafs manage to keep the Rocket out of play. Both sides, furious and passionate, are striving to block the opponent, to weaken him, to wipe him out. At the end of the third period it's a scoreless tie. The game will go into overtime.

In Maple Leaf Gardens, emotions are running so high that even the fans are gasping for breath. The Canadiens are struggling like shipwreck victims: if they swim vigorously the shore will come towards them. Each spectator is exhausted by his own desire to witness a victory, to give more speed to a certain player, to send the puck towards a certain stick. The Canadiens go at the Leafs hammer and tongs. The younger Leafs know that they're unbeatable but they aren't able to prove it. The Canadiens' net is inviolable. The Montreal players are aggressive. Fast. Hard-hitting. They shoot at point-blank range. From all sides. They bombard the goalie. The Rocket is making tremendous efforts. In the past, under similar conditions, he has scored some splendid goals. But the past isn't the present. His team is counting on him. But he can't get anywhere. He feels sluggish. With these Leafs who are keeping him from moving, he's like a horse hitched to a wagon full of stones. The Leafs retaliate shot for shot, breakaway for breakaway. The breathless crowd wishes that the game were over. Suddenly, at sixteen minutes, thirty-six seconds of overtime, Toronto captain Syl Apps scores. The winning goal! God is still on the side of the Leafs—he's given them three consecutive victories. The train that brings the defeated Canadiens back to Montreal resembles a funeral procession.

Before the fifth game, in Montreal, the atmosphere is overcharged. The fans have discovered a scheme of Clarence Campbell's. He doesn't want to give the Stanley Cup to the Canadiens: that's why he keeps laying the blame on the Rocket. Keeping him out of a game was the best way to give Toronto the advantage. During his duel with Ezinicki, Maurice was in a state of legitimate self-defence. Ezinicki had attacked him. "When he hasn't got the puck," claims Maurice, "he's the toughest nut to crack I've ever met on the ice and he doesn't often have the puck." The Catholic religion teaches us that if someone slaps you on the right cheek, you must turn the other one. French Canadians have understood where such submission leads them. In the modern world you don't turn the other cheek to the person who's struck you, you knock him out. Campbell favours Toronto. So the conversations go . . .

The Canadiens' fans know the rules. A game misconduct is imposed only if the player who's been attacked is injured so severely that he can't return to the game. After the brawl, Ezinicki came back on the ice in bandages. Referee Bill Chadwick made a mistake, then. Clarence Campbell should have corrected it but instead he chose to endorse it. Why? Looking down from his English superiority, Campbell wants to humiliate the little French Canadian who takes up too much room on the ice. Clarence Campbell applies two kinds of justice, one for his own people, another for French Canadians. Did Don Metz and Bill Juzda get game misconducts when they attacked Elmer Lach? No.

In houses and taverns, in town and in the countryside, in middle-classes dwellings and farmhouses, in offices and garages, evidence is piling up that Clarence Campbell has decided the Toronto Maple Leafs will win the Stanley Cup.

Before the faceoff, there's revolution in the air. Canadiens fans reimburse the Rocket for the $250 fine that he paid Campbell. The sum was raised by office workers, lawyers, insurance salesmen, grocers, streetcar conductors, taxi drivers. Clarence Campbell deserves just one reply: a Canadiens victory. They've been cheated. Now it's up to them to take revenge. The puck will tell the truth. The fans follow the match as if they were wearing skates. When the Rocket rushes at the enemy net, they're with him. If the Rocket gets shouldered, they're shaken up with him. If he gets a shot on goal, they're the ones who fire it. With such support the Rocket rediscovers his freedom. He gives the Forum crowd a gift of two goals. The Canadiens snatch a victory, 3–1.

Hope has been restored; the Stanley Cup is glittering again in the dreams of fans. First, they foresee the Canadiens taking the next game in Toronto. After that victory they'll come back to Montreal for the final game. And that will be the Stanley Cup! They're dreaming. This time, reality cannot fail to resemble their dream.

The sixth match begins. Twenty seconds after the start of the first period, Buddy O'Connor, recovered from his injury now, wrests the puck from a defenceman and zigzags towards the Leafs' goalie. He shoots. He can't believe it, but he can see the puck slide between Turk Broda's pads as if they were smoke. Dick Irvin tells himself that God has finally decided to speak and he predicts a Canadiens victory. The entire population of the province of Quebec is gathered around their radios. They follow minute by minute, they hope, they wait. In the tone of the voice on the radio they think they can detect signs that victory is nigh. On the other hand, the Leafs have a one-game advantage. God is pointing to the Stanley Cup for them. They work as hard as if there were fifteen of them on the ice at once, on offence, on defence, they attack, they retreat; their defence is impenetrable. Tirelessly, they fire away at Durnan. But the Canadiens are lucky enough to keep the score at 1–0.

At the five-minute, thirty-four-second mark of the second period, Vic Lynn, who's been rather roughly treated by the Rocket, scores the tying goal. The Canadiens are no longer certain of victory. Just as they were about to reach the summit, Vic Lynn's goal has made them feel as if they've fallen back to the foot of the mountain. After a moment of doubt that passes over them like a cold shudder, their faith is restored. Now they're waging war as if the God of Victory were guiding them. Re-energized, the Toronto team feels that victory is close at hand. At the fourteen-minute mark of the third period, a goal by Ted Kennedy gives the Maple Leafs the Stanley Cup.

Defeated, Dick Irvin doesn't understand. Elmer Lach was injured intentionally by the Maple Leafs. Irvin knows it, Juzda knows it, everyone else knows it, God knows it. So why did God let them win? It's a mystery. The Canadiens' fans are sure of one thing: if the Rocket hadn't been unjustly kept out of a match, the Canadiens would have won the Stanley Cup. That's the refrain of an exasperated public. It's the fault of Clarence Campbell that the

Canadiens have lost. As for the role played by God, some think that He's often on the side of the English Protestants. They don't understand.

As for the Rocket, he may be the best hockey player of all time but he's still a French Canadian. Many don't like the fact that a French Canadian is the best hockey player in the world. They haven't been able to demolish the Rocket, so they're trying more hypocritical means. It's through rules and regulations that they want to bring down the Rocket. So many Canadiens fans think.

This spring, though, there are a lot of impassioned conversations. A man who runs a textile company in the Beauce has agreed to take on a hundred young Polish girls who were released from refugee camps at the end of the war. In accordance with an agreement with the federal government, the businessman undertakes to guarantee them jobs for two years, to pay them the salary current in the region, to bring them to Canada free and to house them in a centre run by Catholic nuns. The businessman needs workers and he wants to relieve the misery created by the war.

His good work provokes a stormy debate in the House of Commons. Anglophone MPs accuse him of practising slavery. They accuse Ludger Dionne of dealing in slaves. *Le Devoir* wades into the debate: immigration, the newspaper argues, is very praiseworthy when it increases the number of anglophones in Canada, but it's reprehensible when it brings people who become integrated with the French Canadians.

After giving his fans forty-five goals during the regular season and six during the playoffs, the Rocket has the whole summer ahead of him to try to understand why he hasn't equalled his fifty-goal record. In the middle of his triumph, Conn Smythe comes up with a good one: "Maurice Richard is the three musketeers of the NHL, Athos, Porthos and Aramis." But what team did they play for?

LET'S SET FIRE TO
THE FORUM AND WAKE UP
THE CANADIENS

Maurice Richard, the greatest hockey player of modern times, with three strokes of his skate, before jubilant crowds, could outsmart the toughest defencemen and pierce the most impenetrable goalies. After the game, he spoke English with journalists the way someone skates who doesn't know how to skate. Because he was a shy man, because he felt uncomfortable at not speaking that language well, because he felt ridiculous at speaking it the way he spoke it, he took refuge in a silence that his teammates could break through only with caution. But he applied himself. He listened. He read the English papers. He learned new words.

It was on the ice that he regained his total freedom. There, he didn't need to talk. In English or in French. He talked with his stick and, when necessary, with his fists. The ice was the only place where Maurice felt light. The ice was the only place where he had the sense of being truly free. It was where he was entirely himself: the Rocket, a French Canadian set free of history. With every faceoff the ice becomes virgin territory again. Everyone is equal during a faceoff. Afterwards, each player creates his own destiny.

Little by little, Maurice has learned English. Now he knows how to respond with words to opponents who verbally abuse him. He's better at understanding his teammates' jokes during the long train trips. But his only real friend among the anglophone players is

Kenny Mosdell. He feels safe with him. He has high regard for him. He often says that Kenny is a player who doesn't get the attention he deserves. Lucille gets along well with Madame Mosdell. The tiger from the Bordeaux neighbourhood in Montreal's east end has made his way into the English world with caution. The French-Canadian world seems cramped to him when he's away. In Montreal, he feels in the depths of his soul the extent to which he is part of this small people. He's more confident now. Not so nervous when he has to meet journalists. He can answer their questions. He doesn't need a lot of words.

In the summer, he returns to his francophone environment, in both the city and the country. He forgets, a little more than he'd like, the words and phrases that he's learned. Luckily there are the ball games that the Canadiens play against the local parks' teams. He enjoys speaking English again, even feels an immodest hint of pride at his success in doing so. After the game, they go for a cold beer or two. After they've commented on the events in the ball game as seriously as if it were a hockey match, the talk of course is about the coming season.

The fans look for signs that foretell the future. They're concerned. Training camp is ending, the season is about to begin and Maurice Richard has not yet signed his contract with the Canadiens. Neither has Butch Bouchard. Both are hoping for a raise. The Forum no longer has room for all the fans who want to see the Canadiens. The management safes aren't big enough to hold all the receipts.

Reporters are respectful of the bosses. The Canadiens' management gives them those little gifts that are so pleasing, that make them behave rather kindly. When you're well brought up you show your gratitude. It's better to be polite than to be expelled from the organization. Sportswriters are no different from their colleagues who cover Duplessis's politics.

Do the Canadiens want to get rid of the Rocket and Butch Bouchard? No. At the heart of the matter is money. The Canadiens are a business. Like any other company they want to make the greatest profits possible. What they manufacture is hockey. Their

production costs must be kept as low as possible. To increase reve-
nue they pay their workers the lowest salary they can get away
with. Just like other companies. To the fans, Maurice is a champion;
to the bosses, he's one of their workers. The Rocket should go on
strike! Guffaws. A strike! There are no strikes in sports! Hockey
isn't work.

The Rocket is the very heart of the team, of that the fans are
certain. He himself doesn't wonder whether he's the heart or the
legs or the arms: he wants to play hockey. And that game consists of
putting the puck in the net. Management is treating him as if it
weren't satisfied with his services. His biceps, his wrists, his legs
are restless. He deserves a salary increase but he feels as if he's begging. The bosses refuse. "We're experiencing certain budgetary difficulties." Finally, just minutes before the first game, he signs his
contract. There are some who murmur that he's accepted a modest
salary cut.

He throws himself fiercely into the first confrontation. Elmer
Lach, recovered now, is back in the game. Toe Blake scored the first
goal of the season with assists by Lach and Richard, but the Canadiens are losing momentum. At mid-game, they seem tired. By the
third period the players seem to have aged. The Rangers go home
with a 2–1 victory. A bad omen, say the fans.

Bill Durnan is a different man. At the goal, he's like someone
who doesn't feel like going to the factory. His knee is so painful. An
operation during the summer hasn't fixed it. The pain dims his concentration. He has lost flexibility. His knee can't bend without pain.
As he crouches down to make his chest, his knees and his folded
arms into a kind of funnel to capture the puck, only he knows how
much pain he is enduring. Every ligament in his knee seems to him
like a thorn stuck into his flesh. He wants to cry out like an animal.
But he's a man and he faces up to the puck.

The fans analyze this defeat and others that follow. The Canadiens are weakened. Manager Frank Selke has sold Buddy O'Connor and Frank Eddolls to the Rangers. Everyone remembers
O'Connor's goals against the Maple Leafs at the twenty-second

mark of the first period during the finals. It was the kind of goal the Rocket is famous for. As for defenceman Frank Eddolls, a fighter pilot, he has nerves of steel. He's the kind of man they need. Why did Mr. Selke get rid of these two players? To enrich the shareholders?

Even the Rocket doesn't seem to have the same fervour. He got an assist in the season opener, but for several weeks now he's been left high and dry at the net. Has the Rocket already reached the peak of his career? Once again, he's nursing his knee. In mid-November, the dislocation keeps him out of the game for two weeks. But it doesn't explain how the best hockey player of all time has become ordinary. A diamond never turns into a stone. What's going on? He no longer skates the way the Rocket used to skate. He has lost his appetite for plundering his opponent. His stick no longer performs the conjuring tricks that used to delight the crowds. At the net, he is no longer a relentless streak of lightning about to strike. The opponents have loosened their surveillance systems.

There are injuries that are physical and there are others. Beneath his apparent humility, the Rocket has the pride of French Canadians who pass through ordeals in silence, as if they haven't been injured. If Maurice's muzzled pride contains the power of a hurricane, it is as sensitive as a candle flame. Has the Rocket been thrown off base by management's contempt during his contract negotiations?

The Rocket is not a man to make the fans pay for the horse traders' stinginess. Behind his silence, Maurice doubts every move he makes. He no longer recognizes himself. He feels that he's become another player wearing his uniform, another player who's doing his best to play like the Rocket but can't make it. The harder he tries, the more mediocre a player he becomes. He ruminates over his failures. Is he thinking too much? That's what friends tell him. In the past he scored goals first and thought afterwards. Now, he thinks. He thinks and he doesn't score. In the past, his body fol-lowed his instinct. Now his instinct follows three paces behind his astonished body. The Rocket is thinking too much. He doesn't sleep. He doesn't talk. At home, Lucille sees him only behind a wall of silence. He keeps all his anxiety inside. He's a man: he tends his own feelings. He keeps all his discomfort behind his silence, which is closed as tightly as a safe.

He hates himself when he's impatient with Lucille. He loves his wife as much as he loves hockey. When she sees him deep in thought she loves him like a mother. She dares to shake him up a little. To ask him questions. His replies are impatient. He can't hold them back. Maurice and Lucille quarrel. He's sorry about bringing his hockey problems home. She reassures him. Her understanding irritates him. What can she do? Can she go on the ice and score goals? He's even impatient with his children. He hates himself then. It's not their fault if goalies are no longer afraid of him.

At night he watches himself play on the ice of his imagination. He watches himself try this tactic, make that move—he watches himself fail . . . Especially that. He can't get to sleep. Or else he wakes up early, as if he were already an old man who can't sleep. He thinks too much. That, he knows. When he used to pour pucks into the net like peas into a saucepan, he didn't think all that much; his instincts knew what to do. Everything was clear. His muscles knew how to tense and then let loose a devastating shot. Now the Rocket thinks too much.

When Maurice Richard isn't scoring goals, something seems wrong with the world. The forward march of French Canadians slows down. Maurice Richard isn't scoring and it seems that this province no longer has a future. Clouds are gathering on the horizon. The Rocket's face is sunken. His eyes are set deep under eyebrows scratched with scars. His black pupils are vibrant but you can make out the fever in his gaze. Beneath his eyes are dark stains left by insomnia. Has the angel of doom come back to make the Rocket's puck veer away from its orbit?

The Canadiens have tumbled to last place. How has a championship team become bad in the space of a few months? the impatient fans wonder. If Clarence Campbell hadn't treated Maurice Richard so unfairly, the Canadiens would have won the Stanley Cup. The fans talk, talk . . . But what are genuine champions doing in bottom place?

The wood the Rocket is made of is as hard as the maples in Matapédia, his father's birthplace in the Gaspé, but the Rocket has been injured by the arrogance of the Canadiens' management. His bosses have shaken the barbaric fervour of the young French Canadian who is working himself to the bone to remain the best hockey player of all time.

Some of his teammates are tired of his mediocre performance. What's keeping him from doing his job? No one dares to ask. They fear him . . . And respect him. In a team's locker room, though, no one likes problems. Dick Irvin knows that. The Rocket is the heart of the team. A heart that's no longer beating blithely. He has to find a way to revive that heart. After analyzing the risks of his intended action, the coach has decided to blame the champion. Goaded, the Rocket will be furious. Perhaps in his anger he'll get his inspiration back. Dick Irvin chooses and carefully weighs every one of his words: this season, he tells reporters, the Rocket is resting after the exhausting action of the past few years.

Dick Irvin was right on the mark: in the wake of his remarks, the Rocket fights, he sweats blood; his skates burn the ice, he sweeps the rink like a storm. He passes through walls. The crowds are stirred by the intensity of his efforts, but they have to hold back their cries. The Rocket doesn't score. Maurice isn't offering them bouquets of goals. The fans debate. Instead of blaming the Rocket, maybe Dick Irvin should have looked at himself. The best violin in the world is nothing in the hands of an inept artist. It was wrong of the coach to accuse Maurice.

The Rocket exhausts himself on the job. For naught. Irvin's ruse has failed. Next, it's the turn of manager Frank Selke to swing into action: he fires four players. The others remain indifferent. The team is heading for the reefs, behaving as if they're determined to ruin themselves. It's impossible to change their route; this team seems more attracted to defeat than to victory.

On November 6, the Canadiens meet their esteemed rivals, the Toronto Maple Leafs. Resuming a combat that they didn't have time to finish earlier, Vic Lynn and Ken Reardon box till they're exhausted. Then they stop. To the complete dissatisfaction of the crowd. The combatants are sent to jail. The peace won't last long. The Rocket and Wild Bill Ezinicki aren't going to avoid one another. The Leafs' right wing sends Maurice crashing into the dungeon gate; the hinges are wrenched off under the shock. There is cruelty, stupidity, racism in this fine game of hockey.

In mid-November, the Bruins besiege the Canadiens' strong man. Nine pucks enter Durnan's net. The fans demand that he go. He agrees. He feels washed up as a player. One week later, the Rangers' Cal Gardner rushes fast and aggressive up to his net. Durnan assumes the waiting position. Gardner is about to fire his shot, but he attacks too fast and doesn't have time to take aim or to stop. He crashes into the goalie, who is knocked out by Gardner's shoulder pad. With blood streaming down his face, Durnan is taken to the infirmary. He's replaced by a young unknown named Gerry McNeil.

Bad luck. Some time later, Murph Chamberlain breaks a leg. He can't help screaming. The doctor applies bandages, a cast. Ken Reardon shows up with a saw and pretends to cut through it as if it were a log. The Canadiens are washed up but the sailors still haven't given up hope.

Another piece of bad luck. The Rocket injures his knee—again. And once again he stays behind at home, as his mother says, mulling over his dark thoughts. He's afraid of missing the net. Why is he so afraid? He's so afraid that his movements are hesitant, his shots are losing their acuity. Wanting too much is as bad as not wanting enough. Before, he used to play; now he's working. He will start playing again. The way he did during the good years.

His knee: now he can bend it without too much pain. He's anxious to be back in the game. He'll have fun with the puck. He's anxious to climb back into his skates, to hear the ice crunch beneath his feet, the puck slap against the blade of his stick. Dick Irvin will regret his accusation!

The Rocket is back on the ice, determined to obey only his instincts. Unfortunately, he hasn't been patient enough. He's still bothered by pain. He tries to play as if he weren't feeling a thing. At the beginning of December, he has scored only two goals. On December 4, at the Forum, he scores. His puck hasn't encountered the back of the net since October 27. It's been a long time since Maurice has heard the crowd with one vast voice cry out its joy: joy that is total, short-lived, visceral, essential. The voice of the crowd transforms him into a hero. He absorbs within himself the powerful breathing of his fans. He is its power. When God created Adam, He breathed into the clay, infusing him with a soul. In the same way, through the breath of the crowd Maurice Richard becomes the Rocket again.

His knee, however, hasn't mended. His injury has been aggravated by the two games he played. The pain is so acute that he can't bear it. "Reardon, have you got your saw to cut off my leg?" The doctor sends him home to rest for three weeks. Stay home in an easy chair with his leg stretched out on a straight chair and quietly listen to the Canadiens' games on the radio? He feels like he's in prison. Lucille can hear growls of impatience. She understands. Her man doesn't belong in an easy chair. His nightmare takes hold of him again: he can't find the path to the goal. The Canadiens lose. The Rocket remembers that period not so long ago when he was the top scorer of all time.

The fans talk endlessly. Last year the Canadiens were the best team. This season, they won't make the playoffs. What's happened? Buddy O'Connor, traded to the Rangers, has become the League's top scorer. The Canadiens could use him but, thanks to Frank Selke, O'Connor is now scoring goals for the Rangers. The fans are deserting the Forum. They'll come back when they can see winning games! Why watch the Canadiens being massacred? Despite the little gifts from Canadiens management, reporters allow themselves to think at their typewriters. Frank Selke detects a whiff of revolution. And Dick Irvin's nerves are strained to the breaking point. Then comes Christmas. After another defeat, a journalist shows up in the locker room dressed as Santa Claus. The jolly man with the long white beard laughs his coarse laugh in this funeral parlour. Dick Irvin kicks Santa out as if he's found the person who bears the responsibility for all his bad luck. That night, the reporters don't have to rack their brains to find the subject for their articles.

Even if he isn't scoring goals, the Rocket is still his opponents' favourite target. They're afraid of the moment when the champion will waken. The Rocket is hazardous material; he has to be properly wrapped up. He's still the player who has to be badgered. From the biggest to the smallest, from the best to the worst, each opponent tries his luck against the Rocket. They try to send him off base, to crush him, to shake him . . . But the opposing player who rubs up against the Rocket can feel beneath his uniform a body as hard as rock. The Rocket is patient. Guilty of not scoring, he doesn't want to harm his team further by taking penalties for paying back blows to anyone who attacks him.

One stroke of bad luck brings on another. On January 10, 1948, Bill Juzda overwhelms Toe Blake with a check. Blake's right skate gets stuck in a crack in the ice; his body is thrown forward, his leg is twisted, the ankle cracks, broken. It's just a fracture. Toe Blake, a lordly gentleman who's above any disaster, predicts that he'll be back for the playoffs. The fans like his confident disposition, but with all the bad luck that's been raining down on them, will the Canadiens make it to the semifinals? If only the Rocket . . . Who knows? There is such a thing as the strength of despair. The good luck of the unlucky. Perhaps they'll see the Stanley Cup shining at the end of the tunnel. If only the Rocket . . . Oh, he's not asleep. Watch him fidget! The greatest hockey player of all time has lost his way like Tom Thumb in the forest and he can't find the path to the net.

Toe Blake won't come back. A pensive Maurice covers himself in the protective shell of a tough athlete. He's overwhelmed. A beautiful story is over. Toe Blake won't play hockey again. Accidents happen to those who play this game. As a teenager, the Rocket used to hear about Toe Blake's exploits on the radio. As an amateur, Maurice was inspired by Toe Blake. Then he was admitted to the Canadiens, to Toe Blake's team. And became his partner on the Punch Line. Now the great player's career has been broken. The

Rocket has no desire to forgive Juzda. He'll make him sorry he grappled with Toe Blake. The Rocket is enraged as if he were the one who was injured. Toe Blake can't skate any more? The Rocket will give him his legs. Toe Blake can't shoot at the goalies any more? The Rocket will lend him his arms. Toe Blake's career is over; the Rocket will continue his work. In return, perhaps the spirit of Toe Blake will restore his own lost power.

In Boston on January 18, Maurice flogs Milt Schmidt. The deed does not escape referee Bill Chadwick, who points to the penalty box. The Rocket isn't convinced that he deserves this penalty. The blow was rough, yes, but hockey isn't a game for softies. The blow wasn't against the rules. Yet here he is on his way to the dungeon, as obedient as the young lad who doesn't want to go to school. If he weren't Maurice Richard, the French Canadian, the man who scored fifty goals in fifty games, he wouldn't have been punished. No sooner has he taken his place in the penalty box than he decides that he shouldn't be there. He jumps onto the ice to talk it over with the referee. He has some good arguments, he thinks. In keeping with custom, a player must not argue with a referee. Knowing what arguments the Rocket will use to plead his case, Murph Chamberlain tries to hold him back: this is no time to commit some costly error of judgment. The Rocket argues as if Chamberlain were an opponent. He breaks free and heads for the referee as if he were going towards the net. Chadwick sees a furious bull charging towards him. He moves back, at the same time signalling that he's giving the Rocket a game misconduct that will take him out for the rest of the match. What's more, he calls for police reinforcement to escort the top goal scorer in history to the locker room. On top of that, Clarence Campbell imposes a seventy-five-dollar fine.

Fans comment on these events. Clarence Campbell is an educated man. He studied law in England. Too much education isn't always a good thing. Instead of constantly punishing the Rocket the referee ought to open his eyes; then he'd realize that the Rocket is regularly being hounded, attacked, baited, provoked. There are those who suggest that Campbell and Irvin are cut from the same cloth. For them, French Canadians are hewers of wood and drawers of water in time of peace, cannon fodder in time of war. Neither Campbell nor Irvin can speak French. Dick Irvin has his prejudices: players with names like Rousseau, Pépin and Dubé stay on the bench while English-speaking blockheads are sent into action. And the Canadiens lose . . . One fan grumbles louder than all the others: if Dick Irvin stays on as coach he'll set fire to the Forum! The Canadiens don't blame their coach. Irvin has taken them to five victories in the past and he'll lead the team to new conquests. They have confidence in him. How can they tell him? They show up on the ice wearing big red firemen's helmets. If there's a fire at the Forum, the firemen are ready!

The Punch Line is unrecognizable. Toe Blake isn't there. The Rocket isn't producing. In the past, the coach would order a goal and the Punch Line would drop the puck into the net like a letter into a mailbox. Since the season began, the Punch Line no longer responds to emergency calls.

While Canadiens fans are worrying about the team's predicament, Mackenzie King watches, dumbfounded, as his plan for a national flag sinks into bombast, cultural, regional and ethnic divisions, and historic prejudices. The premier of the province of Quebec has gone on preaching provincial autonomy. What political force a symbol like a provincial flag could generate! King has failed. Duplessis will succeed. Without a hint that something unusual is about to happen, early one afternoon he takes the floor in the Legislative Assembly, as he does every day. In the ordinary tone of an unimportant speech, he reports that the cabinet has unanimously approved the adoption of a flag for the province of Quebec. And he announces that even as he is speaking, an employee is on the roof of the building, unfurling the fleur-de-lys flag in the breeze rising off the St. Lawrence River. "Duplessis shoots, he scores!" Opponents and fans are stunned. Opposition leader Adélard Godbout can't resist an exultant "Now we're going to feel more at home."

At the end of February, Bill Durnan is once again booed by the fans. Another defeat, 5–2, by the Red Wings. He can't put up with this blame any more. He didn't come into this world to receive the contempt of the crowd. He's playing despite the unbearable pain in his knee. He has never blinked before a puck that could blow up in his face. In the locker room, surrounded by his uncomfortable teammates, he bursts out sobbing. He really does want to give up hockey.

Dick Irvin tries to console him. This is no time to desert ship. Irvin can see some hopeful signs. When things are going better they'll soon forget these minor tensions. The Canadiens can still win the Stanley Cup if every man agrees to do his part. Bill Durnan must not leave. They have no one to replace him. Dick Irvin needs his goaltender. Despite his fatigue and despondency, how could he desert? In the next game he prepares himself to fend off the hard flash of rubber. And the Rocket has started scoring goals again.

However, bad luck does not desert the Canadiens. Towards the end of a game with the Red Wings, the Canadiens are going to win. Faceoff in the Canadiens' zone. The puck swerves towards defenceman Roger Léger. He makes a rush to the red line. The defenceman, playing like a forward, will cross the red line to the blue line, which doesn't seem to be very well defended; he'll cross it, move in on the goalie, shoot . . . Terrible Ted Lindsay comes along, heavy as a tank, and, as he is throwing the mass of his body onto Léger, elbows him in the face. The defenceman starts jumping up and down. His dance makes the fans burst out laughing. Léger coughs, spits. Writhing, he strikes his stomach. The players approach him. What's going on? The puck is there, in front of his skates. He chokes, slaps his head, contorts himself. Turning his back on the puck, he rushes to his team's bench, gesturing desperately. Incomprehensibly. Finally, someone figures it out. In his collision with Lindsay, Léger has swallowed his dental plate. A volunteer rushes to remove the cumbersome object from his throat. The referee hasn't stopped the play. The Red Wings realize that they're getting a chance that can only have come from God. They seize the puck where Léger left it and attack Durnan, who is now alone and absolutely vulnerable. The score is tied.

The Rocket's knee is mended. His magical power has been restored. He's not worried any more. He plays. His shot on goal is devastating. The fans are jubilant. Things are looking up in the province of Quebec. The Rocket knocks down the best goaltenders. The defencemen look clumsy when they move towards him, heavy, with massive shoulders and moves like loggers. The Rocket passes through like the wind. The Canadiens will make the semifinals. They have to win. The Rocket is scoring goals. The Stanley Cup is within their reach.

Early in March, the Rangers break down. In seven consecutive games they can't win a single victory. Their rout favours the Canadiens. The gate to the playoffs opens a crack. The Rocket is like fireworks on ice. Unfortunately, in spite of all their efforts and their combative spirit, the Flying Frenchmen are no faster than turtles. The Rocket is still hopeful. Defeat devours them like a wicked dragon; the Rocket goes out, attacks, head down, fearless, reckless, with the unshakable certainty that he can win his battle.

At the end of the season the Canadiens will be eliminated like genuine losers. There's one more game, the final one, against the Rangers. But it won't have any consequences. Win or lose, the Canadiens won't be in the playoffs. The Rocket makes an all-out effort as if the Stanley Cup were nearly within reach. Despite the difficulties, he's still the Rocket. The Rocket is a fire that burns to the last twig of his energy. He's playing for Toe Blake who can no longer play. He's playing to restore their pride to the fans. He's playing because a French Canadian is experiencing calamities and continuing on his way, wounded but with his head high, fearless and strong. The Rocket is giving generously of himself because there is ice beneath his skates, because there's a puck to conquer and because at the other end of the rink stands the opponents' net. This game is important only to him. Because it's a game. In the first period he scores a goal. At the final-minute mark of the second period, the New York coach pulls his goalie. The Rocket shoots into the open net. In the third period, the Rocket scores another goal. Hat trick!

But it's pointless. The Canadiens have been eliminated. The fans, though, are celebrating! The incredulous have seen that the

Canadiens are the strongest. With Maurice Richard's hat trick the Canadiens are the true victors. The Rocket is not abandoning his people. Thank you, Maurice! A hat trick is a genuine feat but the fans want another goal. For the joy of it. For the art. To avenge the angel of doom. Their cries make the Rocket feel strong; he ravages the defence. Goal number four! A triumph! A pointless triumph. French Canadians, so hungry to be loved, have an incredible capacity for love.

Contrary to the famous fable, the tortoises don't make it to the finish line before the hares. Once again, gloom settles over the province of Quebec. The playoffs are going on elsewhere, far away. After an unproductive first half of the season, the Rocket has racked up twenty-eight goals and twenty-five assists during the second half.

All is not well in the province of Quebec. Everywhere, the atmosphere is pervaded with uneasiness. With discomfort. People sense that they can't win this game. Production is slowing. Workers are being let go. Rumour has it that some plants might even shut down. The workers' unions are concerned: what has happened to that fine economic strength of recent years? There are some who fear a backlash of unemployment. People have mortgaged their houses. And there are some new diseases. Apparently miners have died from breathing harmful dust. Silicosis. There's talk about entire villages that have been poisoned by asbestos dust. The unions are perturbed. The bosses deny that there's any danger. They, of course, don't have to breathe the dust in their offices. Why should they worry? It's the workers who are sick. It's not hard to replace a worker. It's not hard to replace a French Canadian. The bosses' health is good. They rake in profits while the hewers of wood, the cannon fodder, ruin their health. That's what people are saying as they wait for hockey to come back.

CAN HOCKEY REMAIN THE SAME WHEN THE LANDSCAPE IS CHANGING?

1948. In July, the province of Quebec comes alive for the festivities of an election campaign. Maurice Duplessis promises to save our province from being drowned by the federal government. Autonomy is our last hope. And what is autonomy? He explains to the people that if they don't have it, they lack something important. So they vote for autonomy. And Duplessis sweeps back into power with eighty-two of the ninety-two seats.

With its sunny days and the scent of autonomy in the air, summer erases the icy memories of winter. People forget about the problems the Rocket has experienced. The more the days move them away from the defeats suffered by the Canadiens, the less important they are. And the Rocket appears just as he is: the best hockey player of all time. For us children, the Rocket with his stick resembles the Genghis Khan of our comic strips on the vast Mongolian plains. In terrifying cavalcades, the Rocket conquers enemy rinks, brandishing his stick like a sabre, and he shoots the puck with the precision of an archer. Tactics, endurance, recklessness . . .

Because of the modesty in which his inordinate will is wrapped, because of the timidity which hides his irrational bravery, French Canadians identify with Maurice Richard. When he steps onto the ice, a new chapter in our lives is beginning. We follow every one of his moves with religious devotion. We don't have many heroes to admire. Our society hasn't produced any scientists, great artists or authors. Hockey has been the National Grand Theatre of Quebec. A few big businessmen? They're considered to have gone over to the side of the conquerors. As for the politicians, they are powerless. Poverty has created an egalitarian people. Poverty and ignorance are a soil in which talent has not thrived.

This year, however, crowds are rushing to the theatre to see a play by Gratien Gélinas entitled *Tit-Coq*. They identify with the poor orphan who has failed at everything. Tit-Coq has signed up because the war was the only job he was offered, as was the case for thousands of French Canadians. He signed up because he was desperate. In the army, in England where he was shipped, like many French Canadians, he was uncomfortable under the orders of the English. The discipline was unbearable to him, as it is to French Canadians when they're required to obey. Lucky because he didn't lose his life, he comes home only to discover that while he was away his fiancée has married someone else.

The newspapers celebrate the birth of a national theatre. Universities declare that Gélinas has understood the French-Canadian soul. The people are touched. Tit-Coq, the impetuous little bastard, makes them laugh and cry. Tit-Coq's awkwardness is familiar to us. French Canadians are one big family. Everyone is a cousin. We know ourselves too well to admire ourselves. Yet Maurice Richard stirs ripples beneath the consciousness of French Canadians. "Nothing changes in the land of Quebec," we read in *Maria Chapdelaine*, a 1914 novel that's known to everyone who has gone to school. The quotation is no longer true. The province of Quebec has entered a new season.

Immigration is a constant topic of discussion. Between 1946 and 1950, Canada took in a total of 430,489 immigrants. Of them, a mere 5,573 were of French origin. The federal government, it seems, is still following the advice of the Durham Report: it wants to "block the progress of the French element," a nationalist historian insists.

In a tiny bookstore on St. Catherine Street near St. Lawrence Boulevard, dividing line between the anglophone and francophone communities, there are stacks to the ceiling of books forbidden by the Catholic church or by Duplessis's police. It's a den of iniquity where readers come to sin delightedly as they taste some forbidden literary fruits. On the evening of August 9, a few dozen artists and intellectuals come together to launch a mimeographed pamphlet entitled *Refus Global*. This manifesto, signed by seventeen artists, painters, dancers and poets tackles the conservatism of their society, which has remained French and Catholic as a way to resist the conquerors, out of an instinct for survival, out of nostalgia. Today, the authors of the manifesto maintain that "the frontiers of our dreams are no longer the same."

Like the Rocket, they want to overthrow the defencemen who are blocking the way to their freedom: "The shame of hopeless bondage gives way to pride!" The manifesto delivers a blasphemy against our quaint, caricatural Catholic church which controls consciences, education, history, politics: "To hell with holy water and the tuque!" The young artists promise to obey their dream: "Joyously, we shall pursue our brutal need for liberation."

Attacked by this modest document, conservative circles react like executioners. Those signatories who have jobs are fired. Those who do not won't find any. They are denounced in the press. Ridiculed.

Maurice Richard doesn't read the *Refus Global*. He barely reads the contract that will bind him to the Canadiens for another year.

Maurice Richard starts training camp. He practises his shot. Obsessively, he starts over and over. Though he can hit the precise spot in the net that he's selected with his eyes shut, he is training like a rookie who wants to stand out on the team. He's the fastest skater in the NHL, but he spends long moments circling the ice, pushing his legs ever harder, ever faster, demanding that every one of his muscles make a maximum effort. He experiments with ways of applying the brakes. He takes abrupt detours, without slowing down, as if he were following a straight line. With the Punch Line he repeats the repertory of passes, invents others to make the magic appear. The season is longer now, with seventy games instead of sixty.

The Red Wings come along with a new formation made up of Sid Abel, a tough left winger named Ted Lindsay, and Gordie Howe: the Production Line. Seven years younger than the Rocket, Howe is, like him, a proud fighter. He clears away anything that blocks the path he has chosen. Like Richard, he imposes respect. If opponents are afraid of his bodychecks, he thinks, he gains more space around him, more freedom to manoeuvre. Like the Rocket, he has an explosive nature. Like the Rocket, Gordie Howe grew up poor. Both have struggled to survive. Both have also gone for days at a time without taking off their skates. Both have played flashy games on the frozen surface of the street. Both have worked at developing their muscles. Maurice pedalled his bicycle; Howe, to strengthen his shoulders, let himself hang from the lintel of the door. And both wear number nine. Is it a sign of admiration on the part of Howe? Or a subtle provocation?

The Canadiens present an impregnable defence with Doug Harvey, who joined the team the year before, the rugged Butch Bouchard and the fierce Ken Reardon. Bill Durnan, whose knee is healed now, also seems to be cured of his anguish. At training camp he defends his net the way he did when he was the best goalie in the NHL.

Last year the Canadiens suffered the indignity of not making the playoffs. This season they're going to fight for their lives. They take blows. And repay them like compound interest loans! Resentment accumulates. The atmosphere is one of explosive rivalry when Montreal and Toronto meet. Just a little friction and unbridled power is unleashed. The Rocket pulls out all the stops. In game after game he brushes aside the doubts that gnaw at him as soon as play is over and that last till the next game begins. Only action can drive away anxiety.

The Canadiens are host to the Black Hawks. Fans are wild: will the Rocket score his two-hundredth goal tonight? They want that goal. The Rocket's two-hundredth goal has to be recorded at the Forum. Tonight! They're waiting for that gift, clamouring for it.

The party has already begun. When the Rocket goes up to the enemy blue line, the cries drive him the way a gust of wind drives a sail. The Rocket zigzags through Chicago's defence. The fans are on their feet. This is an exploit they don't want to miss. The eyes of fourteen thousand people are on the puck. The magician will make it disappear. The Rocket goes up to the net. The Forum crowd of fourteen thousand, everyone in the province of Quebec, have their feet in the Rocket's skates, their shoulders in his pads, they're holding his stick, they're the best hockey player in the world. He shoots. Hocus pocus! No. We go back to our seats. He shoots again. This time, the puck will go in the net! We're on our feet. No. We sit down again. The Rocket is going to score his two-hundredth goal. He's driven by an epic inspiration. He bombards the goalie. He has already given his fans a bouquet of three goals. Those who aren't at the Forum, people of all ages, old men and children, even some women, are gathered around a radio where the static crackles like hot fat on the stove. Kenny Mosdell passes him the puck and the Rocket fools the Black Hawks' goalie. A huge howl from a victorious tribe explodes: the Rocket's two-hundredth goal. Fans who know hockey as well as a rabbi knows the Talmud make an observation: to get to his two-hundredth goal, Nels Stewart played 340 games; the Rocket has played only 308. Fans congratulate one another. We've scored our two-hundredth goal! It should be a good week.

This Monday, January 17, 1949, people open their newspapers, listen to the radio. The Catholic lay teachers are on strike. Teachers on strike! It's immoral. Will the priests go on strike too? People thought that teachers had too much education to come down to the level of workers. And now they dare to go around with placards instead of teaching children how to be good French-Canadian Catholics. The population is shocked. The archbishop, recalling the duties of educators, pleads with Duplessis to bring discipline back to the schools. The strikers, parents declare, are endangering our children's future. The wily Duplessis waits till everyone has had time to express his dissatisfaction. Now the saviour can appear and declare the strike illegal.

From grade school to university, the Catholic church has a monopoly on education. Lay teachers are junior employees. Positions of responsibility belong by divine right to individuals in religious uniforms. This strike by lay teachers has shaken the earth. A few cracks appear in the fortified castle of the church. There is revolt beneath the ice of the province of Quebec.

By mid-season competition is tight. Just eleven points separate the first team from the last. Every encounter is a desperate attempt to get ahead. No backward steps allowed. We have to win. The players are making tremendous efforts. Every faceoff is a collision. Every second is burned up by the will to win. Instinctively these young males are fighting to establish their supremacy. Professional hatreds, sometimes personal ones, fester. Bruises. Pain. The smallest step backwards is fatal. The slightest advantage is precious. The Maple Leafs, who won the Cup in 1947 and 1948, are in a slump. How humiliating for champions! The Leafs are in fifth place. Will they be able to pull themselves up to the semifinals? Conn Smythe has learned the art of war. He must invigorate his troops. He must increase his firepower. What player could strengthen his offensive?

Conn Smythe goes on a Rocket hunt. His chances of success are fairly good. The Rocket isn't very happy with the salary granted him by Frank Selke. Even if Smythe fails, he'll have disturbed the harmony of the Canadiens. In fact, he's stirring up the lukewarm ashes so the Leafs' fire will be reborn. And the press and the radio are taking an interest in his Leafs. What an inspired horse trader!

Two years earlier, Conn Smythe offered Lucille a gift if she could persuade the Rocket to move to his team. This time, he delegates his coach, Hap Day, to come to an agreement. Money, Smythe makes clear, shouldn't be an obstacle. Hap Day knows that the Rocket isn't easy to manage. He knows that the Rocket has been wounded by the parsimony of Canadiens management. He also knows that, once again, Maurice's goal-scoring machine has broken down. In Day's opinion, the Rocket needs a change of scene: he should leave Montreal. Toronto is the best possible destination. He's hated there because of the damage he's done to the Leafs, but hatred will turn to adoration as soon as the Rocket—a Leafs forward—demolishes the Canadiens!

Will the Rocket leave Montreal for Toronto? There are suspicions that Maurice and Frank Selke aren't the closest of friends. Hockey bosses, like factory bosses, aren't in the habit of paying a French Canadian what he's worth. The Rocket will endure. He wants to play for his own people. He won't betray our race. But in kitchens, in barbershops, in bowling alleys, people are concerned. Some think that management will trade him; they have good financial reasons to do so.

Frank Selke analyzes Conn Smythe's offer. Never in history has so huge a sum been offered for a hockey player. The offer seems serious. Is it? Could it be a ploy by Smythe to infect the Canadiens' esprit de corps? Is he just trying to get some free publicity for his team? Frank Selke is wary. The financial proposal is interesting. Maybe he could get a little more; no one has beaten Maurice's record of fifty goals in fifty games. Would his fans accept the Rocket's exile? Between the Rocket and French Canadians there are the same ties as between a maple tree and the soil. Does someone want to move the tree? They'll have to move the soil as well. If the Rocket leaves the Canadiens to join the Maple Leafs, fans will demolish the Forum. And Selke and Irvin will be hanged on the ruins.

The Globe and Mail runs a rigged photo on the front page, showing the Rocket in a Maple Leafs sweater. According to the caption it's a good fit.

What does the Rocket think? He feels tired. The fans want him to be perfect. They hope for a feat of arms the moment he brushes against the puck. As soon as his skate touches the ice, fans welcome him as if he were the miracle-working Brother André. And if there's no miracle? Then the fans reproach him. And their disappointment is noisy. It's not easy to have Canadiens fans as masters. On the other hand, though, their dictatorship is exhilarating. Maurice is fuelled by their terrible demands. When the Rocket dashes down the ice, French Canadians see a legendary warrior who is recreating the battle of the Plains of Abraham and reconquering lost territory.

Could their soldier switch sides? And could he come back like a traitor to play against the Canadiens, and his people?

Maurice talks it over with Lucille. They agree that what the Rocket needs to do is to play hockey. After Montreal, Toronto is the best city to play in. Give Torontonians good hockey and the crowd applauds like crowds at the Forum. Of course the Leafs' fans boo him but he still commands respect. And sometimes the crowd applauds him, too. What does the Rocket really think?

It would be tough to play against the Canadiens. He would hate to hear his fans booing him because of the Leafs uniform. He should not leave just because he is not happy with his contract. Selke has tight pockets? But sometimes he gives him good advice, like a father. Finally Selke and Irvin decide that the Rocket is more important than the money offered by Conn Smythe.

On February 3, the Maple Leafs are assured of an advantage over the Canadiens, who have allowed a weaker team to surpass them. The Punch Line tries to fill the gap. The Rocket does his utmost, as if he were alone. Yet he's not alone. The defence is secure, mobile at the blue line. His teammates are ubiquitous. The puck passes from player to player; when it gets away from them they rush at it, tireless. With the surges and retreats, the attacks and the flights, with the impulsive back-and-forth movements and collisions, the spectators, like the players, are out of breath. The Maple Leafs don't let their advantage get away from them. Wherever there's a radio in the province of Quebec, there is also a circle of silence punctuated with worried faces: how is this going to end? A few years earlier, people gathered in silence like this to listen to the war news.

Hockey is a tapestry that is constantly being woven and then picked apart. You can only make out the movements of the shuttle. The tapestry is finished off with a final knot in the opponents' net. The Canadiens apply themselves to the task. No one hates the Leafs' momentary superiority more than the Rocket. He multiplies himself, he toils like an ox that has sprouted wings. Wild Bill Ezinicki sticks to him, as usual. Canadiens fans criticize him: *"Sangsue!"* Or sometimes in English: "Bloodsucker!" Ezinicki curbs the Rocket's movements, blocks his breakaways. How long will the Rocket keep his anger in check? The two players collide. An intentional collision. A vicious collision. Two sticks sizzle. With both hands, Ezinicki and Richard joust. The sticks break. Disarmed, they fight with their bare hands. Maurice, who knows some wrestling holds, shackles Ezinicki's neck with his arm. A stranglehold. Ezinicki can't breathe. His arms stop waving about. His body goes limp. Suffocated. He drops to his knees. Richard doesn't let go. Someone intervenes to separate them. Richard doesn't give in. He's going to kill Ezinicki! Break the hold! The referee sends them away to do penance. The Rocket follows Ezinicki. They're within an arm's length of one another. At the end of each arm is a fist. A boxing match. The blows hit home. Each man absorbs them like a punching bag. A punching bag doesn't bleed, though. Now the blows are landing like bricks. Ezinicki and the Rocket are facing one another for the national boxing championship. The crowd has forgotten that it's at a hockey game. They egg on the boxers. They celebrate the blows that devastate. Boo the Toronto boxer. Cheer the French-Canadian boxer—pride of the race, the nation's pride. A maniacal hand-to-hand combat. Finally, Ezinicki crashes to the ice. The Rocket triumphs! Now Toronto knows what Montrealers are made of.

Ezinicki struggles to his feet. He's dazed. His legs are wobbly. Butch Bouchard appears, bends over, hoists the limp body onto his shoulder and, in front of the stunned Toronto team, drops it over the boards. The fans are jubilant. Their triumph, unfortunately, is not complete. The Leafs win the game, 4–1. By outsmarting Turk Broda, the Rocket has spared his team the humiliation of a shutout.

On February 9, the Canadiens and the Maple Leafs are back in Toronto. Several of them, limping, aren't up to facing the hostilities. Dick Irvin asks the Rocket to play despite an injury to his ribs. His troops have been devastated. The Leafs become aware of the situation. They'll take as much advantage of it as they can. The Canadiens, less numerous, will tire more quickly. Their defence is weakened; their morale can only be weakened as well. They must doubt their ability to win. Confident and implacable, the Leafs roll over the Canadiens like the big rollers that tamp down the gravel on the roads Duplessis is building in the countryside. The Maple Leafs take the lead, 2–0. They don't ease their attack. Pitiless, they want to dismantle the Canadiens, break up their tactics, shatter their hope of making the playoffs.

Despite the pain from his injury whenever he contracts a muscle, the Rocket doesn't abandon ship when the enemy boards it. Courageous, he defends himself bravely and breathes vigour into the Punch Line. The mission seems impossible; that's when the Rocket is at his best. His teammates let him have the puck. The Maple Leafs circle him. Twice, the Rocket eludes them. Twice, receiving passes from Murph Chamberlain and Kenny Mosdell, he breaks away. General alarm! The opposing team bars his way. Twice, he goes up to the goalie, who twice sees a flash of lightning. The Rocket has avoided a shutout. He has given his team a tie. But for Maurice, not to win is a defeat.

———

All sorts of new things are being invented. Even new diseases. The air in factories contains deadly dust. Workers are being poisoned. The priests were right when they denounced the cities. They preached that towns and cities are the damnation of the French Canadians. On the farms, the good Lord's air doesn't make people sick. In factories, though, French Canadians are being poisoned with deadly dust and Communist ideas. In the very centre of a small town no one's ever heard of—Asbestos—there's a mine shaped like the crater of a volcano. The town breathes in the poisoned dust that rises from this mine. People die young. The doctors call their sickness asbestosis. The Johns-Manville Company that exploits these mines is interested in nothing but profits. Duplessis does nothing. He doesn't want industries fleeing to Ontario. He tolerates this waste of human lives. But the traditional servility no longer exists. Cannon fodder? No. Company slaves? No. Workers are men. Mankind is a species that stands erect. No one wants to surrender his life to a company for a handful of dollars.

The workers and their union leaders are hockey enthusiasts. They talk, they discuss this check, that pass, successful or failed, this rush at the net, that shot. On one point they agree: the Rocket doesn't let anyone intimidate him, not bigger players, not stronger ones. He doesn't waste his time thinking before he defends himself. He returns blow for blow and a little more. He stands erect and makes no apologies for it. He knows what he wants. And what he wants, he takes. If he wants a goal, he scores it. "The time of the docile French Canadian is over. Look at Maurice Richard!"

In Asbestos, the workers are demanding a salary increase, a bonus for night work, and two-week paid annual vacations. Given the hard times of families whose fathers are sick or have died because of asbestosis, they ask the company to establish a fund for social assistance. The company, of course, considers these demands excessive. On February 13, the Asbestos workers declare a strike.

I am twelve years old. My parents have sent me to a small seminary as a boarder. Our history teacher tells us how fine life was in Canada before the arrival of the English in 1759. Suddenly he closes his book and his voice changes. "Do you know what's going on in Asbestos? That strike is a revolution," he assures us. Is it like the French Revolution? All I know about it is that they cut off heads which they stuck on the ends of pikes for their parades. A revolution? Our teacher explains that this strike is inspired by Communist agitators in the pay of Moscow who are sabotaging the religion of the French Canadians. Fortunately, Duplessis won't let the Communists act as if they were in Moscow. He orders the workers back to work immediately. We clench our little fists; we're ready to fight the Communists. Instead of obediently going back to the mine, the strikers march with drums, cars with blaring horns and placards covered with slogans. Duplessis delegates a hundred policemen to protect company property that's under threat from Communist saboteurs and the strikers they've perverted. We try to understand. The story of Julius Caesar in Gaul seems less complicated.

Taking their time along the road to Asbestos, the policemen arrive late. They know the bars along the road. They drink; you don't get a chance to beat up Communists every day! It's something to celebrate. The road is bumpy. The journey is rather long. They get thirsty; they stop; they drink some more. Eventually they arrive in Asbestos, slightly the worse for wear and determined to restore order and make the rebels in this village grovel at their feet.

The following day, in a unanimous vote, the town councillors deplore the bad behaviour of these officers of law and order. Witnesses have seen them commit violent and even indecent acts.

Duplessis blames the union leaders, claiming that they're damaging the town's industry. The strike drags on. Families with many children are desperately poor. They used to scrape along from one payday to the next. They piled up debts. Now there's no more pay. Their fate moves others to pity. In the churches, collections are taken up for these unfortunate families.

The company for its part isn't too upset about the strike. Thanks to the scabs they hire, production continues. To slow it down, strikers blow up a railway track with dynamite. The company reacts. To respect its production agreements, it takes on more strikebreakers. Every morning they enter the mine under police protection, between rows of starving, angry strikers. Most of them live in accommodation rented from Johns-Manville; now the company orders the strikers to clear out.

Our history teachers tells us that these deplorable events resemble a great novel from France, *Germinal*, which is set in the mines and was written during the nineteenth century. It's a novel that we aren't allowed to read because it is banned by our Holy Mother the church.

Despite the revolution, the priests in our small seminary don't deny themselves the pleasure of listening to the Canadiens' games in their common room, around the radio, smoking as they leaf through *Le Devoir* or *L'Action Catholique*. The following day, when we file in for 6:30 Mass, the youngest priests whisper the result of the match to us. We pass on the information.

"We beat Boston. Maurice Richard scored the winning goal."

"We're going to win the Stanley Cup!"

"Silence in the ranks!"

The hockey season has been difficult. All the teams were affected. The top scorer is the Red Wings' Sid Abel, with twenty-eight goals. That total is far from the Rocket's fifty-goal record. The Canadiens are in third place. Last year they didn't make the playoffs. In the semifinals they face the Red Wings.

The Red Wings' goalie is Émile "The Cat" Francis, with his glove that looks like a first baseman's glove. The Production Line has sworn that it will demote the Punch Line.

But isn't it already weakened? Toe Blake, its backbone, is no longer there. This year it's done nothing spectacular. Without Toe Blake, the chemical composition of the line is less explosive. The Production Line takes advantage of its vacillation. Both sides want to intimidate. In this jungle where the referee looks like a lost missionary, only bloodthirsty beasts survive.

In the first game, Elmer Lach is struck in the face with a stick. He wipes up the blood. He can't move his jaws. The doctor's verdict: fractured. Did Black Jack Stewart want to break up the Punch Line? Speaking to reporters, Dick Irvin offers an indisputable argument: "Lach didn't have the puck between his teeth but Stewart hit him on the jaw." At the end of a tight match, there is no score. The teams have to get through three periods of overtime. Finally, Bill Durnan doesn't move quickly enough to stop a shot by Max McNab. It's a victory for the Red Wings, who continue to wreak havoc.

The Canadiens are shaken but they don't surrender. In another game, Gordie Howe delivers a blow to the Rocket that knocks him out. The Rocket isn't fully unconscious when he hears Sid Abel ask, "How'd you like that, Frenchie?" The question reinvigorates him. He gets up. Without a word he responds to Sid Abel. The blow is powerful. Abel's nose is broken.

"Give 'em hell, Maurice!"

Elmer Lach, deciding that he's been hit often enough, announces his imminent retirement. Murph Chamberlain, who was recently left unconscious after a bodycheck, confesses, "That ice is starting to feel pretty hard." The injured list is growing: Butch Bouchard, Normand Dussault, Ken Reardon, the Rocket. The Red Wings swoop down like a conquering horde. Despite his injuries, the Rocket does his utmost to win every second, every time his skates hit the ice, every bodycheck, every pass. Inspired by his confidence, the Canadiens don't back down. Don't they have the best defence-men in the NHL—Butch Bouchard, Ken Reardon, Doug Harvey? Isn't their net defended by the ambidextrous Bill Durnan? The Canadiens resist. After seven matches, though, the Production Line has imposed its law.

A deep sadness spreads over the province of Quebec. We've lost. This does not bode well . . .

With the Canadiens eliminated, the race for the Stanley Cup is no longer interesting. The confrontation between the workers and the Johns-Manville Company is worsening. The dust of Asbestos is falling on the entire province, according to two young journalists who've shown up in sports cars and intellectuals' sandals to investi-gate the miners' situation. Their accounts produce another wave of sympathy for the strikers. One of the journalists, the one who looks a little pretentious, is called Pierre Elliott Trudeau.

The president of Johns-Manville runs a warning in the news-papers: if the Asbestos strike doesn't end, several other factories will close; one hundred thousand employees will be out of work and nearly half a million men, women and children will be affected. This threat is employer's blackmail: "A little more misery or a little less . . ." The misery spreads and tightens its grip. Newspaper photos of the people in Asbestos remind readers of certain photos from the war a few years ago.

In our seminary, the debates are impassioned. Do the workers have the right to stay out on strike when their children are starving? Who owns the mine, the bosses who collect the profits or the workers who do the work? Why is the company stronger than the premier elected by the people and the archbishop named by the pope? Our adolescent minds wear themselves out trying to understand a world that's more complex than a hockey game, where the solutions never come as quickly as a goal by Maurice Richard.

From all over, trucks filled with food and clothing head for Asbestos. The strikers picket outside their factory. Mercenaries have replaced them at their machines. Once again, on May 5, 1949, the strikers block the access roads. When the scabs turn up, insults are traded, the strikers get their backs up. People have run out of patience. And tolerance. Tempers rise. There are confrontations. Blows intended to injure. Soon there will be killing. The strikers are struggling to eat. The fighting is vicious. The injured bleed. Bodies are stretched out on the ground. Automobiles are on fire. Duplessis orders the police to make peace. They show up, pointing revolvers and machine guns. Grenades hang from their belts. A fire hose knocks down some strikers. Tear gas rains down. Women join the melee, reciting their Hail Marys from the rosary. There are a dozen unknown men, plump, wearing clean suits. They talk rather loudly. The strikers don't like these strangers. They rough them up the way scabs deserve to be roughed up. They are policemen. Duplessis wants order. The riot act is read.

The following day, three hundred zealous, powerful policemen arrest the 125 miners they've rounded up, shoved with their rifle butts, with night sticks, beaten with their fists. These policemen are violent like the police in poor countries. Terrorized, the population of Asbestos calms down, but the strikers continue the struggle.

Two months later, on July 1, during our summer holidays, the strike ends. The strikers have lost. The Rocket hasn't won the Stanley Cup. There will be other strikes. There'll be another hockey season . . .

THE HOCKEY HALL OF FAME

Maurice Richard

This is the first NHL photograph of le Rocket. Doesn't he look small and frail? He seems to be impressed by the photograph. Who would have predicted a glowing future for the young man in this photograph? Dick Irvin, his coach/instructor, was convinced that he had never met a youngster with such a desire to excel.

THE HOCKEY HALL OF FAME

The Rocket and Toe
Blake in the locker room.
Before a game the
Rocket did not like to
talk. These two friends
did not need many words
to understand each other.
Blake was Maurice
Richard's hero when
he was an adolescent
amateur player. Later,
Richard and Blake played
together on the "Punch
Line" for the Canadiens.
Finally, Toe Blake became
the Rocket's coach.

The Rocket, and his wife,
Lucille, met when they
were adolescents. She
never missed a game he
played in Montreal. When
he was playing out of
town, she would wait for
him at the train station.
Had he lost, he would not
speak a word during the
trip home. Sometimes,
when an injury was too
painful, he would cry. One
day, someone will write
Lucille's story.

CP PICTURE ARCHIVES

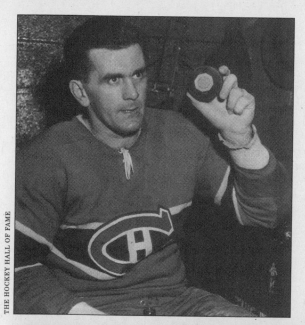

THE HOCKEY HALL OF FAME

The Rocket exhibits the 324th puck that he had just catapulted into the net. He matched the record set by Nelson Stuart fifteen years previously. He should be celebrating, but watch his eyes— he is looking towards the next summit to climb.

TIMEPIX

Maurice Jr., "le Petit Rocket," works hard to score against the Great Rocket, now a dad and goaltender. Playing as well as Maurice was our dream. Playing against him was something we could never even dream of doing.

When he felt he was
being treated unfairly or
unjustly, the Rocket
could become furious.
Boarded illegally by his
foe Bob Bailey, Maurice
responded with the fist
of an aggressive boxer.
The linesman Georges
Hayes intervened to
calm him down, but the
Rocket, feeling that he
was also being assaulted
by Hayes, slashed him.

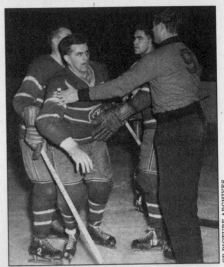

CP PICTURE ARCHIVES

CP PICTURE ARCHIVES

The Rocket has been suspended by Clarence Campbell, the president of the NHL. The consequence: no Rocket, no Stanley Cup. That's what one of the placards says. Ten thousand people gathered around the Forum to protest the suspension. If the Rocket made a mistake, he should be forgiven; Campbell should act as a good Christian. The police force could not calm the demonstrators who ravaged the neighbourhood.

It's not the first time that the Rocket's fans see him taken out of the skating rink because of an injury. This time, in 1957, when they learn that his Achilles tendon has been cut by a sharp skate blade, many believe he will not come back onto the ice. It's not the way the Rocket wants to exit. His leg will heal.

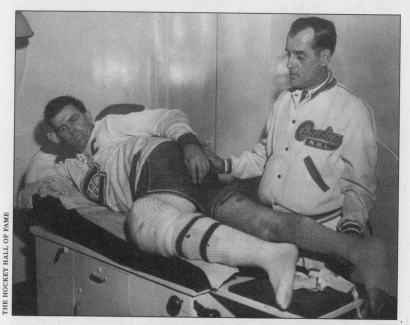

THE HOCKEY HALL OF FAME

To stop the Rocket was to stop the Canadiens. On each opposing team, some tough player was given that responsibility. Here, in the second game of the Stanley Cup finals against the Boston Bruins, on April 12, 1958, it takes two players to slow down the Rocket: Jerry Toppazzini and Leo Boivin.

CP PICTURE ARCHIVES

THE HOCKEY HALL OF FAME

When he joins the Canadiens, Henri Richard, fifteen years younger than Maurice, knows the Rocket less as a brother than as a famous hockey player. Soon he is a shining star in his own right. At the end of his career, Maurice was very disappointed when the Richard Line, made up of Maurice, Henri and Claude, a younger brother, was dismantled after only one game. There were high expectations for the three Richards (the Rocket, the Pocket and the Vest Pocket Rocket) playing together.

THE HOCKEY HALL OF FAME

1959. The Rocket knows that he is close to retirement. In this game against the Maple Leafs, two tough defencemen are waiting for him: Tim Horton (number seven) and Allan Stanley (number twenty-six). These two solid walls did not give the attacker a lot of room to manoeuver. Not visible on the photograph, another adversary the Rocket has to fight against—time. But the Rocket goes to the goal!

At one time when the injured Rocket could not play, he was invited to visit Prague, Czechoslovakia, where the World Amateur Hockey Championships were being held. It was during the Cold War. For many people in America, going to a Communist country was going to hell. Maurice went. He was greeted as a hero. He gave some hockey workshops, and he came back with a white Skodo sports car.

BETTMAN/CORBIS

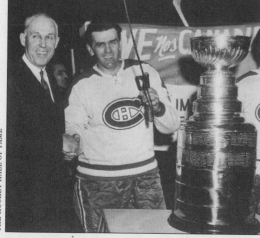

THE HOCKEY HALL OF FAME

The Rocket between his two obsessions: Clarence Campbell, the NHL president (the boss, who, Maurice feels, is unable to give fair and just treatment to a French-Canadian champion) and the Stanley Cup, the Holy Grail, the cup that avenges all the injustices.

BETTMAN/CORBIS

Here is the Rocket heading for the net, lightning fast. We practised to look like him, pushing the opponent away with the
power of our eyes. Years later, when visiting the Molson Centre
where this great picture hangs, I was told that the Rocket had
posed for this photograph. I was very disappointed.

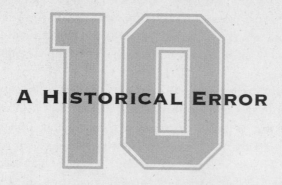

A HISTORICAL ERROR

And so the Maple Leafs won the Stanley Cup three years in a row. Before my eyes I have the dates, the statistics, the photographs. I shouldn't question the superiority that's been demonstrated. Yet still today I have trouble bowing to this verdict by history: three times in a row Toronto won the Stanley Cup and Montreal didn't.

At the end of the 1940s I was ten years old and, like my friends, I believed that the Canadiens could never lose to Toronto. When we talked about the last game with Toronto, it always seemed to us that the Canadiens had won it. Like my friends, I believed that when the Rocket came onto the ice the Leafs were flattened. When we talked about hockey on the way to school, the Rocket had always scored the winning goal. The Leafs had never learned how to score. That was how life was imprinted on our childish minds. Maurice Richard, our hero, triumphed over all adversaries, especially the Maple Leafs.

We walked along the snow-covered street in our village, making our way towards the world, towards life, confident. We had learned from our hero how to vanquish obstacles. Like the Rocket, we were going to score goals.

When I became an adult, through work, writing, travel and the disarray of life, I often went back to the land of childhood to recapture certain attitudes that it's good to have when life becomes hard to grasp. With its fine and tranquil assurance, my memory would tell me that the Canadiens grouped around Maurice Richard were an unassailable fortress. The Maple Leafs couldn't even get close.

I wrote a story called *The Hockey Sweater*. In it there's a sentence that echoes the memory of that fine certainty: "The Toronto team was always being beaten by the triumphant Canadiens." It was neither a charming irony, as some people said, nor an athletic tease. It was an absolute conviction. I was remembering indisputable facts. When I wrote with such great pleasure those words that I am rereading today, I was a man trained to the caution that grand declarations demand. Writing those words I never at any moment experienced a hint of doubt. I didn't even think of checking the facts. A certainty is a certainty.

I believed that for fifty years. Hundreds of times, when I read *The Hockey Sweater* to children of all ages and all generations, I repeated that declaration. And never did anyone rectify my historical error.

Today, after writing about those three consecutive Stanley Cup victories by the Maple Leafs at a time when I believed our Canadiens to be invincible, I accept the facts, even though it hurts. Do you think that it's easy to turn over a new leaf? I feel like someone who, at the threshold of old age, turns his back on a faith he has practised fervently and adopts a pagan religion.

Such was the power of the Rocket: he captivated our childhood. We invented that Rocket, our dauntless and irreproachable hero. That's what all the peoples of the earth do when they feel small in the face of a world that's too big. When the ancient Greeks created the gods of Olympus, they needed them. Gods are the wind that blows in sails as they unfurl.

For isn't truth our memory of facts? And aren't facts the memory we have of them? Aristotle dared to declare that legends are truer than history.

During the summer, Maurice con-
tinues to play hockey. The sun that beats down on Montreal beats
more gently on the shores of Lac l'Achigan. Maurice is smiling
when a family photo is taken in front of the modest chalet where
they spend several weeks. He's smiling because you're supposed to
smile for a photo with the two children and the wife you love. His
eyes are looking somewhere else. The Rocket can't tear himself
away from the hockey rink of his imagination. He replays the games
of the past season. He recalls every one of his moves. And of the
opponents'. He replays them the way he played, the way he should
have played. He hasn't been able to climb to the summit of fifty
goals. He hasn't even got close.

Despite his failure, the fans' affection has continued to grow.
His magnetism fascinates them. His eyes are two black bullets that
are silently shot at his opponents. His hair is disciplined steel wire.
His face, an angular meteorite. Under his Canadiens uniform his
breath is like the fire in a locomotive's belly. Even sitting motionless
on the players' bench, he attracts more attention than a lot of players who are out on the ice sweating blood.

At the end of the 1940s, for French Canadians torn between
submissiveness to the past and the temptations of the future, the
Rocket is a dream that's coming true when so many others have
been smothered. A few years earlier, for instance, a young pianist
was delighting music lovers. At barely nine years of age, André
Mathieu was presenting his compositions in the Salle Gaveau, the
concert mecca of Paris. "At his age, Mozart had created nothing
comparable with what this extraordinary little boy performed for us
with stunning brio," one critic exclaimed. In 1943, this Canadian
Mozart performed at Carnegie Hall in New York.

Then André Mathieu is nearly twenty. He's only heard in sad
pianothons or in bars. Like André Mathieu with music, Maurice is
obsessed with hockey. He gives to it all the strength in his body. He

obeys it. Fans admire Maurice because he is ruled by his genius. In order to obey his genius, he has the strength of an ox. A strength that perhaps the Canadian Mozart didn't have.

Elmer Lach had announced that he was retiring. During the summer he changed his mind. He's coming back to the game. That's good news. Maurice likes having this capable partner playing at his side. The Black Hawks are starting the new season at the Forum. The gate opens. The Rocket leaps onto the ice; he's a starving tiger showing his claws. The fans are quivering. As soon as his skates touch the ice, sparks fly! Tonight, on the offensive, the Canadiens are irresistible. Their defence is faultless. Bill Durnan is invincible. The Rocket scores two goals. The season is looking good.

In game after game, the Rocket scores goals. Will he finally beat his own record? The more enthusiastic the fans are, the more they feel entitled to demand even more. The failed-poet-turned-sportswriter has too much inspiration and not enough words to celebrate properly the Rocket, who is "dynamite," "a thunderbolt," "a star," "the god of a new religion." The Rocket makes children dream, he amazes crowds, he gives wings to the failed-poet-turned-sportswriter. But people aren't talking only about hockey. The Montreal police have just made a spectacular arrest. A young bearded artist, probably a Communist, named Robert Roussil, has exhibited a wooden sculpture with rather abstract forms, called *The Family*. *The Family* seems to be dressed like our ancestors, Adam and Eve. Emergency! Public danger! Like films, books, calendars, songs, unions and Communists, *The Family* will contribute to the devaluation of traditional French-Canadian virtues. Police! Protect us! A commando of six policemen seizes the statue, which gives in without any resistance.

In Chicago on November 2, a spectator grabs Ken Reardon by the sweater as he's brushing against the boards. Reardon turns around, hammers him with his stick. Another spectator jumps onto the ice to avenge his friend. Racing like firemen on their way to a blaze, Léo Gravelle and Billy Reay come running. Threats turn into blows. The blows into a brawl. The brawl into frenzy. From the stands, spectators push their way onto the ice. The referees, power-less against this tidal wave, call for the police. The Rocket fights like a valiant knight. This time he's lucky: no penalty.

Send the Rocket to the penalty box: the other teams dedicate themselves to this task. For the Red Wings, Terrible Ted Lindsay enjoys the responsibility of being the Rocket's shadow enemy. He needles him relentlessly. He pushes the Rocket to despair. He wants to see him pull the pin out of the grenade of his anger. Lindsay knows the risks of an explosion. What a pleasure it is to watch the Rocket glide, with a sour look, towards the penalty box! In November, badgered by Lindsay, the Rocket explodes. His twirling stick could slice open necks. His fists stun. The referee is ruthless: a five-minute major penalty.

The hands of the clock aren't moving. The Red Wings score twice. Helpless, Maurice rages at himself. Two goals. Never have five minutes passed so slowly. The Canadiens are wearing themselves out. If he weren't out of commission, his teammates wouldn't have to work so hard. He should be helping them, not cooling his heels on this bench. If he'd been on the ice the Wings wouldn't have scored those two goals. He is responsible for those two goals. If the Canadiens lose, it will be his fault. The minutes aren't passing. Will he be able to restrain himself from jumping over the boards? He can't let the Canadiens lose. Time has stopped. Head down, revolted, he's turning in circles within himself.

After five interminable minutes, the tiger roars. The crowd shudders. Maurice emerges from his cage. Famished! He swipes the puck. Fury. Without flinching he absorbs bodychecks, shoulders, elbows, sticks on his body and his legs, he rushes towards the goalie, hypnotizing him with his gaze. The puck doesn't stop till it's inside the net. And there it is! The harm that his penalty caused the team is half put right.

A few seconds later, he receives a pass from Elmer Lach. With a backhand, Maurice sends the puck into a crack that wasn't blocked by the goalie. Goal number two! The Rocket has erased the damage done to his team. Dick Irvin decides that after such an effort, he's entitled to a little rest. For Maurice, it's not enough to correct his error. He has to win. "I've just had a five-minute rest." No one is going to take him off the ice till the Red Wings cave in.

The faceoff. Elmer Lach makes the puck swerve towards the right winger. The Rocket keeps it on his stick. Already his feet have started the race towards the net. Terrible Ted Lindsay is waiting for him, planted on his path. Here comes the Rocket; he doesn't try to avoid Lindsay; crashing into him head-on, he pushes him out of the way. With one hand he handles his stick and the puck. His other hand pushes opponents out of the way. And as he continues his race towards the net, he fires a missile. "Maurice Richard shoots—he scores!" It's the Rocket's third goal! Victory for the Canadiens.

November again. The Forum. The Canadiens against the Maple Leafs. The game is nearly over: forty-nine seconds are left. The Canadiens have the advantage. Victory is assured. In a corner of the ice, the Rocket is battling for possession of the puck. He wouldn't be more impassioned if he were trying to save his team from defeat: he needs that puck. Sticks fly. Skates too. Elbows. Jolts. Rebuffs. The Rocket defends himself as if they were trying to tear his heart out. Gus Mortson won't let the Rocket stroll in his zone as if it were a strawberry field. He charges. At his back. The Rocket crashes into the boards. Propped on his skates, Mortson keeps him pinned there like a butterfly. Butch Bouchard rushes to his rescue. A right to Mortson. Who returns the compliment. One by one, players appear. Punches are exchanged. Everyone joins in the dance. And it becomes an out-and-out brawl. At one and the same moment, hockey is offering a movement as inspired as the brush stroke of a great painter and as brutal as the bite of a carnivorous beast.

The Rocket has absorbed Mortson's shock. He holds back his impulse. He mustn't get a penalty. He controls himself. Glances at the clock. A few seconds remain. Short. Long. Then, at last, the siren! The game is over. Where's Mortson? The Rocket wants to put the final touches to the settlement of their battle. It mustn't be delayed. When things calm down, Maurice is jubilant. He has relieved himself with a few punches to Mortson. With no penalty.

Conn Smythe has to distract the newspapers and radio from the Leafs' setbacks. If his team isn't winning, he declares, it's because they're too fat. In the first period, they're already at the end of their tether. Turk Broda is too fat. It's not enough to block the net with the mass of his body; he has to be able to move. Smythe orders his players to go on a diet.

The Rocket takes pains to avoid penalties. When playing the Rangers, he puts up with the brutality of Tony Leswick. The pressure in the boiler is going up. He holds it back. He remembers his collision with Mortson. The siren announces the end of the game. There's no referee now, no penalties. The Rocket lets fly at Leswick like a tornado. The crowd is leaving the stands, anxious to avoid a traffic jam. But the action isn't over! The Rocket is putting on a boxing exhibition! The fans stream back to their seats. On his knees in front of the Rocket, Leswick begs for mercy. The Rangers appear and surround them. With fists and sticks, the Canadiens force their way through the Rangers and set free the French Canadian who fears no one. When it's over, the players go back to the locker room, the fans to their buses.

Everywhere in the province of Quebec, even in those regions where Duplessis hasn't installed electricity yet and radios run on batteries or on electricity produced by windmills, the people get to their feet along with the fans at the Forum when fighting breaks out. No one complains about the violence of the game. That's hockey. For the priests in our seminary who preach love thy neighbour on Sunday, it's a real treat when the Rocket sends his fist into the face of another Christian. That violence isn't shameful; it's noble.

By mid-November, Maurice is credited with eleven goals. A few days before Christmas, after twenty-seven games he's rung up twenty-two—one-third of all the goals scored by his team. He's insatiable. He wants to surpass his own record of fifty goals in fifty games. Connoisseurs maintain that the teams are stronger now than when he set his historic record. Yes, scoring goals is harder. Defence systems have improved. But the Canadiens have also improved. And he himself has become a better hockey player. With obsessive perseverance, with irreversible determination, he repeats the same movements, makes the same efforts, demanding that his muscles accomplish them always faster and more precisely. He's anxious, slogging away as if he weren't scoring.

And the opponents don't let up. In Toronto on December 14, thirty-seven seconds before the end of the first period, Bill Juzda collides with Maurice, who goes flying, his skate slashing the Herculite glass panel that protects the spectators. The unbreakable glass explodes into fragments, the Rocket falls to his knees, and five fans report to the infirmary for cuts to the face, hand and knee.

To inaugurate the year 1950, the second half of the century, Prime Minister Louis St. Laurent organizes a federal-provincial conference. He hopes to obtain the agreement of the provinces to the principle of amending the Constitution here, in Canada, instead of needing London's approval. It would be a step towards the year 2000.

I am thirteen years old. At the seminary, we listen to our teachers. This question of the Constitution is very confusing, but we guess that the federal government is trying to find some trick to slash away at the rights of French Canadians. Duplessis will defend us. As usual, the provinces squabble. One demands a right to veto, the other a new definition of an absolute majority. Suddenly, on the political rink, Duplessis grabs hold of the puck: he asks for nothing less than financial autonomy for the province of Quebec. "Without the power to levy its own taxes, the province of Quebec is like a Rolls-Royce without an engine or gas." Duplessis shoots—he scores!

It's not by chance that Duplessis used the metaphor of an automobile. That's a subject that touches voters. In the province of Quebec there are only half as many cars as in the rest of Canada. The desire to own one is powerful—complete with engine and fuel. Duplessis lets fly words that blast into our consciousness like one of the Rocket's cannonballs into the net. Duplessis admires the Rocket and envies his popularity a little. He goes to see him play as often as he can. He's given him several invitations, written personal notes to congratulate him on some success.

The priests in the seminary allow us now to read *Le Devoir*, the newspaper that defends our people. I'm educating myself. Pax Plante, a former assistant director of the Montreal Police, is denouncing debauchery in the city: four-hundred-odd houses where gambling, betting and prostitution flourish. What are they? I can guess that they are distractions that aren't kosher. Pax Plante accuses the police of being as corrupt as the people who run those branch plants of hell. And in a French-Canadian Catholic province . . . Corruption is creeping through the city streets, declares Pax Plante. How does Duplessis react? He replies: "Let's not look for perfection. Perfection came to earth two thousand years ago and it hasn't been seen since." Duplessis needs the income for his war chest.

The people still respect honesty. That's why they get to their feet when the Rocket, without cheating, quite straightforwardly, like an honest worker, without handing out bribes to the referees, without scheming, without double-dealing, knocks over obstacles and places the puck in the net. Every move, every stroke of his skate is the impulse of raw honesty. Give 'em hell, Maurice!

━━━

On January 28, the Rocket scores his 235th goal. He saves the puck. It's the number of goals scored by his old companion Toe Blake, the hero of his youth. But he doesn't waste time on nostalgia. He must surpass his hero. What matters is to shoot the puck to a place where the goalie's arm or his pad can't stop it. The Rocket doesn't pay much attention to sportswriters' comparisons. He reads what they write but the words hardly matter. Maurice is proud, modestly proud of what he has accomplished, but the next goal is the only thing that matters. Actually, the Rocket should have done better. If he hadn't had those injuries . . . Why so many excuses? The Rocket puts himself back in the game, as voracious as a young player who hasn't yet scored his first goal. To honour his hero, he must surpass him.

This is a fertile period. He tots up goals with stunning speed. Then, abruptly, it stops. Why? On the one hand, the opponents have declared open season on the Rocket. On the other hand, could Maurice simply be tired? As an ancient Greek writer whom I studied at the seminary noted, a bow that's always taut loses some of its firing power. The Rocket's bow is always stretched taut. He's not a machine for bombarding the goalie, nor is he a god. He is just a French Canadian from the Bordeaux neighbourhood of Montreal. Maurice confides in no one about the doubts that are muddling his thoughts and perhaps his action.

Not so long ago, the puck would obey him. Now it's rebelling. He works relentlessly. Testing his arms. Testing his heart. He starts over again and again. By dint of trying, he's going to succeed. But when he takes off for the enemy zone, the net moves away. The ice slopes. Where do such imaginings come from? The ice is horizontal, the goalie's net firmly in place. In spite of his stubborn persistence, in twenty games he scores only five goals.

At night, as he waits for it to get light, he sees again the match that he's just played, sees how his opponents accosted him, how they kept him from executing a pass. He observes his teammates. He examines himself. His evasive action is successful but his shot doesn't break away quickly enough. He changes the way that he lures and gets around the defence. He feels like turning everything upside down. He doesn't do it. Lucille is so good. The children are so good. He's lucky to have this house. He wants to be good to them the way that his father, Onésime, was good. It's just that he's nervous. His skin feels too tight on his body. Everything irritates him. If he realizes that he's been harsh with the children, he'll be too gentle next time.

Long before the game he shows up in the locker room. What could he do to skate faster? He shoots at the goal. Starts again. Lobs a backhand shot. He aims at the top of the net. Starts over ten times. Without looking, he can hit the point he aims at. He starts over again. Doggedly. How to shoot faster, harder? He skates. He fires. Skates some more. Fires.

The Rocket shoots and doesn't score. After a bad game, Maurice mopes as if it were all over. Yet he's playing with the passion of a winner. He darts around. Oh, he pulls off some good passes but he doesn't put the puck where it's supposed to go. He's in a slump. When the fans are on their feet, mouths open to cry out, hands ready to applaud, the Rocket hates going back to centre ice empty-handed and seeing them, hearing them return to their seats grunting and clearing their throats, disappointed. After an unsuccessful shot he hates to see the expression of his teammates. He has to keep going. Flat out. And the time of high scoring will return. He mustn't wait. He has to make it come. The sportswriters are using words like *lethargy*. Though it annoys him, Maurice blames no one but himself. By dint of repeating the movements that used to produce goals, good results will come. Between the Rocket's successes and his failures, there is a wall to break down, a wall that will be demolished if the Rocket bashes into it with all the determination in his muscles and his soul.

In mid-February the Rocket suddenly comes out of exile, scoring seven goals in seven games. His recovery gives rise to delirious celebrations. At the close of the season, which ends with a 4–0 shutout of the Black Hawks, he's still offering his fans a goal per game. A bittersweet detail: once, the Rocket scores on a pass from Bill Durnan. The happy crowd has never seen a goalie get an assist. Durnan smiles. In fact, he'd rather be somewhere else. Dick Irvin pleaded with him to stay there facing volleys of shots. He's anxious for it to be over. So many projectiles have hit him. He is shaken. He has seen too many pucks flying towards his unprotected face. He's taken too many. Instead of waiting for them he'd rather run away. His courage has eroded. He's afraid. His muscles have tensed themselves so often for a move as precise as a surgeon's, and now they're reacting more slowly. Bill Durnan is tired.

At the end of the 1949–50 season, the Rocket has forty-three goals and twenty-two assists on his record. No one has driven more pucks into the enemy net. He has also earned himself 112 minutes of penalties.

The Red Wings end the season in first place. The Maple Leafs are getting ready to conquer the Stanley Cup for the fourth

consecutive time. On March 28 they're in Detroit. The Production
Line—Abel, Lindsay and Howe—is waiting, backed up by Red Kelly
and Leo Reise protecting goalie Harry Lumley, who is sometimes
replaced by young Terry Sawchuk. The semifinals get off to a very
rough start. With Toronto leading 3–0, Ted Kennedy takes the puck
along the boards and out of his zone. Howe approaches at the speed
of light to flatten him. Kennedy doesn't slow down. Howe arrives.
Kennedy applies the brakes at the last moment. Howe goes past
him and crashes into the boards. He's taken to the infirmary, then
to the hospital. He has a fractured skull, a broken nose. The indig-
nant Wings vow they're going to make life miserable for the Leafs.

The games that follow bear a faint resemblance to the Normandy landing. Injuries mount up. The players spend more time in
the penalty box than on the ice. It's a goaltenders' duel: Turk Broda
racks up three shutouts, Harry Lumley two. During seven games in
which no one is blameless and nothing is forgiven, the players do
battle like the damned who want to enter paradise. In the end,
Toronto backs down.

Meanwhile the Canadiens are squaring up to the Rangers. In
front of the net Durnan is porous. The Rocket is rendered helpless
by the implacable surveillance of Pentti Lund, who won't let go of
him. The province of Quebec has been waiting for a fine war against
Toronto. The Canadiens lose the first battle. Unhappy fans are calling for Durnan to go. They have no pity for the tired athlete who
has given them so many victories. They boo him as energetically as
they once acclaimed him. The Rocket is uncomfortable: he can't
bear the sight of a vanquished man in tears.

Dick Irvin replaces Durnan with the young Gerry McNeil. The
Rangers want to take advantage of his inexperience. McNeil guards
the fortress. An overtime goal by Elmer Lach brings victory. It's a
goal that the Rocket wishes he had scored.

Following Gerry McNeil's victory, Dick Irvin doesn't bring
Durnan back. In the next game, the young goalie shows himself to
be unassailable. Near the end of the third period, it's a scoreless tie.
Suddenly, energized by some magic potion, the Rangers send a vol-

ley of shots at McNeil, who caves in. The final result: 3–0. In the locker room, pensive and frustrated at his own way of playing, the Rocket looks up from the floor. The new goalie and the old one are crying. Toronto has been eliminated, Montreal has been eliminated: the war that people have been hoping for won't be fought.

The Rocket would have liked to win the Stanley Cup to celebrate the birth of a son on May 1, 1950. His mother-in-law notices his wobbly legs and his eyes filled with tears when he holds his son in his arms. Yet on the ice, this man fights on his own against ten. All the children in the province of Quebec know immediately the first name of Maurice Richard's son.

THE HOMER OF
THE PROVINCE OF QUEBEC

1950. Summer holidays begin with
the St. Jean Baptiste procession on June 24, the feast day of French
Canadians. The newspapers are full of photos of the youthful St.
John the Baptist, with his blond, curly hair like a girl's, his chubby
cheeks, one little shoulder bare under the sheepskin he wears as
both shirt and pants. That boy will never have a beard. He's St.
John the Baptist as a child. Apparently he represents the French
Canadians. There's not one of us who looks like that monster, half
little girl, half sheep. Our mother, our grandmother, our friends'
mothers swoon over his photo. If he and his curls ever put in an
appearance at our seminary, he'd get the living daylights beaten out
of him! At the toddler's feet is a lamb—the symbol of our people's
aspirations.

I'm thirteen years old. I hate it that this fake little girl is supposed to represent me. Why should our people idolize a lamb and
not an eagle? Our history teacher explains: the lamb is a very
ancient Christian symbol. In Florence, in Italy, he says, there's a
fresco dating from before 1355 where you can see at the feet of the
pope some Christian lambs that the pope, the emperor, the cardinal
and the priests are protecting from the heretical wolves.

When the Rocket isn't playing hockey, people complain that
there's not much of interest in the newspaper. But there are a

hundred or so people who probably never read the sports pages who are curious to open a modest publication called *Cité Libre*, published by some young people no one's ever heard of. One of them, though, attracted some attention during the Asbestos strike: Pierre Elliott Trudeau. The few readers of *Cité Libre* read with horror or delight a denunciation of the Catholicism that's forcibly imposed on the province of Quebec by an all-powerful church.

The *curé* of our parish, a genuine soldier of God, bellows from his pulpit to persuade farmers and loggers to avoid that unhealthy publication like the plague. When I go back to the seminary in September, I dig out this intriguing magazine that you have to hide to read, like the ones where grown-ups can see naked women.

That summer should be called the summer of the broken windows. The origin of all that havoc was a trip the insurance agent made to Montreal, home of the Forum and the Canadiens. Like everybody else, he probably went to one of those houses where you can rent a girl, but he doesn't brag about it. Then a cousin took him to the Oratoire Saint-Joseph; reciting prayers along the way, he climbed its steps on his knees. After that the cousin showed him the Sun Life Building, the tallest in the city, and finally, the Forum. The cousin knows Montreal so well that he even knows where Maurice Richard lives: "A house like yours and mine." The Rocket ought to live in a castle.

The insurance agent doesn't believe that his cousin is really going to show him the residence of the greatest hockey player in the world. He knows his cousin. He's a show-off. He'll show him some ordinary house.

"This is the Rocket's street."

A street like any other. The car slows down. The insurance agent is afraid the police will think they're thieves. The car barely moves. Stops.

"Here it is, this is Maurice's house."

The insurance agent looks but he's so excited that he can't see anything. His heart is pounding. He will remember this moment when he's on his deathbed.

"There he is," says the cousin. "There's Maurice."

A few metres from the house is a man busy with a hockey stick.

"That can't be Maurice," says the incredulous insurance salesman.

He can't believe that with his own eyes he is seeing the Rocket, disguised as an ordinary man. He'd like to yell something at him but he can't think of what to say.

"Maurice is practising his shot," says the cousin; "he slams the puck against the foundation of his house. That's how he makes his shot more powerful. It's his secret. No goalie is as solid as a foundation!"

The car starts up again and glides slowly past the Rocket's house.

"We mustn't disturb Maurice; he's getting ready to win the next Stanley Cup."

The insurance agent can't help shouting:

"Give 'em hell, Maurice!"

Back in the village he tells every living person what he's seen. Several times. And thus the Rocket's secret is revealed.

"I saw him as plain as I'm seeing you, right there. Seeing Maurice that close is like seeing the apparition of the Blessed Virgin at Fatima! Better, even: the Blessed Virgin never won a game against Toronto! I even saw Maurice practising his shot against his foundation. He does it every day. It's his secret. His house moves back a foot a year."

This story is picked up, repeated, then repeated again. Soon there's a rumour going around that Maurice's house collided with the neighbour's.

We, the children, understand what we have to do to become genuine Maurice Richards. We practise our shots against the house. When our mother runs out of patience and orders us to stop the bombardment, we practise our shots on the neighbours' houses, until their mothers run out of patience.

Aside from the shattered windows, some statues of the Sacred Heart knocked off living-room shelves and a few terrorized babies, our pucks haven't caused nearly as much damage as our parents claim they have.

═══

At the end of September it's the turn of Duplessis to welcome the prime minister of Canada and the premiers of the other provinces to Quebec City. Instead of "patching up" an old constitution, Duplessis suggests drawing up a brand new one. The idea sounds interesting, but the hockey season is about to start.

The Canadiens have lost the fiery Ken Reardon, who is out with a back injury, but they've also been rejuvenated by the arrival of some new players. Bernard "Boom Boom" Geoffrion, who feeds on dynamite, is definitely a future Rocket. A few years ago, Maurice was taking long bicycle rides by way of training. He stopped at a restaurant. A teenage boy, the owner's son, told him, "Monsieur Rocket, you're my hero. I'm going to be like you." It was Geoffrion. After much negotiating, Jean Béliveau has joined the Canadiens. He plays hockey as if it were a game for princes. Doug Harvey has gained experience; he's a defenceman who doesn't mind attacking when the time is right. Dickie Moore is a tough one; at training camp, the young recruit wasn't afraid of defying the Rocket to impress the recruiters. Maurice liked that attitude. And Bert Olmstead: he's quiet, but he's powerful and effective! They're all young people who want to put the puck in the net.

In the opening game, against Boston, Maurice Richard scores his team's two goals. In ten games, he scores nine goals. Is he on his way to another record? The journalists launch a debate: who is the best player in the NHL? Some consider that Gordie Howe surpasses the Rocket. Since he joined the Red Wings at the age of eighteen, in 1946, he has gained weight and sharpened his tactics. He skates with masculine elegance. Ambidextrous, his shooting is unpredictable. His bodychecks are devastating. He doesn't hesitate to cheat a little to hold back an opponent or make him run out of patience. When his team is afflicted with a penalty, Howe has the gift of a boundless imagination for killing time: he moves, he spins, he kneads the puck . . . Will this player, who is seven years younger, catch up with Maurice Richard? For him, Gordie Howe is just another opponent in front of the Red Wings' net.

Faced with an obstacle, the Rocket is like a Catholic saint: he is consumed by a fire that lights up the lives of believers, he is immolated by the fire of hockey. When the Rocket began his reign on the ice, he stood as firmly on the ice as French Canadians do in history. Duplessis yells at the federal government, "Quebec was the first province to be inhabited by the pioneers of Canada. If you think we've been an obstacle to progress, we're ready to pull out. The province of Quebec can get along on its own and fend for itself." Duplessis shoots—he scores!

Our history teacher explains Duplessis's words: we can speak French and practise our religion without submitting to the English Canadians who don't like our language or our religion. We're thirteen years old. In our blue-and-grey uniforms, our lanky bodies stand erect. We shall be worthy of our gallant ancestors!

In January 1951, with goal number 271, the Rocket outstrips the great champions of the past, Howie Morenz and Aurèle Joliat. In few words, he celebrates his success: "There's always somebody ahead of you." One summit conceals another. With exceptional pride, but with sincere modesty, the Rocket sets out to conquer the next peak. Nels Stewart scored a total of 324 goals during his career. Only fifty-three goals separate him from that all-time record. And Gordie Howe? He refuses to talk about that subject. Journalists have to fill their pages . . . The Rocket's page is the ice . . .

At the start of the season, the Rangers inflict defeat after defeat. Now, all at once, these losers have become invincible. No other team can stand up to them. Rumour has it that the coach gives them a magic potion that makes them wince, but since they've been ingesting it they've imposed a dozen victories on their opponents.

Are they really invincible? On January 10, the Rocket hammers them with a hat trick and a 3–0 shutout. Young Gerry McNeil's nervousness is transformed into agility. An overnight train trip to Chicago and the fatigue of the journey don't slow down the Rocket. Against the Black Hawks the next day he scores two goals for the Canadiens' 4–1 victory. Bert Olmstead has replaced Toe Blake at left wing on the Punch Line. The confident Rocket reinvents himself every fraction of a second. He modifies play, both his own team's and the opponents'.

On January 13, he goes to the locker room after the game, eyes blackened, nose slashed, dragging his leg. He has been kneed in the thigh. Muscles snap. The leg refuses to bend. As soon as he puts any weight on it, he's shot through with pain. He doesn't want to miss the next game. Little by little he forces his leg to support his weight. He practises walking without bothering about the pain. And he shows up in the locker room pretending that he's not limping. He wants to go on the ice; when his skates glide along it the pain will vanish.

Faceoff. He starts as if he weren't suffering, even more eager than usual. The pain lacerates his leg. To deaden it he's going to stun himself by playing; action will lull the agony. The injured muscles rebel. His efforts have worsened the torn muscles. After a cautious examination, the doctor sentences him to a four-game rest. The injury doesn't heal as quickly as he'd like. Just over a week later, he shows up at the Canadiens' practice. His leg, which has undergone various ordeals, doesn't obey as it should. With the appropriate protector, he'll be able to plunder the Bruins. Following these few days of forced rest, he's like water that has been held in check when the dam opens. At the end of the first period he has fired three pucks into the opponents' net. A hat trick in less than five minutes! The Canadiens win, 4–1. The Rocket has been stronger than his pain. Going back to the locker room he limps like someone wounded in a war.

When he's on the ice no world exists except hockey. There is no past, no future, there is only this moment when he's racing towards the net. His heart thumps, his breathing is a gasp. This fraction of a second is his entire life. Solid as rock he is on his skates, and light as a butterfly.

1951. When the Rocket dresses for a game, it resembles a religious ceremony. In the seminary, I'm an altar boy and I watch the priest get dressed for Mass—amice, alb, stole, cingulum. I see our monitor become a man of God. He lives now not on earth but in heaven. He has been transformed by the certainty that soon he will perform a miracle. Something identical happens when Maurice Richard dons his leg pads, shoulder pads, elbow pads, skates and sweater. He becomes the Rocket. And then, sitting on the bench and leaning against the wall, he enters into meditation. He lives no longer on earth but on the planet Hockey.

On this February 17, nearly seventeen thousand people are here, quivering with fervour, to honour Maurice Rocket Richard in the way that they honour, with pious processions, the saints of heaven who have poured their favours onto the people. The luminaries have concluded a political truce. Present are Prime Minister Louis St. Laurent, Premier Maurice Duplessis and Montreal mayor Camillien Houde. They who see eye to eye about nothing agree to pay homage to "*un p'tit gars de chez nous*," one of our own little guys, who has become the greatest hockey player of modern times.

"Give 'em hell, Maurice!"

The air in the Forum is fragrant with the ladies' perfume and the gentlemen's cologne. When Maurice comes out, there's a roar that makes the roof shake. No one in Canada has ever received such an ovation. The fans applaud, chant his name. He'll make a brief speech. The management has prepared a statement for him. He doesn't like to talk. He doesn't like speaking in public. Before this crowd, he would rather play hockey. He's not a politician. The fans demand a speech. Not goals. So he'll make one. It's hard. He'll make a serious effort. His paper is in his back pocket. To get it out he has to drop his gloves onto the ice. The crowd guffaws and applauds hard enough to bring the roof down. Usually when he drops his gloves it's to whack somebody! Maurice makes his way to centre ice. The ovation dies down, silence returns. The walls are still vibrating.

He starts to read. Diligently. He's uncomfortable with writing. Speaks hesitantly. The words are too slow for him. He has trouble with anything that doesn't move. The only writing he's comfortable with is the line he traces on the ice on his way to the enemy net. It's to celebrate that writing—brave, fiery, inspired—that the crowd has come here tonight.

That writing makes Maurice Richard the Homer of the province of Quebec. The poems that his skates improvise on the ice express the passions, the hard times, the dreams and the strength of the French-Canadian people. Like the blind poet of ancient times, he gives the people lessons in bravery, in courage. The Rocket creates his adventures with the muscles in his body, with the fire in his soul. His poems on the ice are the only literature that this small people recognizes as its own. It recounts the true story: that of the present moment. Those poems inscribed on the ice will endure as long as if they'd been carved in marble.

The words on paper that he is deciphering don't seem real to him. The Rocket reads them. He folds his paper and stuffs it back in his pocket. Will the Forum building stand up to the ovation? The Rocket is uncomfortable. He doesn't deserve this noisy admiration. He hasn't scored a goal.

The luminaries are watching Maurice Richard. What is it about him that elicits such applause after a speech? Maurice would like to go back to the players' bench. He's embarrassed at being alone at centre ice, skating in circles before the crowd without a puck to pursue. Someone behind him shouts his name:

"Hey, Rocket!"

He turns. It's Gordie Howe. The Rocket doesn't think very highly of this sly adversary. Even in Montreal there are those who maintain that he's a better player than the Rocket. He's a dangerous scorer of goals. The Rocket's not afraid of him but he stays out of his way. The Rocket is bare-handed; he hasn't picked up his gloves from the ice. Gordie Howe skates up to him. The crowd holds its breath. Gordie Howe pulls off a glove . . . and extends his hand. The silence becomes heavier. Will the Rocket shake it? They look at one another. They glide on their skates a little. The Rocket hesitates, then takes the proffered hand. The crowd resumes its interminable hymn. The Rocket is the greatest! Gordie Howe has shaken his hand!

The evening has been awe-inspiring. But on the way home in his car with Lucille, the Rocket isn't happy. He's gruff. Doesn't want to talk about the ceremony. All the important persons delivered speeches in his honour. Camillien Houde announced that "He is an example for young people." The fans have given him an automobile. He couldn't give them a single goal and the Canadiens lost 2–1.

＝＝＝

Saturday, March 3, at the Forum. The fans are already dressed for Sunday. Many have rested during the day. They haven't sweated at work. They've taken a bath, soaped themselves. The women are wearing their finest hats. This crowd knows the meaning of hard work. These people struggle to survive. They work hard, expend a lot of energy on the job: they recognize Maurice as one of their own.

The face of Red Wings goalie Terry Sawchuk bears the marks of the pucks, the sticks, the elbows and the skates that have injured him. Tonight, he repels shots in the manner of a boxer looking down on punches that are too weak. The Rocket wants to tear open this rampart in front of the net. Exasperated, he fires another shot. The puck bounces off Sawchuk's stick. The Rocket reaches out to grab it on the rebound. Red Kelly charges. The Rocket is thrown forward; his face hits the goalpost. Already furious, he brings his hand to his forehead. The viscous warmth of blood. He doesn't let himself lose his temper. The Canadiens mustn't lose their advantage because of a penalty. They simply draw the referee's attention to the cut and the blood. Red Kelly won't be punished. The referee closes his eyes. It's unfair. The Rocket clenches his fists but he keeps himself under control. He mustn't do anything to harm his team. "This is the worst goddamn state of affairs I've ever seen," he says. The referee won't tolerate any comments on his decision. Ten-minute penalty!

Stunned as much by this sentence as by his collision with the goalpost, the Rocket heads for the penalty box which is already occupied by the Wings' Leo Reise, who greets him in his own way. The Rocket responds with a few punches. Exchange of courtesies. The Rocket, as vicious as a trapped animal, threatens to devour Reise and the linesman who steps in between the sparring partners. Referee Hugh McClean restores peace: the Rocket is suspended for the rest of the game.

A roar of disapproval in the Forum. Objects come raining down: overshoes, fruit, programmes, newspapers, coins, handkerchiefs. Why is the Rocket being punished and Red Kelly not? The Canadiens lose the game. The fans are furious. One day somebody's going to pay for the injustices to the *"p'tit gars de chez nous."*

Immediately after this frustrating defeat, the Canadiens board the train for New York. Maurice can't digest his meal, can't even doze off. He has caused the defeat of his team. The drone of the wheels gets on his nerves.

The next day, someone warns him that Hugh McClean is in the lobby of the Piccadilly Hotel. The Rocket rushes at him the way he crosses the enemy blue line, grabs him by the collar and in his finest English begins to express all the shadings of his sentiments. Some journalists are delighted.

The NHL president, Clarence Campbell, gives himself a week to investigate these events and prepare his ruling. During that time, the Rocket plays in three games, scoring four goals and five assists. In the conclusion of his report, Campbell approves of the referee's sentence to the Rocket. The Rocket's behaviour at the Piccadilly has shown a lack of respect. On top of that, his language, in the presence of several ladies, was not appropriate. The whole thing costs him a five-hundred-dollar fine.

Here's what we think in the province of Quebec: Maurice Richard will never be treated fairly by Clarence Campbell. The priests teach us that a good Catholic has to love his neighbour; although if we hate Clarence Campbell, we understand that we aren't obliged to confess it.

On March 21, the lighting at Maple Leaf Gardens in Toronto is much brighter than usual. Television cameras are positioned all around the ice. Is it possible to transmit a hockey game onto a television screen? Will it be possible to watch the screen throughout the entire game? To follow the players? To follow the puck?

During the Christmas holidays I looked at television in the window of the local store. I wasn't very impressed. All I could see was falling snow. Granules that couldn't organize themselves into pictures. Anyway, a television is expensive. Only people who have contracts with the Duplessis government can buy one.

The Red Wings have suffered only thirteen defeats. The Canadiens are far behind them. The two teams meet in the semifinals. On Tuesday, March 28, the first game ends in a 2–2 tie. It's been a trying game. Gerry McNeil had to fend off sixty-four shots on goal. Both teams are exhausted. After one period of overtime the score is still 2–2. The players, who would rather crawl than skate, go into a second overtime period. Though they move heaven and earth, neither the Rocket nor Gordie Howe can find the back of the net. Neither one stands out. Each man seems to be the reflection of the other; each man seems to kindle the strength of the other. Each man struggles to erase the action of the other. Stubbornly, they refuse to feel exhausted. Neither one would be the player he is without the other, who cancels out his moves. The score remains 2–2. There will be a third overtime period.

Muscles are sore; tired lungs don't take in enough air; numb legs have trouble supporting the weight of bodies; arms are heavy, feet weigh too much, skates get stuck. Even the spectators are out of breath. Amid the physical exhaustion from which they carve out the next effort, a certain giddiness settles in. They feel slightly stunned. Every move is flabby. After three overtime periods, the score is still 2–2.

Dick Irvin wants that puck behind Terry Sawchuk. In the locker room, he gives his players his assessment: Butch Bouchard scored the first goal, Bert Olmstead scored the second on a pass from the Rocket. The Rocket hasn't scored a goal yet . . .

Generally, in the households of the province of Quebec, people go to bed early because they have to get up early. This night is special. Father and children are gathered in front of the radio. The voice from Montreal is fairly clear, despite the snatches of English or music that come through. People are exhausted from wanting the Canadiens to win. Children are yawning. No one knows what to do next. They're ready to drop. On the sidelines, the mothers don't understand why it's so important to follow some men who are chasing after a puck. They do their mending but they've been doing it for so long that their eyes sting. What is it about hockey? Usually, the men fall asleep when supper is over.

Old folks reminisce about the longest game in history, between the Montreal Maroons and the Red Wings, which ended on the night of March 24, 1936, at the Forum. Six overtime periods! It wasn't until the sixteen-minute, thirty-second mark of the sixth period that a rookie drove the puck into the net of the Maroons' Lorne Chabot. Some people didn't see the goal because they were snoring in their seats. It was 2:25 A.M.

"Don't talk about that, you'll bring the Canadiens bad luck."

"Lorne Chabot was mad enough to chew nails . . ."

In the Canadiens' locker room, the air is as thick as molasses. The sweat-soaked leather and felt equipment gives off a smell of overworked animals.

"Rocket," says Dick Irvin, "it's your turn!"

It's past midnight when the fourth overtime period begins. Maurice has left his fatigue behind him like a piece of clothing in the locker room. The ice beneath his skates bears him up like the air beneath the wings of a bird of prey. The puck slaps against sticks. The Rocket intercepts it. The net is down there at the end, far away. Propelled like a puck shot by an invisible stick, the Rocket crosses the blue line, slips between the defencemen; it's as if they've gone to phone their mothers. He comes within ten feet of Terry Sawchuk, who stares at him defiantly: you won't score! The Rocket respects Sawchuk. Shooting into his net demands special precautions. Sawchuk is a good goalie; goals scored against him are fine goals.

The Red Wings come running. The Rocket takes his time. His black eyes are focussed on Sawchuk's. The tremendously silent collision of those two black gazes reverberates. Two visceral passions, two unshakable resolves. For the Rocket as for Sawchuk, eternity is this instant. Both were put on Earth for this moment. The one was born to shoot the puck, the other to stop it.

The Rocket's concentration is absolute. His gaze, locked with Sawchuk's, slowly shifts towards a corner of the net that's not blocked by Sawchuk's body. Launched by the relaxation of an arm and wrist, the puck follows his gaze. And vanishes. The Rocket's gaze connects with Sawchuk's. "Did you see that?" The puck becomes visible again at the back of the net: a 3–2 victory for the Canadiens!

Two days later, Maurice Richard, Elmer Lach and Bert Olmstead again encounter Sid Abel, Ted Lindsay and Gordie Howe in Detroit for the second game in the semifinals. The Red Wings should have won in Montreal; luck was on the Rocket's side, they claim, apologetically. They're going to set matters right. Sawchuk promises himself that he'll erect an iron curtain in front of his net. With their victory, the Canadiens now have dominion over the Red Wings. This second game will be fought even more fiercely. The Canadiens have to calm their nerves or they'll be tired already when they get off the train. Mustn't smoke too much. Sleep. None of them must show a single second's weakness. At every moment, they must be superior to the Red Wings. Avoid errors. Each of them knows his own weak point. Don't give in to bad habits. They have to convince their opponents that they can't cross the Canadiens' blue line. They have to convince their opponents that the Canadiens will cross their blue line as often as they decide to do so. Victory will go to the Canadiens again. All that has to show when the Canadiens get off the train.

In the province of Quebec, families are once again gathered in front of the radio. Now and then a hand will reach out and slap the contraption to help it get its voice back. The game begins. The situation is the same as two days ago. After three turbulent periods, the score is 0–0. After one overtime period, it's still 0–0. The players are numb as they go into a second overtime period. The scoreless tie is immutable. The teams are equal. The Production Line is equal to the Punch Line. Gordie Howe is equal to Maurice Richard: Sawchuk is equal to McNeil. It's nearly midnight. No one is asleep. The Earth has stopped turning. Time is frozen. Everyone is waiting for the denouement. Mothers are impatient: once again the children will be sleepy at school tomorrow. Only hockey can keep the men awake. Soon one of the teams has to give in. It won't be the Canadiens. This victory belongs to us. The Rocket is going to drop the puck into their net. If Maurice takes too long, Gordie Howe could hurt us. The good Lord will give a French-Canadian Catholic a helping hand! And we'll win. We waken those who are asleep. The third overtime period is beginning.

Two minutes and a few seconds later, the Canadiens' Billy Reay receives a long pass from a defenceman. Coming up to Sawchuk, he notes a crack; there's room for the puck to get in. It will take precision. Rocking slightly as he prepares to shoot, he sees the Rocket coming. Reay directs his puck towards him. It belongs to him! The thirteen thousand spectators at Detroit's Olympia Stadium and two million people in the province of Quebec are on their feet. The Rocket dodges Red Kelly, who tries to hook him. From the middle of his net, Sawchuk moves to the left. His padded body completely blocks the nearest part of the net. From this angle, the net is inaccessible. But not for the Rocket. A backhand shot. The puck slides across the ice. Terry Sawchuk can't even see it. We've won! The lights go out in the windows. It's been a long day and it was one well worth living.

The next two games are played before fans at the Forum. Alas, these two get away from the Canadiens. Why has the good Lord abandoned us?

At the beginning of the fifth game, the Red Wings are leading. Terrible Ted Lindsay needles the Rocket, mocks him for being French Canadian. He'd love to set off his anger. With the Rocket in the penalty box, the Canadiens would be weakened for a few minutes. One of his darts hits a nerve. Reaction: a straight right.

Lindsay drops like an ox in the slaughterhouse. Satisfied at having silenced this loudmouth, the Rocket awaits his sentence. He doesn't like to fight. It makes his children unhappy. All he wants to do is play hockey. But if he's attacked, he defends himself. The sentence doesn't come. He's amazed. Since he hasn't been driven off the ice, all he has to do is play. When he knocked out Ted Lindsay, did he stun the entire Red Wings team? The Rocket scores twice! The Canadiens win, 5–2.

Sixth game. Neither players nor fans can remember such arduous guerrilla tactics. Are the two teams more or less matched? In the locker room, they've already started to play. They're nervous, tired. Some can't get to sleep. The Rocket has spent long nights with open eyes, waiting till it was time to get up. The matches have been relentless, interminable. Muscles ache, bodies are bruised. If they could still dream, the players would summon up the pleasure of simply sleeping.

Called onto the ice at the Forum, they seem supple and light. The puck is more precious to them than all the gold in the Klondike. They will defend their net as if it were their family house. It's a rapid ballet, but you can sense that at any moment the players could switch from dancing to boxing. At the start of the third period, the score is 0–0. The game is tense. Something will break. At the six-minute mark, Billy Reay scores the Canadiens' first goal by deflecting a shot from Boom Boom Geoffrion. Less than one minute later, Sid Abel counterattacks: 1–1. Next, it's the Rocket's turn: 2–1. Then Kenny Mosdell consolidates the Canadiens' lead: 3–1. The fans start to celebrate the expected victory. Barely forty-five seconds before the end of the game, Gordie Howe receives a pass from Ted Lindsay and Gerry McNeil isn't as fast as his drive: 3–2. The fans stop singing. The Canadiens still have the lead. Only forty-four seconds of play remain. A trick of fate mustn't steal it from them. Carefully, Dick Irvin sets up an impenetrable defence, at the same time preparing for a raid on the enemy. The Canadiens are ready.

Those forty-four seconds are hours that never end. The Canadiens fear some mishap. Suddenly the fans have doubts about their team. Both teams have doubts about themselves. When the siren announces the end of the game they've been so afraid that they're slow to acknowledge the Canadiens' victory.

Unhappy because he didn't stop that insulting last-minute goal by Gordie Howe, the Rocket undresses in silence as if he had suffered some irreparable defeat: coming so close to defeat is like actually living it.

After that, Montreal plunges into the frenzy of its rivalry with Toronto. At the very beginning of the finals, a disappointment: the Leafs win the first match, 3–2.

During the next game in Toronto, the Canadiens outstrip Toronto 2–0. Then Sid Smith outsmarts Gerry McNeil: 2–1. In the third period, while the Rocket is serving a penalty, Ted Kennedy wipes out the Canadiens' advantage: 2–2. The Rocket takes responsibility for that goal. Therefore he has a moral obligation to wipe it out during overtime. The Leafs are even tougher than the Red Wings. The Rocket is impatient to correct his mistake. At two minutes, fifty-six seconds, the Rocket has slipped like a snake to the blue line, where he picks up a pass from Doug Harvey. The silence of the crowd becomes religious. He's across the blue line. Behind him, the defence is working hard. Cautiously he advances on the goalie. Without excessive haste, Turk Broda comes out to meet him. The Rocket keeps his eyes on the puck. Broda tries to guess what his next move will be. The Rocket pushes the puck. Broda reaches out his arm to sweep it away with his stick. That move throws him off balance. The Rocket has already got it back. Skating around Broda, he lets it slide delicately into the net. The Rocket has mended the damage. Canadiens three, Maple Leafs two. The entire team surrounds the man who's given them the victory. The Toronto crowd stay in their seats, crushed. The Rocket goes up to the stunned spectators and offers one of them the stick with which he scored the fatal goal. In an uncontrollable burst of admiration, the crowd gives him an ovation that wouldn't have been more frenzied if the Leafs had won. This triumph belongs to the Rocket. His teammates withdraw.

The teams are evenly matched. Every moment of play is a border skirmish. In the third game, Ted Kennedy scores the winning
goal. Will the Canadiens recover?

Fourth game, the Forum. The Canadiens aren't ready to lay
down their arms. Toronto takes the lead. The Rocket ties the score.
Toronto gets the lead back. Elmer Lach wipes it out, sending a pass
from the Rocket into the net. Hope is reborn at the Forum and
around radios all over the province of Quebec. Once again, the tie
sends the game into overtime. After five minutes and fifteen seconds, while everyone is waiting for a miracle from the Rocket and
he's wearing himself out to accomplish that sought-after miracle,
Harry Watson scores for the Leafs. Toronto now has three wins.

The Canadiens have to take the fifth game; if they don't, it's
elimination, humiliation. At the first faceoff, Ted Kennedy, checked
into the boards, falls to the ice unconscious. He has a pinched nerve
in his neck. And the Rocket delivers the first shock to goalie Al
Rollins: 1–0. Toronto ties the score, 1–1. The Canadiens get back
the advantage: 2–1. Then they don't let the Leafs get near Gerry
McNeil. The Canadiens get a whiff of the scent of victory. Unfortunately, it seems to intoxicate them. Just thirty-nine seconds before
the end, the faceoff is in their zone. Back on the ice, Kennedy grabs
the puck and transfers it to Tod Sloan. The Canadiens let it pass
and the puck lands in Gerry McNeil's net, wiping out their victory:
2–2. It's Sloan's first goal.

After the break, the Canadiens come back for overtime shaken
by their costly error in the third period. Their skating is disorderly.
They seem already submissive to bad luck. They don't seem to be
rebelling against their fate. Their defence is incoherent. Howie
Meeker shoots the puck into the Canadiens' zone and rushes after
it. Arriving first behind the net, he picks up the puck and whips it
over the blue line to Watson, who sends it to Bill Barilko. To catch it
he'll have to plunge; he stretches his arm and dives as if into a river.
The blade of his stick catches the puck; he fires it, then flattens
himself on the ice. After just two minutes, fifty-three seconds of
play, he scores the winning goal. And the Leafs win the Stanley Cup!

In the Canadiens' locker room after the defeat, both veterans and rookies shed tears. During eleven playoff games, the Rocket provided nine goals and four assists. During the regular season, he scored forty-two goals (one fewer than Gordie Howe) and was credited with twenty-four assists. He is silent. He's done his best. Everyone on the team has done his utmost. His silence resembles a storm. His third-period weakness can't be justified. When you want to win you can't be weak. This defeat is more painful than all his injuries. He avoids looking at certain teammates who can guess what he thinks of their flabbiness.

And there's Gerry. He was nearly always excellent, but the Rocket can't really reproach him for being distracted when Barilko fired his shot: the goalie's wife is in the hospital, about to give birth. Gerry wants a boy who will play hockey. His wife wouldn't be surprised if it's a girl. Has the child already been born? He must have been thinking about that while he was waiting for the puck. It's a girl, he learns later.

Montreal has been knocked out by Toronto and the Canadiens don't feel proud. People start talking about politics again. The federal government has just announced a $7 million investment in university education. Duplessis protests: Ottawa wants to take control of teaching. Then it would have the power to make our French culture disappear. We feel blessed because we have such a *chef* to protect us. During the summer the sun, birds, flowers, brightly coloured dresses, bike rides, ball games assuage all our fears.

I am fourteen years old. Like my friends and my parents, I'm proud that Duplessis is standing up to Ottawa. As our history teacher tells us, Duplessis is a beacon on our small French, Catholic island which is constantly being battered by anglophone, Protestant waves. Fourteen: in my village, that's the age at which a boy begins to work. At fourteen, if you work you become a man. You're entitled to smoke. You're entitled to drink beer. You're entitled to curse.

My father has friends in Duplessis's party. That's why I get a job in the roads department. At 6:30 A.M. I climb on board a truck with my new workboots and my new overalls to join my group of workers. My shovel is sparkling, without a single scratch. The others are older than I am. They're hefty men. I, a young student with white hands, am proud to be with men. I feel free.

We arrive at a mountain of gravel. Our job is to shovel that mountain into the truck. My companions set to work, obedient like animals who are accustomed to their fate. I struggle to lift a shovelful whenever they do. Before long the gravel is so hard that I can no longer lift my shovel. My hands on the handle of my shovel are burning.

But I have to work. The boss has warned us: anyone who doesn't do his share today won't be here tomorrow. We sweat. The gravel barely forms a small bump in the truck. We'd like to rest for a while.

"Boss," says one of the old men, "remember that night when the Rocket grabbed the puck?"

"Do I remember!" he exclaims. "I can still see it as if I were there."

And the boss launches into a description of one of the Rocket's magnificent breakaways. Shovels are laid down. I understand. If our fatigue demands a break, we just have to activate the mechanism of the memory box:

"Boss, remember when the Rocket . . ."

A RESURRECTION
ON THE RINK

Hockey is a sport that you play in armour. The player trains for the horrors of war, but like a ballet dancer, he never stops refining his strides, his splits, his dégagés, his sets to partners, his vaults. Stuffed into pads, feet armed with sharpened blades, holding a stick, he moves with vigour and elegance. His legs are excessively powerful. His legs must guess in what direction to propel his body before his brain has decided what the next sequence in his choreography will be. In the manner of a karate expert, he knows how to immobilize an opponent. He knows the art of fencing. He's a champion runner. In his padded equipment he has to demonstrate the powerful stupidity of a tank. At the same time, he masters the art of the tightrope walker. He has the intelligence of a chess player, the precision of a javelin thrower. He must have the faith that moves mountains. He is endowed with the patience of a tamer of wild beasts, because the puck is a cantankerous animal. He professes a piety towards the puck as fanatical as that of certain believers in the Middle Ages: they would carve up a holy hermit who was still alive in order to have the privilege of owning a relic that would bring them his favours in heaven. Finally, the hockey player must desire the conquest of the Stanley Cup as fervently as those ancient knights who would give their lives for the Holy Grail. This war on the ice is a dangerous game.

When the hero goes back to the house, he's just a father coming home from work, tired out, sometimes injured, untalkative and preoccupied by the next day. He takes the time to play a little, to help the children with their school work if he can. Perhaps he'll read them a story?

Maurice Richard is starting his tenth season with the Canadiens. He likes the young people around him. Some have grown up trying to emulate him. Their respect for him is touching. Like him, they're convinced that hockey is the great game of life. A number are French Canadians. It's good to hear the French language in the locker room. Geoffrion, who has a fiery temperament, who scores spectacular goals, is also a joker. On the Punch Line, Maurice is back with his old comrade-in-arms Elmer Lach; young Dickie Moore, tough and shrewd, is in Toe Blake's place. All of them are hungry to win. As for the Rocket, his arms and legs must be weighed down by fatigue, aching from bruises, but he's as young as the rookies. Even more than they, he has that fervour that inspires them all.

On October 11, the season begins well. In the first game, the Rocket collects a goal. A good sign. Three days later, two goals, one after the other in less than fifty seconds. It won't be long before he scores number three hundred. The next day he inflicts a winning goal on the Rangers. We're walking gloriously towards the future.

At the end of October, employees are repainting the seats in the Forum. They build a platform of honour. A long red carpet is unrolled that the fans are forbidden to walk on. The brass band of the Van Doos polishes its instruments. Princess Elizabeth of England and Prince Philip will be greeted with great pomp and ceremony.

At the seminary, our history teacher teaches us that Princess Elizabeth, the daughter of King George VI of England, is a descendant of King George II, the king of the English who defeated Montcalm on the Plains of Abraham in 1759, then seized Canada, burned Catholic churches along the St. Lawrence River and, before that, would even have taken hold of France, our motherland, if Joan of

Arc hadn't driven the English out. Besides that, Princess Elizabeth is a descendant of King Henry VIII, the founder of Protestantism, who persecuted Catholics.

Why then is my father called Georges, like the kings of England? Why do my mother and my grandmother, like many women in the village, collect photos they cut out of newspapers of Princess Elizabeth, her sister, the Queen and George VI? I, the patriot, even mixed the flour-and-water paste to glue the photos in the album.

When the princess and her prince enter the Forum, the brass band strikes up "God Save the King." French Canadians don't like that anthem but the fans are polite. After that, they attack the first note of "O Canada." Chests swell to sing the French words to the princess.

The presence of these highnesses requires a certain refined behaviour. Rangers and Canadiens management have ordered their players to play refined hockey. "If it's refined it ain't hockey!" joke the players. Referees and management will not tolerate uncouth behaviour. In other words, it's forbidden to commit a murder tonight.

The opponents are disconcerted by the fine manners of the other team. The play is hesitant. The period is riddled with dead moments. The bosses have said "refined." Hockey isn't a game for princesses. The players feel the way the strippers on St. Lawrence Boulevard would feel if the highnesses were to visit their nightclub.

The Rocket is uneasy with all this civility. He'd prefer less etiquette and more hockey. He doesn't even get a shot on goal. An ill-mannered lout treats him roughly. The Rocket hands out a few refined whacks which are not, however, approved by the formal code. Camillien Houde, the mayor of Montreal, who adores the Rocket, fears that the pastoral image of his city will be strained by one of his escapades. He recommends that Dick Irvin send the Rocket out to pasture. When the mayor speaks he has no doubt that people listen. He is, after all, a mayor of a city that has four hundred brothels.

The impetuous Rocket isn't invited back on the ice till the third period. Stand clear! Furious at being sidelined, he's determined to send the puck right through the goalie's body. At the thirteen-minute mark he scores his 298th goal! Forty seconds before the end of the game he spies a gap. Another goal: number 299! The crowd gives him an ovation unlike the one for their highnesses. Will the Rocket offer his three-hundredth goal to the prince and princess?

"Give 'em hell, Maurice!"

The fans are jumping up and down. Ah! To show the prince and princess that we've survived the defeat on the Plains of Abraham! The fans' voices urge him along like a rolling wave. The clock shows five seconds of play remaining. Maybe that's long enough for number three hundred. He shoots. Misses. The crowd chants as if he'd been successful. The prince and princess leave. Have their highnesses grasped the subtleties of the game played by the Canadian tribe?

Maurice's three-hundredth goal is inevitable. The puck is already in orbit. It's going to land. No one knows where. No one knows when. During the next game? No goalie wants to be the victim of that shot. On the alert, the threatened teams get their protection ready. They're going to tie up the Rocket.

On November 1, the Leafs are at the Forum. This isn't a courtesy visit. Several players owe the Rocket a few punches. Altercations multiply. The Rocket defends himself and now he's being punished. Then one of his parasites, Bill "The Beast" Juzda, jeers at him for being French Canadian. The Rocket leaps out of the penalty box and onto Juzda. The Forum is dancing with joy. But the Rocket hasn't given his fans the three-hundredth goal that they're hoping for.

In the next game, Terry Sawchuk sees the Rocket approaching the net. He crouches down, sticks out his torso and spreads his arms, creating a funnel in which the puck will be trapped. To spread out the volume of his body even more, the goalie leans towards the left; he extends his right leg while his hand protects the upper part of the net that has thus been sealed. Along comes the Rocket. Sawchuk, eyes glued to the puck, awaits the shot. Rather than fire, the Rocket makes a turn that sends up powdered ice and turns his back on the net. What trick is he getting ready to pull? He steps on the brakes. Danger! Sawchuk is ready. Knees bent by effort, body twisted as he continues to scrutinize Sawchuk, the Rocket stretches out his arms to push as far as possible the blade of his stick where the puck is still clinging. Every muscle in his body is strained, then that magnificent slingshot relaxes. The puck enters the goal as precisely as a scalpel into flesh. Number three hundred!

In case Jack Adams and his swaggering Red Wings Abel, Lindsay and Howe still think they're superior, he then castigates them with his 301st. No one will claim that the three-hundredth was a lucky break.

———

Our teachers tell us about the *Odyssey* of Homer, the conquests of Alexander, the era of Charlemagne. Nothing interests us as much as a Canadiens game.

On the top floor of the seminary a hundred beds are lined up. In the middle of our dormitory there's a door. We're forbidden to open that door. Behind it, a narrow staircase leads to the tower. At nine o'clock the monitor recites a final prayer, switches off the lights and retires. We know precisely how long it takes him to fall asleep in his cell. When conditions are deemed to be safe, bodies stir in the narrow beds. Bodies glide along the grey cement floor. The darkness is broken only by a vigil light burning at the feet of a Blessed Virgin. The members of the hockey team get out of their beds. The door hinges creak like the joints of an old man. Will the monitor's light come on? Whispering. Then creaking steps. Rustling against the walls. Finally, the door hinges moan again. The hand of the last of the disobedient students has just closed on the great secret of the night.

The rest of us stay in our beds. We're not allowed to climb into the forbidden tower but we know what ritual is taking place there, unbeknownst to the priests. We don't say a word. It's a hallowed secret. A radio is hidden in a place where it can't be found. An antenna is planted in a spot on the roof where it can't be seen. Someone just has to grab the antenna wire, bring it inside through the window and connect it to the radio, then they can hear the hockey broadcast. In our beds, we're a little sad. Because we aren't on the team we're condemned to stay under the covers. The members of the team are the masters of the tower.

There's an important game against Toronto but it's forbidden to us; we aren't on the team. We're so sad that we can't fall asleep. Why haven't we been chosen? It's hard to get to sleep when you've been rejected by the team.

We try to console ourselves by thinking that we have good marks in French dictation, algebra, geometry, but that doesn't really console us. We'd like to be part of the team.

Tomorrow, we'll practise shooting the puck, skating backwards, applying the brakes. Despite all this practice, we'll never be Maurice Richard. We aren't good. We pull up the covers to wipe our eyes.

And eventually we fall asleep.

Then someone shakes us. We open one eye on the pitch-black night.

"Maurice Richard: two goals!"

We feel better. We'll sleep till morning.

———

The Rocket is an absolute dictator over his body. His anatomy is subjected to the tension imposed by his constant obsession with scoring goals, with winning. Yet there's no respite when he takes part in a game, no rest when he's off the ice. He doesn't sleep well, doesn't digest his food. The farmers who work the rocky soil, the fishermen who haul their nets under a stormy sky have no time for petty concerns. When it is time to go to work, they go. Maurice, son of a working man, knows no other discipline. Despite the wrenching pain that burns his belly, he hunts for the puck. Fans consider him more amazing than ever. Yet his body is sawed by pain.

Dick Irvin suggests that he take some time off. To rest? The playoffs are coming. The Canadiens' position has to be consolidated. Nels Stewart's 324-goal record has to be cut down. And Gordie Howe is scoring goals! The Rocket won't let himself be surpassed. Even on the Canadiens team there are some who challenge him: Geoffrion is trying to have more ambition than he does. Rest? The Rocket doesn't need rest. He's in pain but hockey is a game that causes pain. After two months of torture he finally agrees to see a doctor. The Rocket isn't suffering from indigestion but from a pulled ligament in the groin. Time off? It's Saturday and the Black Hawks are coming to the Forum. He doesn't want to be absent. Like God, the Rocket is everywhere tonight. He's preparing a hat trick for them!

The Rocket doesn't rest. On January 31, 1952, the Canadiens do battle with the Rangers. Dick Irvin has noticed that the Rocket isn't skating the way he usually does. Now and then his face is creased in a grimace. Then all at once he rushes into one of those breakaways that give you goosebumps. The Rocket heads for the opponents' net with zigzags, curves, returns and feints that disconcert them; he'll brake unexpectedly, then resume his race as if he hadn't stopped. Dick Irvin notices that one of his skates seems slower, heavier than the other. The Rocket shoots; it's a goal! Number 317, this season's twenty-fourth. The Rocket is outdistancing Gordie Howe!

The few words that fall from his mouth, the smallest move he makes, give rise to as much analysis and commentary in the press as a passage in the Bible. The pain in the Rocket's groin has become as important as a national epidemic. People are incredulous: the Rocket can't have "a bellyache like a woman." What is the Rocket's real problem? journalists wonder.

At the next practice, his leg goes on strike. The Rocket is sick and the entire province of Quebec is suffering. The Rocket, embarrassed, annoyed, describes for the journalists in few words the pain that has sentenced him to rest. He knows every possible way to lodge the puck in his opponents' net but he hasn't studied the anatomy of the human body. The Rocket, who doesn't understand his pain, has to describe it, explain it. His interviews are prepared in advance.

At the seminary, the radio is forbidden us. However, if we're clever enough to confess to our spiritual director at news time, we can listen to the radio while we list our sins. This little ruse has allowed several of us to hear the Rocket. And we're embarrassed. Hearing him speak makes us uncomfortable the way we feel in the parlour on Sunday, when one of our fat aunties comes to visit wearing a flowered dress that hangs below her coat. We're ill at ease. Someone ventures to imitate him. There's laughter. Suddenly we're making fun of Maurice Richard. The Rocket no longer makes us feel stronger. This man with magic in his skates and fire in his eyes, who taught us to think bigger, to want to go further, to be stronger than our strength, we're now a little ashamed of. Can we still admire a hero who does nothing but push a piece of rubber across the ice? It's ideas that have to be launched! We're only interested in the great men who have statues in Europe and photos in the dictionary. None of them played hockey.

That was when we stopped trying to be Maurice Richard. I neglected the rink for meetings of our patriotic circle. And that was the end of my career as a hockey player.

While he's resting, the Rocket misses about twenty games. The days seem as long to him as if he couldn't breathe. The fans are becoming impatient: he's not supposed to mend so slowly. On March 15, he comes back against the Bruins. The fans know him: after his enforced rest, he'll make up for lost time. The Rocket doesn't let us down. He scores the winning goal.

In Toronto four days later, surrounded by mastodons, Elmer Lach sends him a pass. The Rocket flexes his knees, bracing himself, and then, twisting his waist, he reaches out to collect it. Despite repeated checks by Jim Morrison, he holds on to it. Head down, he gores his opponents. He charges through their sticks. Wrapped in opponents, he still controls the puck. Between crossed sticks and tangled legs, he shows it what direction to go. Docile, the puck obeys him. He scores!

The fans are dreaming of the Stanley Cup, but they're interested in the news of another strike that has just broken out in Louiseville, a small town between Montreal and Trois-Rivières. Textile workers are outraged because, with no negotiations, the company has changed four clauses in their collective agreement. The workers no longer accept their fate like battered animals. Why are French Canadians condemned to suffer a fate decided by others? Why are decisions always made by others? Our politicians? They let the corporations run the country. Even Duplessis. To the corporations he says, "Yes, sir!" We need a Maurice Richard in politics!

Our history teacher explains: "A society is like a body; you're healthy if your brain, your stomach, your heart and your arms do what they're supposed to do. Your body is like a hockey team. What would happen to the Canadiens if Maurice Richard decided not to play? What would happen if your brain or your feet or your stomach refused to do their job? Our society is sick. But like the people in France who brought about the Revolution, French Canadians are waking up . . ." Adults are lucky that they have the right to strike. A strike seems like a vacation. But why do the strikers look so miserable?

The playoffs are starting. In the first game, the Canadiens wipe out the Bruins 5–1. The Rocket has imposed two goals on them. The Canadiens win a second victory, 4–2. The wind has shifted, though, as the fans say to explain the inexplicable: the Canadiens lose the next three games. In the sixth, the Bruins are continuing their triumphant march. Gerry McNeil can't resist them. The Canadiens struggle. The Bruins' defence is insurmountable. Eleven minutes into the third period the Rocket, like a great vulture, looms out of no one knows where, grabs the puck from Milt Schmidt and takes it away in his talons. Stunned, the other side hesitates. The Rocket forges ahead. Twenty feet from Jim Henry, he fires. The puck is in the net: the score, 2–2.

The overtime period is endless. The Bruins want to finish off the Canadiens tonight. The Canadiens have to survive, tonight. The seconds drag on. The air is scorching. The players are exhausted. Just as they feel like giving up, their energy is restored. No one creates the goal that would put an end to it. They have to go into a second overtime period. The two teams are evenly matched. Will a third overtime be needed? At seven minutes, forty-nine seconds, rookie Paul Masnik snatches the puck as it rebounds on a shot by Doug Harvey and sends it into the net.

Each team has three victories. The Canadiens now have a future. The seventh game will decide the outcome of the semi-finals. On April 8 the most important thing in the world is what's going on at the Forum. The playing is rough. In the second period, the Rocket tries again to rip apart the Bruins' defence. Léo Labine, who skates as if there were no blade under his boots, moves in front of him. With his broad shoulders and big arms, Labine crashes into him. Maurice loses his balance and drops to his knees. Bill Quackenbush sees him coming and knees him in the head. The Rocket collapses onto his back, spread-eagled, arms outstretched. Fans think of the crucified Christ. At this time of the year, in the Catholic province of Quebec, thoughts are on Good Friday, the day when Christ died on the Cross. The silence in the Forum is distressing. The people would like to get down on their knees. Easter, the day of His resurrection, isn't far away either . . . Suddenly, the Rocket moves. The crowd explodes. Christ is resurrected! Painfully, his face red with blood, held up by the doctor, he heads for the clinic, to applause. He has no memory of what happened. He's fixed up with the necessary stitches. He wants to go back to the players' bench.

What's the score? he asks: 1–1. A few seconds later, he's forgotten. What's the score? Toe Blake observes him. There's fog in the Rocket's eyes, but behind it there is a flame. The Rocket has been shaken up but now he's seething with impatience. He's still dazed. Toe Blake pretends not to notice. He knows his player. The opportune moment is coming. The crowd too knows their Maurice. The Bruins have been sentenced to death for the crime committed by Léo Labine.

The third period is well under way. If the Canadiens don't win this game in the next four minutes, they'll be eliminated. What's the score? asks Maurice. "It's a tie." He has to score a goal. The Rocket wants to score the goal that needs to be scored.

"Give 'em hell, Maurice!"

The opponents have swept into the Canadiens' zone. It's a dangerous moment. Behind the goal, Butch Bouchard quarrels with Woody Dumart and seizes the puck. Surprised to see the Rocket, whom he didn't think would be back on the ice, he passes the puck to him. The Rocket flies to the enemy blue line, where the solid Bill Quackenbush and Bob Armstrong are waiting for him. Though Quackenbush is skating backwards, he's not backing down. The Rocket can't shoot. And he has drifted. From this angle he can't fire a fatal shot, and besides, the tank named Quackenbush is facing him. Instead of trying to find a safe place behind the net to get ready for the next sequence, to the defenceman's surprise he turns towards the front of the net. Jim Henry would let the puck land in his face sooner than he'd let it pass. He waits for the shock. His face is covered with scars. He bends over, the better to see the puck coming. The Rocket takes his time. The enemies arrive. The Rocket crosses swords with them, pushing them away with one hand while, with the other, he stickhandles the puck. Jim Henry is waiting. The puck will bounce off him. Will he shoot? Not now. The savage horde is on him. Jim Henry has moved. A crack appears. The Rocket brings down the blade of his stick on the puck and it splits the air like a sabre. Victory! The Canadiens win the semifinals. They'll win the Stanley Cup! *"Halte là, halte là, halte là, les Canadiens sont là!"*

In the Forum, the fans yell, dance, sing, cry. They applaud. What's the score? asks the Rocket. With his face bloody, seeming drunk, he goes to the locker room and collapses on the bench. His father, Onésime, the humble worker, is waiting for him. He's a man of few words. He puts his hand on the shoulder of his famous son. The Rocket is choking. In him rises the huge flood of emotion brought on by the cries of the crowd, his tension from wanting to score, his anger at being attacked, the suffering he has endured, his constant doubts. His bloody, swollen face is creased; a spasm shakes his body. He bursts out sobbing. The greatest hockey player of modern times is a terrified child, crying in his father's arms. The sobs of this child are like the howling of a wounded beast. The rookies don't know where to look.

That goal was the most beautiful in the history of the world. The next morning, in the seminary chapel, we thank God. Yesterday the priests asked Him to help the Canadiens: "Remember, dear God, that Maurice Richard is a French-Canadian Catholic. It would be hard for us to understand Your justice, dear God, if a French-Canadian Catholic couldn't win against some English Protestants." With all the fervour in our young hearts we thank God for having played with the Canadiens against the Bruins.

Exhilarated by our triumph, did we neglect to pray to God for the finals? The Red Wings prove to be too strong. They win the Stanley Cup.

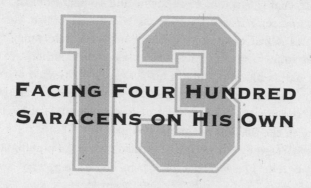

FACING FOUR HUNDRED
SARACENS ON HIS OWN

Like Maurice Richard, I'm
learning English. But at the seminary they teach that language cautiously. If we learn English too well, we'll talk to young English girls; we could fall in love with them, marry them and become fathers of English Protestant babies. We study much more Greek than English. And I'm translating a text by Epictetus, a philosopher who was born in 50 A.D. He was a Ṣtoic. To toughen his resistance, his master twisted his legs in a torture device. One day the limb, which had been twisted too much, broke. He didn't even let out a murmur. His text was written nearly two thousand years ago: "My friend, you want to win glory at the Olympic Games. First of all, study the conditions and the consequences; then you can get down to work. You must submit yourself to a discipline: eat according to the rules, avoid cakes and sweetmeats; you must do your exercises at the appropriate hour, whether you like it or not, whether the weather is cold or hot; you must abstain from cold drinks and from unlimited wine: in a word, you must trust your trainer as you would your physician. Then, during the competition itself, you have a good chance of dislocating your wrist or spraining your ankle, of swallowing a lot of dust, of being severely exhausted from fatigue; and after all that, of being defeated."

In recent times, in remote towns and villages, the people gathered at church on Sunday. At the elevation of the Host, the people
felt that God was within them. Now it's the Rocket, whom they see
on television, who gives them the sense of our power. My grandfather, after a black day in his blacksmith's shop, puts on a white
shirt and tie as if he were going to Mass; but he sits in front of the
TV set to watch the Rocket. That player is as light as a bird and he
perseveres like the sea against the Gaspé cliffs.

Nels Stewart, formerly with the Montreal Maroons and the
Boston Bruins, retired from hockey in 1937, the year of my birth.
Since then, no one in the NHL has scored more goals than his
324. It's obvious that the Rocket, with 322, is going to surpass
that record.

On October 29, the Canadiens are playing Toronto. At 9:00 P.M.,
after one last prayer, the lights in our dormitory go out. Even though
I now prefer politics to hockey, I can't go to sleep without thinking
that in Toronto, a city that to me seems to be in a foreign country,
our Maurice Richard is probably going to break a historic record.
And we aren't allowed to watch it on television! Even the radio is
forbidden. I strongly oppose this education system that came from
France when Quebec was founded, in 1608, and hasn't changed
since, despite the coming of modern times and the atom bomb. The
priests keep us under quarantine, safe from the germs of modern
life. I go to sleep with no news of the Rocket.

At the eleventh minute of play, the Rocket receives a pass from
his faithful partner Elmer Lach. In no time at all, eluding the vigi-
lance of goalie Harry Lumley, he gets ready to score goal number
323. Their team has been humiliated but the crowd can't restrain
itself from applauding, with reservation, this conjuring trick.
Another few strokes of his skates and the Rocket will be standing
with Nels Stewart on the summit of the 324-goal record.

From the depths of their Torontonian souls the fans want a
victory for their team. But they wouldn't want to miss this special
moment when, to achieve that historic record, the Rocket will strike
down the goalie—even their team's goalie. Tonight his energy is

phosphorescent. The fans follow the puck as if they were studying a magic trick. They don't want to miss one moment of this game, just as they wouldn't want to miss one word of a rousing tale. When his stick grabs the puck, the crowd cries out. From fear? From pleasure? Are they encouraging him? Shouting him down? He climbs his way to the net. "Maurice Rocket Richard shoots—he scores!"

When the game is over the journalists want to fill their columns quickly. It's late. The presses are soon going to roll. Maurice would rather be cornered by a pack of defencemen than be questioned by journalists. After a game he comes back from somewhere else, from a journey to the planet Hockey. His body and his mind need to readjust to Earth. He hates to talk after a game. Just as he hates to talk before a game. In English or in French, he doesn't trust words. He's not an actor. When asked questions, he answers soberly, like a plumber who knows that he's made a good connection.

The next morning in the seminary chapel, I dip my fingers in the holy water. A classmate whispers, "Maurice Richard: 324!" Later, during morning recess, the monitor confirms the news. The Rocket's historic goal was scored at the seventeen-minute mark. Maurice Richard has caught up with Nels Stewart. The Canadiens carried their teammate triumphantly on their shoulders. The Torontonians applauded him as if he were the king of England.

"Now he'll go for number 325!"

In the tone of someone sharing a secret, the monitor assures us that Maurice could have shot the puck into the Leafs' net as if it were an open door and come back to Montreal with his 325th goal, but he chose to hold back, to pass the puck to Bert Olmstead and let him score. It's in front of French Canadians that he wants to become the greatest hockey player of all time. The monitor also explains to us that a champion isn't a champion unless God wants him to be. If Maurice Richard has become the all-time champion, it's because in His eternal wisdom the good Lord wanted a French-Canadian Catholic to become the champion. Feeling nothing but pride, we've forgotten how we made fun of him because of his scant knowledge of anatomy and vocabulary.

And so we're heading for our 325th goal. When will we beat the record? Today, of course. Maurice is playing at the Forum. Unsuccessfully. Bad luck. He only plays well when he's away from home, complains a disappointed admirer. Doesn't score. Letdown. Why hasn't he done anything? Another game follows and Maurice doesn't even make it to the goal. Why? It can't be all that hard to come up with one goal when you've already scored 324! His teammates give him all the support he needs. He wears himself thin. The resistance is dogged. No team wants to have its history marked with the scar of that record-making goal. What's holding him back? He's the best. Why is he shooting at the goalie's pads? Three games have passed. Nothing. That goal is anticipated as keenly as rain during a summer drought. Ten days in a row, no goal, endless. Maurice, like the little boats of the Gaspé, has a shivering sail.

November 8, precisely ten years earlier, marked the first time that the rookie Maurice Richard delivered a puck into an NHL net. Since then he has played 524 games. A nervous hope is drifting in the air. The Forum staff is getting ready. What will happen in the stands when the Rocket gives his fans that much-anticipated goal? And how will those fans react if the Rocket runs aground? Will they keep quiet if their champion is injured by the opposing side? If a brawl breaks out . . .

This game won't be like the others. The Canadiens' fighting spirit will be nurtured by the fans. The Black Hawks will barricade themselves. And then the Rocket will try to find the slightest opening. Therefore, he mustn't get anywhere near their blue line. The Black Hawks will work hard at putting him out of commission. The player who brings down the Rocket will become a hero. The journalists write lyrically about the pre-game atmosphere. The air is heavy. Something's going to burst. A celebration? A storm?

When the Black Hawks come onto the ice they're booed like an enemy army. With their spuriously nonchalant way of skating, they defy the crowd. Their smugness is insulting: "Wait till Maurice gets here!"

The boarding is cruel. The rivalry is corrosive. The players hurl themselves at one another as if there aren't supposed to be any survivors at the end. At the same time, there is a perception of something fragile at the centre of this combat: an invisible house of cards that could collapse. It is the dream of a man who wants to succeed at something no one before him has done. The fans hold their breath.

The Rocket sneaks into the enemy zone. He shoots. Superb! A masterpiece of ruse, of speed, of precision. A clamour goes up, then is stifled in the silence of what has not been accomplished. In the first period the Rocket has five shots on goal. Five times the puck is driven back by goalie Al Rollins. Five times the party begins and . . .

The sportswriters start their stories. They're fairly confident. The Rocket is going to break the record. The law of averages is on his side: he has fired at the Hawks' goalie five times already, so he ought to be able to do it again over the next two periods. Al Rollins won't intercept every time. "Tension is so high that the air seems rarefied, as if it were the summit of the Himalayas," writes the failed-poet-turned-sportswriter.

The Black Hawks gain a one-goal advantage. To protect it they tighten their defence. Lach, Olmstead and Richard charge. They weave ingenious passes. They spread out, regroup. They feint. The Rocket opens their defence and shoots! The fans jump for joy. Al Rollins uses his pad to deflect the puck. The fans get back in their seats. Oppressive, disappointed silence. Elmer Lach grabs the rebound, he shoots, he scores! His two-hundredth goal! The fans applaud him decently. His goal ties the score again. It should have been a goal by the Rocket, they think.

No sooner are the fans back in their seats than Butch Bouchard sends a long pass to the Rocket, who diligently carves a path through a forest of adversaries. Doggedly, he doesn't give up the puck. He holds on to it as if it were the prop that keeps him from falling into a bottomless gulf. From that round of black rubber he must take flight, he must project himself higher than Nels Stewart's summit. He looks for an opening. Al Rollins is obstructing the entrance to the net. To fire the puck now would be pointless. Fifteen thousand individuals plead with him, amid a dizzying silence, to give them that goal. The enemy collides with him to make him fall to the ice. The Rocket shoots. The projectile is slow. His backhand was flabby. He needed all his strength to ensure his balance. He collapses. Slowly the puck glides, trickles into the net. "The Rocket shoots—he scores!" Goal number 325! The failed-poet-turned-sportswriter is inspired: "The winds of patriotism have blown onto the puck!"

The Rocket picks himself up, looks for the puck. He doesn't know that it's inside the net. The fans are jubilant. A frenzied dance. Now Maurice understands. Objects rain down on the ice: scarves, programmes, fruit, coins. In the centre of it, he's uncomfortable with this noisy adulation. He doesn't deserve all this fuss. It was a lucky goal. And he wanted to give them a real goal by the Rocket, a straightforward goal.

Modest, very proud, intimidated, the champion turns in a circle under the applause. He bows. Maurice Richard has hoisted the French-Canadian flag on the flagpole of planet Hockey. The story of the small people, defeated, colonized and docile, ends here. We belong to a race that produces world champions! Now we know the taste of victory.

New ideas arrive "on the feet of doves," as the German poet Goethe wrote. They can also come on the muscular legs, padded with felt, of a hockey player.

———

The members of our patriotic circle feel guilty for having turned our backs on hockey this year. Hasn't our people given the world the greatest goal scorer in history? And we plunge back into our books. I intend to use my pen the way Maurice Richard handles his stick. What he accomplishes on the ice, we'll accomplish in the political arena.

Even more than the immortal books by immortal authors, we like *Quick*. It's a magazine written in English. Luckily there's not a lot of text. On every page there's a girl who isn't afraid to show the world the beautiful bumps that the good Lord has fashioned for her.

We marvel at the Americans. They've built the atomic bomb and they turn out these girls. *Quick* is forbidden by the priests. To get hold of it we need to have permission to leave the seminary. After that we go to Première Avenue. At the newsstand we head for the corner where the publication of the Pères Blancs, missionaries in Africa, is displayed. *Quick* is hidden behind it. The forbidden publication burns our fingers. At the cash register, we try not to blush. Before going back inside the seminary we shove *Quick* down our pant legs, into our socks, because when we go past the monitor we have to turn our pockets inside out. It's a kamikaze mission.

Shortly after the Rocket's 325th goal, it's my turn to risk my life. *Quick* is in its place behind the pious publications. I check out the merchandise. This month's girls strike me as more sophisticated than ever. I also take the time to leaf through *Life* magazine, just for the fun of it. What's this! A photo of Maurice Richard! Our Rocket in the greatest magazine in the world, like the pope, Gandhi, Churchill, Elizabeth Taylor. I want to show it to my pals: the Rocket in *Life*, the magazine that talks about the most important people in the world!

Unfortunately my budget won't allow me to buy *Life* as well as *Quick*. I have to choose. I think it over, then replace *Quick* behind the magazines about our missionaries. From my expedition I bring back *Life* with Maurice's photo. At the front door, I slide it down my pant leg.

In the real world, which won't be found in either books or hockey, the strike in Louiseville is dragging on. Idleness ruins the lives of families. Despite the help of charities, children are hungry. While fathers vegetate amid despair and helpless anger, strikebreakers are operating the textile mills. They enter and leave with the protection of Duplessis's police. Every day there's pushing and shoving and insults. One December morning when the cold burns people's cheeks, blows are exchanged. In the resulting confusion, a policeman fires at a striker. The bullet goes through his back. Duplessis decides that more policemen are needed in Louiseville.

Why these strikes? Why these violent strikes? Why these interminable strikes? They're the disastrous result of Communist propaganda. That's what Duplessis explains to the people. Our teachers think like Duplessis. The people argue. Some declare that the bosses treat French Canadians like slaves. Others think that the employees are lucky to have jobs. In our patriotic circle, we try to understand. Why is it that wealth is on the side of the English Protestants and poverty on the side of French-Canadian Catholics? The priests explain that it will be harder for a rich man to enter the Kingdom of Heaven than for a camel to pass through the eye of a needle. That consoles us a little but why is it that we've inherited poverty along with the Truth?

During the first weeks of January 1953, God expresses His love of the French Canadians by choosing one of our own as a cardinal in His church. "How God must love us!" insists the preacher. "He didn't go to unbelieving France to choose a cardinal. He didn't go to Protestant England. He didn't go to the materialistic United States. He didn't go to Communist Russia. He didn't go to Nazi Germany. God came to the province of Quebec to choose a French Canadian."

His Eminence pulls into the station in Montreal on January 29, in a special coach. Thousands fall to their knees when the man of God appears, his coat open so they can see the purple soutane and the impressive gold cross on his chest. Stretching out his arms, he declaims, "Montreal, O my city, you have made yourself beautiful to receive your prince and your King." A number of people can't hold back their tears.

That's what I read in the paper. At a meeting of our patriotic circle, I express the opinion that if Maurice Richard had talked so pretentiously after his 325th goal, he'd have been bombarded with tomatoes. After the meeting, I'm summoned to the principal's office.

"I've been told that you made fun of our cardinal. Have you become a little Communist?"

———

1953. The Rocket is nervous. He doesn't want to see Gordie Howe destroy the best thing he's done. "Goddamn frog!" At the slightest insult he becomes a horseman of the Apocalypse. During the first period of one game, he's sent to the penalty box five times.

Gordie Howe is getting close to his fifty-goal record. Will Howe surpass the Rocket? The fans like to recall that it only took the Rocket fifty games to score fifty goals, while Howe has the advantage of a longer, seventy-game season, making his performance not so valid. Opponents reply that the Rocket established his record when the best players were away at the war.

Detroit, late March, final game in the regular season. Gordie Howe has racked up forty-nine goals; he'll try everything, his team will try everything, to smash the Rocket's record. Though unable to check it, the Rocket has followed Howe's persistent advance towards his own record. In the train at night or at home, he reruns in his head the film of the games he's played against the Red Wings. How could Howe's goals have been prevented? He reads newspaper accounts of games other teams have played against the Red Wings. How did Howe score? The Rocket won't allow Gordie Howe to shatter his record. Tonight he'll be face to face with this player with the hypocritical manners. Determination shines in his bulging eyes. There is such determination stored up in his body that Dick Irvin avoids sending him onto the ice at the same time as Howe. Instead, it's to Bert Olmstead and Johnny McCormack that Irvin assigns the mission of looking after Howe. They carry it out with frightening dedication. The Rocket is moved: his teammates are risking injury to safeguard his record. Gordie Howe doesn't shoot; he doesn't score: the Rocket's record is safe. The province of Quebec can breathe at last.

Jim Norris, who has rebuilt the Red Wings into a powerful team, passed away the previous December. His sister Marguerite has succeeded him. Never before has a woman run a hockey team. How will she control men like Terrible Ted Lindsay, Gordie Howe, Terry Sawchuk? How can a woman expect to run a team of men? The Bruins, very confident, come along and eliminate the Red Wings.

On the other side, Sid "Bootnose" Abel, formerly of the Production Line, has infused the Hawks with a youthful desire to win.

They're formidable. Abel hasn't forgotten that he became "Boot-nose" when the Rocket broke his nose. He has carefully analyzed the Canadiens' style: they attack like firemen racing to a blaze. This spectacular play shakes their opponents, but it leaves them with an open defence. The daring of the Rocket and Geoffrion stirs the crowds but their goalie sometimes feels very much alone. This style of the Flying Frenchmen is their very soul. The Black Hawks intend to dismantle their defence. The Canadiens garner the first two victories; the next three go to the Black Hawks. Dick Irvin, worried, confines to the bench several players he considers lazy. He replaces Gerry McNeil with Jacques Plante, an unknown young goalie with asthma who knits. Finally, the Canadiens win the semifinals.

The Canadiens and the Bruins are facing off for the first game of the finals. The Stanley Cup has not been seen in Montreal since 1946.

"Give 'em hell, Maurice!"

Every Canadiens player understands his assignment: to go out and bring back the Cup. The play is rambunctious, to borrow the journalists' euphemism. The players step up their infractions. The referees step up the penalties. The Canadiens win the first game. The second eludes them. They win the third.

Before facing four hundred Saracens, alone, Roland de Roncevaud, whose epic we're reading at the seminary, vows that he will be "more powerful, more haughty and more fervent and that he will not give in as long as he is alive." Our teacher reads: "They hurled at him countless barbs and serpents devouring babes, pikes, lances and feathered javelins." We think about Maurice Richard.

The Bruins are as tough as the Saracens. The fifth game ends in a scoreless tie. The players, on their last legs, wait for the overtime. The minutes to come will be the most important ones of the season. The players are worn out. Where will they find the energy to draw on? The Canadiens' doctor hands out sugar cubes dipped in cognac. During the war, he once saw French nuns revive the wounded that way. Dick Irvin makes a short speech: they know we're tired; they're expecting us to play defensively. Let's surprise them: let's attack!

The sugar and cognac work miracles. After one minute and a few seconds, goalie Jim Henry deflects a shot with his pad. Defenceman Bill Quackenbush gets ready to clear the ground. The Rocket, looming like an apparition, grabs the puck from him. Henry, puffing himself up inside his equipment, comes to meet him. The Rocket can't shoot. Elmer Lach appears. The Rocket passes the puck to him. Lach shoots—he scores.

Hallelujah! After such a long absence the Stanley Cup comes back to Montreal. And the Rocket's fifty-goal record is still intact.

FIRE, BROKEN WINDOWS, STONES THROWN LIKE AT THE BASTILLE

Watching Maurice Richard conquer rinks the way our ancestors must have conquered America, one feels less like the vanquished and a little more like the victors. The Rocket reverses the current of history. Neither the Catholic religion with its aspirations for the other world nor our political leaders, so absurdly small before the forces of this world, make us shiver with pride at simply being alive the way the Rocket does. Before he came along, our people had no one we could look up to with admiration.

One of our friends who wants to become a sportswriter assures us that Maurice Richard in hockey has accomplished for French Canadians what Jackie Robinson has done in baseball for blacks in that great democratic country where blacks aren't allowed to piss in the same place as whites. He knows everything there is to know about sports.

"To persist . . . to live on . . ." That's the message in the novel *Maria Chapdelaine* which the priests make us read like a prayer. "Persist." That's what Maurice Richard tells us. Persist and score goals!

———

For some months now the Rocket has been delivering his thoughts on hockey to a weekly newspaper. The paper isn't allowed in the seminary, but our friend who wants to become a sportswriter reads the Rocket's column and passes it around, stuck to a page of *L'Action Catholique*.

And I'm jealous. I dream of becoming a journalist. The Rocket, who didn't go to school as long as I have, has gone into journalism as easily as his puck goes into the Toronto net.

In mid-December the Canadiens are wrangling with the Rangers in New York. The crowd is stirred up. There's a little blood. Throwing their gloves onto the ice, players grab each other by the sweater, they shake, they wallop each other with bare fists. Ron Murphy blasts Bernie Geoffrion with a stick to his head. Shaken, the impetuous Canadien hunts down his assailant. Shrinking before him, Murphy tries to fend off his blows. The crowd demands more action. Geoffrion offers rights, lefts. Murphy steers clear of them and his stick comes crashing down one more time. Geoffrion staggers but he doesn't fall. Stunned, in the confusion on the ice he grabs a stick and comes back to Murphy. After an exchange of stick waving and a demonstration of evasions, Geoffrion breaks the stick on Murphy's jaw.

Maurice Richard the sports columnist reports on these events. He defends his teammate. When he was attacked, Geoffrion only wanted to protect his own life in this altercation. NHL president Clarence Campbell sees things differently and suspends both gladiators.

The following week, columnist Maurice Richard denounces the sentence brought down on the victim, Geoffrion, as unfair. He recalls that Clarence Campbell wasn't so ruthless when the Rangers' Mosienko and Jack Evans injured Béliveau. He reproaches Clarence Campbell for his indifference when Gordie Howe nearly caused Dollard St. Laurent to lose an eye. Did Campbell punish Geoffrion because he's French Canadian? wonders the entire province of Quebec. How it all resembles our people's history! The French Canadians are victims of the masters' injustice. Ah, if only my studies were finished. I'm going to write hard-hitting articles too. Maurice Richard isn't afraid to deliver a few home truths to Clarence Campbell.

The NHL president has someone translate this column that everyone's talking about. He doesn't like the Rocket's prose: he fines him and orders him to retract his words in his next column, to give up journalism and to write him a letter of apology. Humiliating the Rocket humiliates the entire province of Quebec.

"One of these days, Clarence Campbell, you'll be hearing from us."

After the holidays, our patriotic circle discusses the autonomy of the province of Quebec. We don't really understand this notion of Duplessis's but when you're sixteen you don't need to understand everything; you just know. All the members agree with Duplessis: the province of Quebec should control its own taxes, that's obvious. However, we discover that in politics, what's obvious for some is not so for others. Workers in the province of Quebec have lower salaries than those in Ontario; they pay higher taxes and they have more children to feed. It's the province's right to levy a provincial income tax, but if the taxpayers can't pay it . . .

═══

1954. Red Wings goalie Johnny Bower is blessed with unfailing self-control. When he's attacked, he doesn't bat an eyelid. He's not afraid of delivering a nudge with his shoulder if an assailant comes too close. Or he'll drop to his belly, sweeping the puck with his stick. If the attacker persists, he'll straighten his stick in his crotch. Harry Lumley of the Leafs has accomplished thirteen shutouts, a record unequalled since the 1928–29 season. When he confronts these teams, the Rocket toils conscientiously. His own fifty-goal record seems out of reach, but he toils away. His fierce doggedness has earned him 112 minutes of penalties, equivalent to missing nearly two entire games. With thirty-seven goals, though, the Rocket is the NHL's top scorer.

The Canadiens' boisterous style of play brings injuries. How will they be able to win the Stanley Cup when their best players— Lach, Moore, Béliveau—are sidelined with injuries? Pain in one knee makes it hard for the Rocket to skate. His body no longer obeys the pugnacity of his soul.

Despite their injuries, the Canadiens' appetite for victory is so insatiable that they win the semifinals against the Bruins. Their fans can dream about the Stanley Cup again.

In the finals against the powerful Red Wings, against Gordie Howe, the Canadiens aren't equal to the challenge. Starting out, they resemble losers. The first game eludes them. Then the second and the third. And like desperate soldiers who won't acknowledge their own imminent death, from one stroke of the skates to the next, from one effort to the next, one minute, one shot, one period to the next, the Canadiens reconquer the lost ground with imperturbable persistence, with tumultuous team play. And go on to win three consecutive victories. Each team has won three games. The Canadiens are no longer losers.

The team that snatches the next game will be crowned Stanley Cup champions. The Canadiens board the train for Detroit's Olympia Stadium. Fans accompany them to the station. And they'll be there to greet them when they return with the Stanley Cup!

The game ends in a 1–1 tie. Four minutes into overtime, the Rocket's old enemy Tony Leswick clears his zone by driving the puck to the Canadiens' end. It flies like a lob in baseball. Landing, it ricochets off defenceman Doug Harvey's glove and bounces into Gerry McNeil's net.

The Red Wings' victory isn't a real victory. The Canadiens' defeat isn't a real defeat. It's luck that has won the Stanley Cup.

I, the adolescent trying to comprehend the truth of the world, ask myself: could it be that luck is an element in all the great successes in history? On this April 16, 1954, luck was not with the Rocket. Yet Maurice Richard has never expected luck to accomplish what he wanted. Not having luck on his side didn't stop him from becoming the greatest hockey player in the world.

Now, at the end of this season, while Maurice can't present the Stanley Cup to the fans, on April 30 he holds in his arms his new son, André. The fans like to see their Rocket—quick-tempered, fiery, an electrical storm on ice, a pitiless artilleryman—transformed into a fond family man. People paste photos of Rocket, of Lucille and their son into their scrapbooks. They go into albums along with family photos. They're taped to cash registers in restaurants and grocery stores. They're pinned up on the walls of garages and shops, displayed in schools among the coloured pictures of saints to be imitated. Dressed up as a family man, Maurice Richard makes me think of Superman when he steps into a phone booth and is transformed into Clark Kent, the ordinary man.

The Rocket too is an ordinary man. He needs an operation on his leg. He's also an artist endowed with a natural gift for obsession. During the summer he goes over the goals he's scored and those he's missed, one by one, correcting this rush, that dodge. He reworks the path he's taken, reweaves his play, questions his tactics, improves the way he handles the puck. He is like Balzac reworking a manuscript. He was wounded by the incident of his newspaper column in *Samedi Dimanche*. Clarence Campbell has humiliated him. The Rocket has never apologized to any man. He made a tremendous mistake when he apologized to a man who looks down on French Canadians. Frank Selke and Dick Irvin made him do it. But the day will come when a French Canadian won't apologize to Clarence Campbell.

<hr>

The faithful companion, the modest Elmer Lach, has retired after so many campaigns in which he and Maurice worked together as partners. The rookies are spirited: Geoffrion, Dickie Moore, the prince Jean Béliveau. Geoffrion is the only man who dares to tease the Rocket. Everyone respects him but they've all set their hearts on scoring more often than he does. These youngsters are gaining in confidence and experience, forcing him to become young again, like them.

I'm seventeen. I can't wait to enter real life. At the seminary I'm like a rookie on the bench, impatient to jump onto the ice. I read. I listen. I observe the world. Politics is a constant thread in the tapestry of our lives. Prime Minister Louis St. Laurent declares that the provinces are less important than Canada as a whole. Straight away, we patriots explode in a fury that must make the Peace Tower shake. For French Canadians, the province of Quebec is the only place where French Canadians don't feel as if they're on foreign territory. Duplessis denounces the prime minister's remarks: if Ottawa dominates the province of Quebec, he predicts, it will mean the assimilation of the French Canadians. Are we going to live our lives always under threat, submissive, threatened with disappearing?

The Canadiens start the new season against the pitiful Black Hawks, who no longer draw any crowds. In an attempt to renew their pool of spectators, they play outside Chicago, in Omaha, St. Louis, St. Paul. In those cities, too, the crowds are sparse. The Canadiens take home the victory. The Rocket: two goals, two assists.

At the beginning of October, the members of our patriotic circle read a rather complicated article by Pierre Elliott Trudeau. Because of our economic poverty and our miserable education, he says, we are condemned to be lackeys. Through politics, we should have won for ourselves the dignity of free men; unfortunately, we've entrusted our fate to religious superstition.

Advised that this text is being circulated, the chaplain calls an urgent meeting. On the day the English seized hold of Canada, he explains, the French Canadians asked the Catholic church to guide them through their adversities. The church carried out its mission. Proof: the French Canadians are still here. We listen. We don't always believe what the priests say. The province of Quebec is changing.

The most modern hotel in America is going to be built in Montreal, announces the Canadian National Railway, which has even obtained an exceptional privilege from the Queen of England: the hotel will bear her name, the Queen Elizabeth Hotel. What? An earthquake shakes the province of Quebec. The name of this new hotel is a slap in the French face of Montreal. French Canadians don't want to see the name of the Queen of England written in English on the most modern building in the city. If CNR president Donald Gordon had even a little respect for us he'd have chosen a

French name for his hotel, for instance that of Maisonneuve, the founder of Montreal. It's already known that the Scottish-born Gordon despises French Canadians. He has stated that there are no French Canadians competent enough to work in the offices of the Canadian National Railway. Donald Gordon is another Clarence Campbell. Thousands of letters of protest pour into the newspapers. Editorial writers fume in their pages and on the airwaves. Thousands demonstrate in the streets. French Canadians will no longer accept humiliation!

The Rocket carries on! To Clarence Campbell's snubs, to racist insults, to the bulldozers on skates who drive him into the boards, he opposes the brilliance of his shots. In Chicago on December 18, 1954, he inflicts his four-hundredth goal on the Black Hawks' Al Rollins. His teammates carry him in triumph as the crowd applauds, extolling his virtues as if he were a player with the Hawks. Never has there been such an ovation in Chicago. Inspired, the organist pours out waves of music. Maurice wishes he were in Montreal.

The following day, the Canadiens will take on the formidable Red Wings. Despite his four hundred goals, in the train taking him to the automotive capital of America, the Rocket doesn't sleep. He is haunted by Gordie Howe, by his bag of tricks; Howe is as solid as a building. His shoulder is as powerful as a horse's kick. He thinks about the tough Terrible Ted Lindsay: a rock that comes rolling towards you on skates, with a stick and fists . . . Even though at five foot eight he's not very tall, he wouldn't yield to an enraged gorilla. The Red Wings' principal line of attack is lethal: Earl Riebel, Gordie Howe and Ted Lindsay. The Rocket has fretted over nothing. The Canadiens humiliate the Red Wings with a stunning 5–0 shutout.

The Rocket's four-hundredth goal. Montreal fans want to celebrate their four-hundredth goal. For the return of Maurice Richard on December 20, at the Central Station near the site where large billboards are announcing construction of the Queen Elizabeth Hotel, a festive crowd is waiting. There are thousands, people of all ages, men, women, children; they are dressed in the clothes of office employees, labourers, businessmen; they wear fedoras, caps, ladies' headgear; their gloves are made of soft doeskin or heavy cowhide. There are women, many women, pretty in their little cloth or fur coats. Some would be very happy to give a kiss to the handsome champion who always looks a little sad, but in the words of a song on the radio, "the Rocket prefers a goal to a kiss." Some hold up newspapers with his photo like banners. A giant papier mâché Rocket dominates the crowd, an amiable guy who doesn't look like a champion.

The moment he appears, the Rocket is lifted up by a sea of shoulders that carries him across the station concourse. The cries are like the ones that greet his goals at the Forum. There's jostling, eyes filled with tears. A forest of hands waves. Hands of children, of young girls, of labourers, old, trembling hands, all try to touch the Rocket, hope to attract his gaze.

Such adulation makes him uncomfortable. Yet without it he knows that his skating would be less vigorous, his shots not so firm. The desire of the crowd is what fuels him, yet he'd feel better if he were on the ice, with a goalie to outsmart. Flashes sputter. The Rocket doesn't shy away.

Four hundred goals: for twelve years it's been an uninterrupted marathon. He works out. He skates. He drives the puck. Always faster. He is attacked. He passes the puck. He fights. He is injured. Penalized. He never gives up. "He shoots, he scores!" The public demands no more of the Rocket than the Rocket demands of himself. This athlete is as powerful as the atomic bomb. The crowd can't take its eyes off this champion who moves with such savage grace. Every one of his goals is a different creation. To surprise the goalie, he surprises himself. His movements are imprinted on the retina in luminescent zigzags. Floating on the waves of his triumph, this man would look like an ordinary man if he didn't have those eyes that see what others don't.

Four hundred goals. It's not over. Behind a conquered net hides another that challenges him. For twelve years he's been like Ulysses wandering on the icy sea of hockey. The distant horizon: five hundred goals.

On December 29, the Canadiens are back in Toronto. The Leafs have built a tight defensive system. Coach Hap Day requires his players to observe certain principles. First of all, the faceoff is crucial. From that moment, the advantage must go to the team. There are a number of ways to neutralize the opponent. His players are trained in every one.

The Rocket is tense. Playing in Toronto means facing Ted Kennedy, whose relentlessness and speed can be compared only with his own. Like the Rocket, Kennedy doesn't hesitate to use his stick like a sword. His speed is impressive, though the Rocket thinks that he doesn't know how to skate. The fans stir up his ardour: "Come on, Teeder!" Playing against Toronto also means having to extricate himself from the tough Bob Bailey, a rookie whom the Rocket thinks has as much talent as a third-rate butcher. At one point this rookie, travelling at his top speed, hurls his two-hundred-pound mass against the Rocket's back. A tremendous crush into the boards. Punch-drunk, the Rocket picks himself up, turns towards the referee, suppressing his instinct for revenge: Bailey will be punished. The Canadiens will have the advantage. The Rocket waits for the sentence. Referee Red Storey doesn't react. Is he closing his eyes to the assault? The Rocket was attacked from behind. The check was illegal. The referee isn't assuming his responsibility; the Rocket will take the law into his own hands. Like Zorro or Robin Hood on television. Who attacked him? Someone tells him: Bailey. In a few strides he crosses the ice and accosts Bailey, smacking him with his stick so hard that Bailey loses a tooth. The strongman staggers, falls. Carried along with him, the Rocket trips over his legs and lands on him. The two exchange the usual courtesies. Bailey, gripping the Rocket's head in the vise of his arms, sticks his fingers in his eyes. Maurice explodes. He wants to wreck everything. With his stick he mows down whatever is standing on the ice. Five times Red Storey disarms him. Five times he comes back with a stick. Finally, the referee expels the Rocket.

Back in Montreal he is summoned before Clarence Campbell, who hands down another fine. It's the same old story: an opponent does something reprehensible and the victim, Maurice Richard, is punished. Not the assailant. The fans' fury is rising. They recite whole rosaries of the injustices the Rocket has suffered.

At the newsstand on Première Avenue, it's not *Quick* that attracts my attention. Of course I glance at the photo of a beautiful French actress you'd think was the Blessed Virgin if she wasn't totally naked. I'm more interested in the French novels that are on the list of books forbidden by the church. I buy two. I'll smuggle them in past the monitor by hiding them inside my pant leg. At his cash register, the owner is talking with a customer:

"You can't say the Rocket was right to do what he did, but you can't blame him, either."

"Time after time you put up with these things, but you can't put up with them forever."

The Rocket responds to injustice: "He shoots, he scores." The day after the incident with Bailey, he scores a hat trick. One day the French Canadians will rise up. All the Clarence Campbells who head the NHL, the textile mills, modern hotels, factories, finances and the government will realize that French Canadians no longer want to be a "people on their knees," in the words of a famous Christmas carol.

In our patriotic circle there is anger. Donald Gordon is building the Queen Elizabeth Hotel in the world's second-largest French city, its population more than 60 percent French-Canadian. Donald Gordon maintains that his hotel will be named for the Queen of England. And to add insult to humiliation, that name will be written in English. We've read more than a hundred articles on the subject. Jean Drapeau, the new mayor of Montreal, is calling for a French name. Demonstrations at the construction site multiply. We collect money to support this patriotic war. None of us has ever been in Montreal. Because it's French, it's our city. This time the English won't win.

The Rocket continues his climb. On December 30, he scores another hat trick. And another on January 20, 1955. At the beginning of February he crowns a hat trick with a fourth goal.

At the Forum on Saturday, March 12, the hospitality being shown the Bruins isn't warm. The Canadiens almost feel that they can touch the Stanley Cup. The Rocket also wants to become the top scorer in the NHL: that is, the player who obtains the highest total of goals plus assists. To date, this championship has escaped him. This season he's in first place, but Béliveau and Geoffrion are hard on his heels. As usual the Bruins try to exasperate Maurice: "French pea soup!" "Goddamn Frog!" "French bastard!" Blows from sticks, knees. Finally, he's toppled into the goal; his back crashes into the goalpost.

The next day, the Canadiens meet the Bruins in Boston. The Rocket feels a biting pain in his back. He's tired, too. Six months of playing and travelling. This game will be a tough one. It's the season's last meeting with the Bruins; some accounts are going to be settled. In the past five games he hasn't scored a goal. At a certain point in his career a player comes up against a wall and can't advance any further. Has he reached that point? He has to work. He has to break down that barrier. The Stanley Cup is waiting on the other side, and the scoring championship.

The Bruins try to demoralize the Canadiens. Sticks are flying high. Certain kinds of clubbing hurt. The crowd is excited. Are the Bruins going to take the lead? Dick Irvin urges his players not to let themselves be intimidated. Nobody knows yet that he is suffering from bone cancer. It's his secret. For some time now he's been looking unhappy. He's always impatient. He wants the Stanley Cup. His last one, maybe.

Defenceman Hal Laycoe tackles the Rocket. The referee points to the penalty box. The game goes on. The Rocket doesn't forget that Laycoe has tried to crush him. The Canadiens take the assaults. They're impatient, spitting sparks. The crowd spurs on its Bruins. Stimulated, they redouble their efforts. The Rocket resembles a furious bull in the arenas of Spain.

In the third period, Hal Laycoe and the Rocket are face to face. The Rocket tries to get the puck away from him. Laycoe puts up a fight, pounding with his shoulders, his elbows. The Rocket is solid.

Finally, with both skates wedged into the ice, he swipes the puck from Laycoe and pushes himself towards the net. He feels as if he's flying again. And he'll score!

Laycoe, on his trail, can't catch up with him. Reaching out his arm he lashes the Rocket's face with his stick, near the eye. Was it an accident? Was it intentional? The Rocket rages and goes on, skating around the Bruins' net. A sensation of heat travels down his nose. He takes off his glove, brings his hand to his face. His fingers come away red. He drops his stick, his gloves, clenches his fists. Spitting with rage, he rushes at Laycoe. The defenceman's glasses go flying; he looks for them on the ice. The powder keg has exploded. Everyone joins in the brawl. The Rocket grabs hold of his stick and goes back to Laycoe, armed. Cliff Thompson, the linesman, wants to prevent a murder. Grabbing the Rocket's arm, he twists it behind his back like an accomplished wrestler. The Rocket resists. Laycoe comes up to the immobilized Rocket and smacks him several times. The Rocket, held back, squirms, rolls onto the ice with the linesman, frees himself. But the linesman resumes his wrestling hold. How to get rid of him? A punch in the face! The Rocket has struck Thompson . . . Everyone knows that he has the sharpest punch in the NHL.

Laycoe mounts a fresh attack, his stick in the air. The Rocket invites him to fight like a man, with his fists. Laycoe turns down the invitation. Referee Red Storey sends the Rocket to the locker room for the rest of the game. The doctor gives him the five stitches he needs. The next day the Boston papers call for a stiff penalty for the Rocket, who struck a linesman.

In the train taking them back to Montreal, Dick Irvin and the Rocket can't bring themselves to go to their berths. Hal Laycoe has made the Rocket bleed. With his response the Rocket has caused a major upheaval. The coach, riddled with cancer, sees his Stanley Cup drifting off to sea . . . Will he still be standing behind the players' bench next year? Maurice has no regrets. His anger was warranted. But his rage did nothing to help the Canadiens. Silent, head bowed, all he has left is his pride.

League president Clarence Campbell summons Maurice Richard, Dick Irvin, Ken Reardon, Hal Laycoe and his coach, Lynn Patrick, who accuses the Rocket of opening the hostilities. At 2:00 P.M., Campbell informs the press of his disciplinary action: the Rocket is suspended for the rest of the season.

The province of Quebec is incredulous. The Rocket was simply defending himself: he can't be punished for that. Later, people realize that the punishment is irrevocable. And then they face up to reality: without the Rocket, the Stanley Cup won't be seen in Montreal. Once again the Rocket is punished for being attacked. Strongmen like Laycoe will never slow down the Rocket. Maurice will always be far ahead of them. Clarence Campbell would like to see him stretched out on the ground. The Rocket is standing on his feet. He defends himself like a man. People are no longer afraid of the bosses. They've lived through strikes in the factories, in the mines, in the textile mills. Now they will organize a strike against Clarence Campbell, who has always looked down on French Canadians. During the war he sat in his neat and tidy office while French Canadians were fighting in the mud. That's what people are saying. Clarence Campbell is indulgent towards players who have strong arms and slight talent, like Ezinicki, Leswick, Murphy, Bailey, Laycoe, but he's always been pitiless towards the greatest hockey player in the history of the world. That's what people are saying. Clarence Campbell is trying to crush a little French Canadian who has wings. That's what people are saying. Anger is rumbling in the province of Quebec like the water held captive in the rivers by the winter ice.

The time of contempt is over, Monsieur Clarence Campbell. Ever since your ancestors seized hold of our country two hundred years ago the people, with tremendous patience, have been swallowing their anger. It has grown; now it's immense. That's what people are saying.

The Rocket comes home, livid. Lucille has never seen him so furious. He's back from the hospital. With good news. Ever since he struck the enemy goalpost, his back has been scorched with pain. The X-rays have shown no serious injury. In a little while it will be gone. Today, it's Clarence Campbell who is making him suffer. Lucille wishes she could help him. She's familiar with her husband's silences. He's desperate. The phone rings again and again. People are calling from all over. All kinds of people. They promise Maurice their support.

In Clarence Campbell's office the telephone is just as feverish. Voices are protesting. Insulting him. Some issue threats. The tone of the voices is worrying. Telegrams pour in: the entire province of Quebec is crying out its disagreement.

Everywhere fists are pounding tables. Everywhere, faces are red with anger. From everywhere, insults are flying towards Clarence Campbell. Everyone has his own story of indignity to tell. The old folks talk about the time when they were cutting wood in the logging camps, slaving from one darkness till the next. They talk about the time of the war, in the army. They remember a boss who cheated when he added up the hours of work. They mention a cousin who used to work for somebody like Clarence Campbell. They talk about places where a French Canadian couldn't get in because he was French Canadian. Maurice Richard has never accepted humiliation. Humiliating the Rocket means humiliating the entire people. This time we won't bow our heads.

Messages from admirers pile up at the Richard home. The phone rings so often that the young children are terrified. Neighbours lend a hand to Lucille, who is run off her feet with all this commotion. Maurice's mother, Alice, comes to help. And some neighbours. "We're with you, Maurice!"; "Give 'em hell, Maurice!"; "Keep it up, Maurice!" A slogan spreads: "Boycott Campbell's soup!" The product has the misfortune to bear a hated name on its label. Fearing a popular uprising, Montreal mayor Jean Drapeau insists that the NHL re-examine the matter, while Conservative MP Léon Balcer demands an emergency debate in the Commons.

Clarence Campbell has informed the police that hooligans intend to blow up his office. Others have issued death threats. Some policemen hint that this time, they'll have more sympathy for the murderous horde than for the victim.

Early in the morning, the curious show up outside the Forum. They sense the storm about to break. At noon, demonstrators hold aloft placards with awkward inscriptions: "Outrageous Decision!"; "Campbell Is A Jerk!"; "Campbell Out!"; "Campbell's A Pig!"; "Long Live Richard!"; "Injustice to Richard = Injustice to French Canadians"; "Richard the Persecuted"; "Campbell the Greedy Puppet."

At home, Maurice is on the phone. "We'll set up Campbell for you!" an admirer promises. Maurice tries to calm him: "The Canadiens still have a good chance of winning the Cup." He's not convinced that what he says is true. When he soothes the fury of his admirers, he lets them down. They don't want to be calmed. Should he go away with his wife and children to escape all this? Lucille reminds him that Maurice Richard has never fled before anyone.

Early in the evening the crowd makes its way to the Forum. Saturday night is a big night out. The men's neckties are carefully knotted. They're wearing hats. Their gabardine coats are buttoned. The women are lovely in their pretty little felt hats trimmed with flowers. Some are wrapped in fur coats. They don't dress up like that for Mass. Some bring along bags filled with eggs, some of them rotten, and tomatoes . . .

St. Catherine Street in front of the Forum is blocked by demonstrators: men and women, bosses and employees, office workers and factory workers, young and old. There are women with children, even pregnant women. The police are keeping an eye on this human tide. A few hooligans are there in leather jackets. People perch on cars that are parked or paralyzed. Some sit on phone booths, on newsstands, on "No Parking" signs. Others have climbed onto hydro poles or trees in the park. In English, in French, placards inveigh against the president of the NHL: "Campbell, Drop Dead!"; "*Dehors*, Campbell!"; "*Boycottons la* game!"

Inside, the Forum resembles a heart that's swollen from too much emotion. To avoid the throng, Maurice and Lucille use a private door in the back. When they appear the cries meld into one victorious rumbling: it's as if the Rocket has just scored the finest goal of his life! Tears pour down the cheeks of a number of people. Yesterday, when Clarence Campbell handed down his judgment, they felt powerless. Tonight, together, they feel strong. Maurice and Lucille take their places behind Terry Sawchuk's net. These two adversaries respect one another. It's no dishonour to have your shot stopped by a magnificent goalie like Sawchuk. Nor is it a dishonour not to catch a puck fired by the top scorer of all time. The Rocket is worried; will the Canadiens lose their faint edge over the Red Wings? He'd like to flatten Clarence Campbell's nose. But he won't touch the man. His body is condemned to stay in his seat, but his soul will be out on the ice, in his skates. All the seats are occupied save two: those of Clarence Campbell. Will that "dictator," that "hater of French Canadians" as some placards call him, dare to show his face?

Among the fans a young man is shaking. In his pocket there's a tear gas bomb that he'll launch when the moment is right. He's very nervous. Luckily, he's not alone. Friends are with him. They know his secret. These young people don't accept the injustice done to the Rocket. They demand Clarence Campbell's resignation. Starting at seven o'clock tonight, they've been arriving at the parking lot armed with projectiles: tomatoes, eggs and that tear gas bomb. One of their friends, a policeman, didn't hesitate when they asked if they could borrow a tear gas bomb. Who will throw it? The friends draw lots. Gendron will throw the bomb. He's never done anything like this before but he'll do it gladly. Campbell . . . Some time later, he pulls out. He's too nervous. Desmarais will do it. Gendron exchanges his bomb for Desmarais's tomatoes and now it's his turn to be upset. Other fans in the crowd make bets: if a member of their group manages to hit Campbell, they'll give him a hundred-dollar reward. The sounds of breaking glass. Bottles are being thrown against the front of the building. Shattered glass falls like snow onto those going inside the Forum. A demonstrator throws a lead weight into a store window.

The Canadiens and the Red Wings come onto the ice. A heavy silence greets them. The game begins. The Canadiens are moving slowly. Nobody feels like watching this game: it's a different contest that they've come to see. Maurice grits his teeth; never has he seen his team so inconsistent. His feet move as if they were in skates. His hands clench as if they were holding a stick; the muscles in his arms contract as if he were about to shoot the puck.

Clarence Campbell and his secretary, Phyllis, walk along St. Catherine Street, go through the demonstrators without being recognized, and now who should appear at the Forum but His Majesty, Clarence Campbell. His manner is stiff and disdainful. He looks like a snob with the white handkerchief in the breast pocket of his coat, like a boss. Staring into space. Maurice doesn't remember Campbell ever looking him in the eye. Slowly, the president takes his seat. He wants the fans to see that he's not impressed by this circus. He was right to punish Richard. And he takes out his opera glasses.

At first there was only silence in which cigar and cigarette smoke were suspended. Then, whispers. And the crowd's voice is raised. Cries flagellate him: "Long live Richard!"; "Shoo, Campbell!"; "We want Richard!" Phyllis, terrified, asks to leave. He sits there, impassive.

Hardly more than a minute after his arrival, the Bruins score. Is Clarence Campbell going to bring them luck on top of everything else? Two minutes later, the Bruins drive in another goal. Very calmly, Campbell watches the Canadiens lose through his opera glasses. What contempt! What disdain! "Campbell Out!" As if it were the rallying cry people have been waiting for, on all sides fruits, vegetables, fresh eggs, rotten eggs, overshoes, hot dogs, ice cubes, pickles, potatoes, tomatoes go flying. Under these projectiles Campbell remains imperturbable. He was right to punish the Rocket. His exemplary sentence was fair. In the past, the Rocket has been reprimanded for giving officials a hard time. In the past, he's been warned by the League not to use his stick like a weapon. Clarence Campbell has done his president's job well. His decision wasn't an easy one. He acted in accordance with his responsibilities. Tonight, the president is seated in his box, despite the death threats, despite the advice of the police, despite the insults, the projectiles. He has acted reasonably according to his own best judgment.

When the first period is over, the crowd comes down from the stands. Through the melee security agents hurry to Campbell's rescue. A young man hurls tomatoes at his coat. The president remains impassive, but there's terror in his eyes. Can the security agents prevent him from being lynched?

Desmarais, the young man with the bomb, pulls it out of his pocket, tears off the ring the way his policeman-friend showed him and throws it in Campbell's direction. He was overwrought. The bomb doesn't fly very far. Instead, it rolls down through the stands. A thick cloud of yellowish smoke emerges from it and spreads. The acrid smell is horrible. People choke. Cough. Weep. Suffocating, blinded, with handkerchiefs over their mouths, they try to find the exits. The Forum empties. Firemen demand that the game be ended. The announcer declares that the victory is conceded to the Bruins.

Outside, terrified, unhappy fans mix with the demonstrators who are covering St. Catherine Street and spreading under the trees in the park across from the Forum. Hurling abuse at Campbell, carried away by the same rage, the two crowds join forces to lay siege to the Forum. There's plenty of ammunition: chunks of ice, stones, bricks, bottles. Fires are lit here and there. Bonfires? Fires to warm the chilly air of this early spring? Fires to throw at the Forum? Demonstrators overturn police cars. They kick dents into cars parked along the sidewalks. Derail streetcars immobilized in the frenzied traffic jam. Pull panic-stricken passengers out of taxis. They shatter windshields. Smash windows. Break television lights. Demolish newsstands because they need wood for their fires. They need paper too. The wind blows pages of newspapers into the air and they take flight like fiery birds. If policemen grab a demonstrator, the crowd sets him free. Madness reigns in the street. The Forum refuses to catch fire. The demonstrators can't get inside to wreak havoc there, so they go where there are store windows to smash, stores to loot. Is this the great anger of a small people? Is it a barbarian celebration?

Policemen in long coats, in close order, striking their hands rhythmically with the white sticks they're holding, advance on the demonstrators and push them towards the east end of town.

The next day, the Rocket learns the extent of the damage. Some fifty store windows smashed. Those businesses looted. The Rocket is shaving at his mirror: he is responsible for that mess. He is guilty of all that disorder. He caused that violence, the like of which has never been seen in Montreal. In the street, fans were imitating things that he'd done on the ice. Will today's violence be worse than yesterday's? Vandalism is smouldering like fire beneath the ashes.

At the demand of Frank Selke, the Rocket goes on television to urge the population to be calm. Ill at ease, he reads the speech that's been written for him. His misbehaviour, he says, merited punishment. The penalty is severe. He accepts it. He reads the words but his heart isn't in them. The Canadiens can still win the Stanley Cup, his prepared speech declares.

In our country seminary we don't understand this urban hysteria. What frenzy has taken hold of the people? We argue. Did they want to destroy an environment in which they felt like foreigners? Have the people treated themselves to a free celebration? Were they just sports fans expressing their disagreement with the referee? Were they cries of protest sent up by our small people for the injustices that we've suffered? After being held back by history for so long, are the French Canadians now beginning to react like the Rocket on the ice?

An English newspaper, the *Montreal Star*, which we hate with all our soul and have never read, upbraids us for suffering from emotional instability and lack of discipline. The paper's bosses must be something like Clarence Campbell. Aristocrats in the time of the French Revolution also saw as unattractive the discontent of the people who demonstrated against them in the street.

In the semifinals, the Canadiens without Maurice demolish the Bruins in five games. Then, still without him, they try to survive the finals against the Red Wings. The seventh game is fatal. And so ends a terrible season.

Maurice Richard watches helplessly as his team goes down to defeat in the last two games against the Red Wings. While he's just a spectator, Bernie Geoffrion is playing with all his might, scoring goals, surpassing the Rocket's total and becoming the scoring champion. That championship was stolen from Maurice, not by Geoffrion but by Clarence Campbell.

Maurice is bitter, unable to forget. Unable to sleep. Lucille doesn't know what she can do to calm him. Even with the children he sometimes runs out of patience. He snarls. He can't stand the western songs he's fond of. He has just one thing in mind: if Clarence Campbell hadn't got rid of him, the Stanley Cup parade would have been held in Montreal . . . After this disastrous season, he no longer dares to show himself in public. He wishes he could make himself invisible like Mandrake the Magician in the comics.

His teammates have no trouble persuading the taciturn Maurice to join them for a trip to the Florida sun. They're fond of this lone wolf. The vacationing athletes wrap him in their rough friendship. Jean Béliveau used to follow his exploits on the radio, dreaming that one day he'd play like him. He has inspired them all. With the Rocket on the team how could they not believe that a defeat is the end of the world? For him there's only one option: to win. No one dares to be mediocre next to him. Béliveau, Geoffrion, Mosdell, Moore like this family man who doesn't need to talk to tell them what he thinks: one look is enough. They respect this legendary hero who sometimes laughs at a story but doesn't know how to tell one.

THE RETURN OF TOE BLAKE

1955. In Canada, May 24 is Victoria Day, but in the province of Quebec we celebrate instead a legendary hero of New France named Dollard des Ormeaux, who along with his companions resisted for long hours an Iroquois attack on his fort at Long Sault. Just as the Iroquois were entering the fort, Dollard drove them back by setting fire to a powder keg. He sacrificed his own life, we're taught, to save New France, the Catholic religion and the French language in America.

Our patriotic circle has delegated me to deliver the traditional speech to the assembled students and priests. I exalt the courage of Dollard, symbol of the French-Canadian people who no longer accept quiet submission. Don't the events at the Forum prove it?

Have I touched the hearts of my comrades? They applaud me. I'm a little bit proud of myself. The principal asks to see me in his office. Is he pleased with me? He doesn't look up when I'm introduced. He says only:

"Your trunk is out on the balcony."

I don't understand. I repeat:

"My trunk is on the balcony?"

"Take it and go. There's no room in our seminary for someone who reads unclean books."

I understand. The monitor has been snooping. That illiterate has found the two masterpieces of French literature that I bought instead of *Quick—Germinal* and another one.

"If an apple is rotten you don't leave it in the fruit bowl," the principal insists without looking up from his paper.

I feel dazed. A minute ago I was applauded; now I'm an outlaw.

"I'm being expelled like Maurice Richard?"

"Like a rotten apple," snaps the principal, "but there won't be any mob supporting you."

Pathetically, I go back to my village. My parents don't know what to say to a rotten apple. If the only wrong I've done is to read books, it can't be all that serious, declares my mother, the former schoolteacher. She'd have liked to have had books to read.

On June 24 comes the feast of St. Jean Baptiste, patron saint of French Canadians. I'm watching television. The people of Montreal seem calm now after shaking up their city. Lined up peacefully along the street they watch with tender affection the young saint on his float, that insipid fair-haired child with his curls and his sheepskin. St. John the Baptist, failed boy, failed little girl, insipid depiction of our identity that the priests have invented and taught us to venerate.

One day, the people will knock that pitiful idol off his pedestal. That's my prediction: no doubt such a wicked thought comes to me from the wicked books I've read. My mother's heart turns upside down at the sight of the human lamb. My father is more realistic:

"Instead of daydreaming, find yourself a college that will take you next fall."

═══

Toe Blake rejoins the Canadiens to replace Dick Irvin. Toe played at Maurice's side for six years. Six years of joint efforts, of mutual support, six years of injuries, of victories and defeats. Six years of constant dialogue in which they didn't need a lot of words. Six years when those two men on the ice struggled to be more than players: to be winners. Six years when their speed, their sang-froid, the way that they gave of themselves made crowds go wild in all the arenas of America. Six years when they agreed on the same game plan: "We'll score more goals than the other team." Imagine the ties that unite these two men.

What's more, Toe Blake is half French-Canadian; he'll speak French to his French-Canadian players. Like the Rocket, though, Toe Blake isn't talkative either in French or in English. During his days on the Punch Line, if a tactic aborted, if a play fell apart, if one of the wings wasn't where he should have been, Toe Blake didn't "give hell to the universe," as the poet Rimbaud said. It was through silence that these two players communicated. Together they amassed so many victories. Now those days are going to return. Toe Blake talks to Maurice about the future. "If you want to win, you have to control your temper like you control the puck. Get a grip on yourself. Put your anger into shooting the puck." A few words, a few truncated sentences, a few looks. They don't need complete sentences. Yet the coach wants to make something clear: "Maurice, you and me, we've played some games together, we know each other a little. If you don't agree with me, don't say so in front of the others." Maurice doesn't say a word, only nods. Toe merits his respect.

Frank Selke is a businessman whose first thought is for the Canadiens' earnings. Sometimes, though, he talks to Maurice like a father: "You're thirty-four years old. You're the most famous player in the NHL. You've got your records. I'm not saying take a rest. The crowds come to see you. You're at your peak. What I'm saying is, you've got teammates. You aren't the only one out there. You shouldn't take all the responsibility on your shoulders. Leave some for the others. At the end of the last two seasons the Canadiens were the best; we should've had the Stanley Cup. In '54 a shot veered off Doug Harvey's glove and Gerry McNeil didn't see a thing. Last spring, your fight with Laycoe hurt the team. Rocket, I don't want to talk about the past. I'm talking about the future. Get a grip on yourself. Don't create conditions that'll make you lose. What's important isn't winning a round of boxing; it's winning the Stanley Cup."

At training camp, Toe Blake observes his rookies. These young-sters understand that it's not enough to dream about playing for the Canadiens. They have to earn their places. And he marvels at the sight of his veterans fighting as if they were trying to hold the attention of the scouts. He can't remember seeing the Canadiens so strong. The puck streaks across the ice. Among the youngsters is Maurice's brother, Henri. The little player's fierceness is reminis-cent of the Rocket's. For a long time in the minors he's been paying the price of being the Rocket's brother. His opponents like to pit themselves against Maurice's kid brother. During his time as a sports columnist for *Samedi Dimanche*, Maurice encouraged Jean Béliveau to leave the Quebec City Aces and join the Canadiens. Friends of the Aces didn't appreciate this pilfering. When Henri turned up in Quebec City, he suffered the consequences of his brother's words. Those experiences have taught him courage. They've toughened him.

Henri, fifteen years younger than the Rocket, doesn't know him very well. Mainly, he knows the great hockey player. When he was five, Onésime took him to the Forum and sat him on his knees to watch the game. Already he knew the names of all the players. He shouted when Maurice got the puck. Maurice is his hero. And Henri's style, like his brother's, attracts attention. People can't take their eyes off this rookie. Maurice is spectacular even when he's lacing his skates, while Henri's movements fascinate the way a candle in the dark does. Ten thousand people would come out to watch him play in the Junior League.

One morning at practice Henri makes a breakaway towards the opponents' net. He shoots and, without taking his eyes off the puck, heads behind the net. At the same time, Maurice positions himself behind the net to prepare for the next play. Bottleneck. They collide. If the two brothers were cars, they'd be accordions. Cut faces. Blood on the ice. The trainer arrives. The Rocket regains consciousness. He recognizes his brother, who's also come back to earth.

"Watch out, Henri, you might get hurt!"

On a three-game tryout, Henri impresses the management. He's only nineteen but the little devil on skates is ready to fight for the puck with anyone he wants. The fans recognize a Richard. Some recall the arrival of the young Rocket thirteen years ago: Henri is a new Rocket. The opponents keep an eye on Henri the way they keep an eye on a Richard. Maurice is never far from his brother if anyone shows him a lack of courtesy. The girls like this fast little player. They've noticed that during warm-up he circles the ice twice as often as the other players.

On October 15 the Rocket scores twice and Henri registers his first goal in the NHL. One fan in particular is silently proud: their father. He left his native Gaspé because there was no future. He has worked hard. He's been strict with his boys. Now two of his sons are playing for the Canadiens. Maurice is the best player in the NHL. Henri will perhaps be even better. To reporters who ask how he feels, he says, "Those two boys of mine aren't bad!" Don't expect speeches from him.

Frank Selke, the businessman, wants his show to be as appealing as possible. Toe Blake wants to win the Stanley Cup. The two are in agreement: Maurice and Henri will play together on the same forward line, with the capable Dickie Moore at left wing. What firepower! When they need rest, they'll be relieved by a second, equally awe-inspiring line: Béliveau, Geoffrion and Bert Olmstead. And a third line will be waiting in the wings: Floyd Currie, Claude Provost and Don Marshall. On defence, Doug Harvey and Butch Bouchard. In goal, Jacques Plante, who's as lithe as a cat. All are hard workers, skilful skaters, who know how to use their shoulders when necessary; all are convinced that the puck has no reason for existing unless it ends up in the enemy net. Each man knows his responsibility. Each man carries it out as if he were going to save the country.

Boom Boom Geoffrion isn't happy. He'd like to leave the Canadiens. Every time he steps onto the ice at the Forum, fans boo him as if he were on the other team. Geoffrion isn't afraid of bruises or cuts or fractures or stitches, but the fans' outcry upsets him badly and sends him to the verge of tears. In the previous season, he robbed the Rocket of the scoring championship. Losing it was hard on Maurice, but he reasons with himself: Geoffrion couldn't take aim beside the net to avoid scoring. The crowd, though, won't forgive him. Their boos affect Geoffrion like fourteen thousand buckets of cold water in his face. He thinks he ought to be playing somewhere else. With his gruff friendship, Toe Blake brings his players back to the objective: to win games one at a time, one goal at a time.

In the same way he tells the Rocket again that he doesn't need to explode every time his anger dial is at maximum. The Rocket listens. He's enraged but doesn't say a word. Shoots furious looks. But he complies. And a rumour goes around that the Rocket is getting soft.

In a short time, Toe Blake has established his authority. The players trust him. He hasn't forgotten what it is to play on the ice. Every member of the team feels respected: never does he reproach a player for committing an error. Instead, he speaks to him in private. He explains how it could have been avoided. Toe Blake sees himself as a father; the Canadiens are a family. Not only Maurice and Henri but all the players on his team are brothers. They listen to the coach: "The objective: to win. To win, first of all you have to score goals. And then you have to score more goals."

═══

Here I am in exile in New Brunswick. Just across the bridge over the Madawaska River lies American territory. My new seminary is a short walk from the United States. My patriotic circle is far away.

I read that the federal government wants some of the street signs in Ottawa to have French words so that French Canadians in the nation's capital won't feel as if they're in a foreign city. The president of the Association of Protestant Women of Canada has declared that "the use of the French language outside Quebec is illegal." That remark flattened me like a check into the boards.

With whom can I share my anger? I like the style of a reporter who writes in *Le Devoir*, the famous Pierre Laporte. I write to him.

Perhaps he could advise an exiled patriot. The great journalist sends a two-and-a-half-page letter in reply: "French Canadians must be like Maurice Richard: never yield an inch, head for the goal and score." I reread the handwritten letter ten times.

I also meditate on another letter that was published in *Le Devoir*, which denounces rock 'n' roll, "that mind-destroying music made to accompany savage jungle orgies." The writer pleads with the government to prohibit concerts of that barbaric music. Rock 'n' roll, the syrupy music of the Platters, Pat Boone, the Four Aces, the Four Lads—American music breaks over us like a tidal wave. There is so much American music that we're shipwrecked. But we like it! Rock 'n' roll makes you want to jump over roofs. With some new friends I go to the States three times to see the film *Rock around the Clock*. We wear zoot suits: a very broad-shouldered jacket with pants very tight at the ankles. Look at us! Thus decked out, my new friends and I cross the international bridge. We're going to the States to dance with girls who wear crinolines under their skirts and stylish white socks with their white shoes. Now and then the rock 'n' roll will give way to a sweet song like "The Great Pretender." In our arms we hold American girls who are plump and perfumed and who like us "Frenchies." But when the fly boys, aviators from the nearby base, land in the hall, we don't exist. If we can grab anyone for the next dance it's a great-grandmother. American music is threatening our culture but the patriot doesn't resist very hard. With a pretty girl in a crinoline in his arms, the great patriot is conciliatory.

Winter arrives. Hockey begins. My new seminary is proud of its excellent team. Here, girls aren't forbidden as if they were wicked books. No one chases them away with a holy-water sprinkler. I've never seen so many pretty girls who are hockey fans. They're like Lucille, Maurice's girlfriend before she became his wife. Between periods here the players are allowed to talk to them. When the game is over, the girls gather at the gate. The players, even the losing team, pass through a bouquet of girls before they go to take their skates off. The girls are for the local Maurice Richards.

Is the Rocket getting soft? He refuses
to box a round with the Rangers' Lou Fontinato. Fontinato holds
the League record for penalties. Little Henri Richard slams him
into the boards. Fontinato pays him back with two punches in the
face. The Rocket is vigilant. He was about to rush to his brother's
defence but he stops. Henri can defend himself. He doesn't need
help. More than Henri, it's the Rocket whom Fontinato would like
to attack. He sets off in pursuit. The crowd eggs him on. He catches
up with the Rocket. Twice, he leaves his official stamp on his face.
The crowd approves willingly. The Rocket falters. Wipes his face. Is
it sweat? No, it's blood! Will the Rocket destroy Fontinato? The
crowd demands a fight. Toe Blake keeps his eye on Maurice, who
finally doesn't return the courtesy but goes to the locker room,
furious and mute.

In the third period, lightning will strike. The Rocket's halberd
is pointed at Fontinato. Toe Blake reminds him: "You get a bigger
payoff from a puck in the Rangers' net than from a punch in Fontinato's face." The players watch. Listen. Say nothing. Doug Harvey
ventures to make a joke. The players burst out laughing. The
Rocket's eyes flash lightning but there's a hint of a smile on his lips.
Is he becoming emotional? Toe Blake calms him down: "Maurice,
you aren't allowed to get mad. But if you do get mad, then slam that
puck in their net."

On December 29, on a pass from Henri, he scores his twenty-
first goal of the season and the five-hundredth of his career, counting both regular seasons and playoffs. No one before him has ever
outsmarted so many opponents, so many goalies. Rousing celebrations in Montreal. In Toronto, the mayor pays tribute to him: "You
represent all of Canada." For the modest and ambitious Rocket,
the summit that matters is the next one. This year he wants to
become scoring champion. The title got away from him last year
because of Clarence Campbell . . . And Boom Boom Geoffrion. Toe
Blake wants the Stanley Cup; his obsession with winning is fine

with the Rocket. To win you have to bash in the net. That too is fine with him.

When they're about to leave for New York, Lucille goes to the station with her husband as she always does. A photographer would like a sentimental snapshot: "Rocket, how about kissing your wife for my camera?" Mischievous, without taking his cigar out of his mouth, Maurice tells the man, "I never kiss her when I'm going on such a short trip!"

The Rocket is getting soft? He plays as if he were putting out a fire in his house. He plays the way a shipwreck victim swims towards terra firma. All of him, body and soul, past, present and future, is in the thrust of his skate that drives the ice behind him, in the tensing of the muscles that fire a shot. The Rocket plays as if only a goal could save the endangered universe. He plays the way a man jumps off a cliff when he's convinced that he can fly.

On March 15, 1956, during the final game of the regular season, the Rocket goes into one of his mesmerizing breakaways. Black Hawks Gus Mortson and Pierre Pilote are waiting for him at their blue line. They dig their skates in. They're going to nab the Rocket. Will he take a detour? Head lowered, he pushes his speed. The defencemen get ready for the collision. Percussion. The three bodies take off. The Rocket glides towards Al Rollins's goal, his head strikes the post, the net moves back. He doesn't get up. Standing in silence, the fans wait for a sign of life. Medics come to pick up the Rocket and take him away on a stretcher.

The Rocket comes back to life. Stitches. X-rays. His scorecard for the season: thirty-eight goals and thirty-three assists. He's not the scoring champion. This year, the title goes to Jean Béliveau. The Rocket races towards the puck as if it were his heart that had fallen onto the ice. Béliveau, who plays as if it were easy, has amassed more points. Maurice is only third. Is he third because he's getting soft? Is he third because he now weighs two hundred pounds, fifteen pounds more than at the time of his fifty-goal record? Several times he's put himself on a diet. He was hungry. Tired. This is no time to feel hungry and tired; the playoffs are about to start.

The Rangers wait resolutely for the Canadiens. Maurice Richard is going to show them that he's the Rocket, not third place. In the first game he administers a beating: a hat trick in a 7–1 victory. The Canadiens have learned Toe Blake's lessons well. Bert Olmstead excels at getting hold of the puck in the corners. He passes it to Doug Harvey. Imperturbable, Harvey protects the puck while his eyes appraise the moving chessboard of the ice. In the whirlwind of moving players he judges who among his teammates is in the best position to send the puck into the net. Then, non-chalantly, he'll dispatch it through a thicket of legs and sticks. He rarely misses his target: it lands on the stick of either the Rocket, Geoffrion or Béliveau, who fires at Gump Worsley.

After winning two games in New York, the Canadiens come back to the Forum swollen with glory to deliver the final blow to Phil Watson's players: 7–0. The Rocket hasn't scored a single goal but he's credited with five assists. An amazing contribution. The fans are disappointed. They wanted to see the Rocket himself send the puck into the net. Is the Rocket slowing down? "An assist," declares one fan philosophically, "is like getting your brother-in-law to do the honours to your wife."

The Canadiens have triumphed in the semifinals. What lies ahead in the finals? Red Wings goalie Glenn Hall is a complex man. In the fall he always shows up late for training camp. His excuse: he hadn't finished painting his barn in Saskatchewan. It's said that he's afraid of the puck. Yet he accomplished twelve shutouts during the regular season. It's said that he hates being a goalie so much that he vomits before every game. Is there any truth to these rumours? Toe Blake points out to his players that when he's in the net, Glenn Hall seems no more nervous than a stump. The Rocket knows his style: he spreads his legs from post to post so they form a capital A. To close the opening completely, he positions his stick between his legs, leaving his other hand free to catch shots in the air. In this way he closes the net like a door.

During the long hours of train travel, some players play cards. Goalie Jacques Plante knits; his mother taught her many children

how to knit so they'll never have to suffer from the cold. Other players tell stories. Some doze. The Rocket tries to read an article in a
magazine but he can't understand what it's about. He's distracted
by his next game. His opponents. Their tricks. It's the weight of his
dreams that makes him so light on the ice. Well prepared, he seems
to improvise. His reflections make him instinctive. They make his
action on the ice luminous.

During the semifinals the Maple Leafs have been cut to shreds
by the Red Wings. Is the same fate in store for the Canadiens? In
the second period they fall behind, 4–2. Toe Blake, unshakable, has
confidence in the strength of his team. If his first line can't score,
he'll call on his second line. And his third. Jackie Leclair reduces
the advantage: 4–3. Jean-Guy Talbot ties the score: 4–4. Béliveau
ensures the victory: 5–4. And Claude Provost confirms the defeat of
the Red Wings. Glenn Hall, terrorized by the pitiless shots, vomits;
he wants to go back to Saskatchewan where it doesn't rain pucks.

The Canadiens rob the Red Wings a second time. Fans are
already celebrating the Victory, the only one: the Stanley Cup. The
third game goes to the Wings, 3–1. The Canadiens come back with a
3–0 shutout.

If the Canadiens win the next game they'll be able to dance on
the ice of the Forum with the Stanley Cup in their arms. Last year,
Clarence Campbell stopped that party from taking place. The
Rocket has promised that this year the Stanley Cup will come back
to Montreal. The Rocket has always given but he's never promised.
This time, he has made a promise; it will be respected.

Fourteen thousand fans have come to witness the transforma-
tion of the Canadiens into Stanley Cup champions. The Red Wings
seem to have accepted that defeat is inevitable. But the will of the
Canadiens seems somewhat limp. The fans are already a little
drunk, but the Canadiens don't give them anything to celebrate.
Luckily, Jean Béliveau, after a clever feint, makes Glenn Hall
unhappy: 1–0. Later, the Rocket grabs the puck. In his well-known
style, which is still amazing because it's never exactly the same,
he improvises a fine solo. The opponents band together. He fires.

A goal! A breakaway by the Rocket is imprinted on people's memories like the passage of a comet through the sky. The fans shudder. Victory! The Stanley Cup! Nearly . . . Duplessis is there, standing among the fans. He, the champion of provincial autonomy, will never receive such an outburst of popular gratitude. No political decision can please the people as much as a goal by the Rocket. Boom Boom Geoffrion drives in a third goal. Alex Delvecchio spares the Red Wings the disgrace of a shutout.

The Stanley Cup belongs to the Canadiens! A tremendous roar of joy goes on late into the night, then starts up again the next morning and lasts all day, during a parade through every part of town on a cold but sunny Saturday. The parade lasts for more than six hours, covering sixty-five kilometres. Following the brass bands and the majorettes, gleaming convertibles transport the heroes, who sign autographs, kiss brides, pat children's heads. Reigning in the Chrysler, a beaming Maurice greets fans, shakes their hands. Their warm friendship always intimidates him. At the corner of St. Catherine and St. Denis, under colourful signs advertising "Bowling" or "Nightclub," the fans rush onto the sidewalks in close ranks. This time, Clarence Campbell, you've lost!

The priests have allowed us to watch the final game on television. We've won the Stanley Cup! The next day we go to celebrate our victory over the Americans by dancing to rock 'n' roll with American girls. On the international bridge between Canada and the States, we walk with the insolence of conquerors. Richard, Béliveau, Geoffrion, Plante, Talbot, Provost: these French Canadians have beaten the Americans. The Stanley Cup is ours! During a slow dance to a song dripping honey, we confide to our pretty Americans that we're cousins of the Rocket. In the music, the crinolines, we triumph till the fly boys arrive.

Whatever the importance of the Stanley Cup, an election is to be held in the province of Quebec on June 20. Duplessis urges the population to resist the pitiless government in Ottawa that wants to eradicate French Canadians' rights and prerogatives. Only autonomy can save us. According to my father, Duplessis has worked miracles. Before him the roads were miserable. Duplessis unrolled fine roads, many of them paved, like carpets. The only villages that don't have a new road running through them are those that voted against Duplessis. They shouldn't complain! Nobody forced them to vote the wrong way. He has also installed electricity in the countryside, even in the stables. My father explains to me that you should be ashamed of voting against Duplessis, who has built 85 hospitals and 3,000 primary schools, created 10,000 new companies, and started to develop mines in Ungava and Abitibi. And that's not all! You should be embarrassed voting against the man who protects his province against Communism.

We don't realize what tricks the Communists use to pervert French Canadians. Fortunately, Duplessis is keeping watch. Lately the Communists have found a way to infiltrate even the most Catholic kitchens. Thousands of dozens of eggs imported from Communist Poland have been discovered at Customs. Duplessis gave the order to seize them all. "Protect your children from Communism. Vote for Duplessis!" During the election campaign, in several parts of the province, Duplessis proudly introduces the man sitting next to him on the platform, his "good friend, Maurice Richard." And the crowd applauds him as if he's just scored a goal. Duplessis nods approval and smiles as if the tribute were for him.

A friend of my father's in Duplessis's party gets me a job as assistant to the assistant to the assistant of a surveyor. During the campaign we lay out the roads that Duplessis will build in the area if the people vote for him. The new road will run through the land of farmers who are Duplessis sympathizers. If the farmer is suspected of sympathy with the opposition, his land will be bypassed. One morning the boss asks me to tidy up the papers on his desk. I know how to read. An addendum at the bottom of a contract mentions: "Usual deduction." The same mention has been added to all the contracts that I file.

"Boss, what does 'Usual deduction' mean?"

"That, you little bugger, you didn't see. Don't get mixed up in politics."

Duplessis is returned to power. The electorate has voted for paved roads, electricity in the stables and autonomy, and against Communist eggs.

In August, *Le Devoir* runs a commentary on the recent election campaign. The authors state that it was dishonest, mendacious, immoral. Duplessis's party bought votes. Paid hospital bills and doctors' fees, fees for delivering babies, repairing cars, buying fridges and TV sets. Promised contracts conditional on how people voted. Stole ballot boxes. Had dead people vote. Had some of the living vote several times. Had sympathizers vote in opponents' places. Kept opponents from voting. Falsified voting results. The authors of this diatribe are two priests. They're accusing Duplessis; could they have been corrupted by Communism? Already it's being rumoured that they have been. They're probably not good priests because good priests support Duplessis. These two even dare to accuse the Catholic church of being obsessed by the "wet sins," which are drunkenness and lust, while it is complicit in the "dry sins," such as economic injustice, abuse of power and the denial of democratic rights.

As for me, I'm reading, studying, writing poems, dancing to rock 'n' roll, but I'm not happy the way someone ought to be at my age. Politics is exciting but the time always comes when politics seems to be corrupt. Duplessis has won seventy-seven out of ninety-three seats, but what is his power worth if it's based on trickery, breach of trust, misappropriation of public funds? What future will our small people have if it sells the right to vote for a few bottles of beer? What is our religion worth if our honesty doesn't resist a little gift from Duplessis? We always accuse the English; when will we accuse those who are guilty of the ignorance that overwhelms us? Those are some of the thoughts I mull over during the summer.

Hockey is simpler. No one can lie. A goal is a goal. A bodycheck is a bodycheck. The game is played openly, before the eyes of the crowd. The Rocket has never cheated. He sends the puck into the net through every kind of interference. During this time of corruption, the Rocket is incorruptible. Can the people be reproached for looking up to a hockey champion when they no longer want to look at their leaders, when they have trouble looking at themselves? While the leaders float like logs in the current that is carrying them away, the Rocket affirms our authority over our destiny.

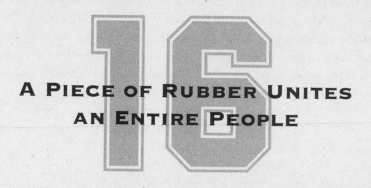

A Piece of Rubber Unites
an Entire People

1956. If politics has its secrets, hockey has its rituals. Every player has his own way of lacing his skates, of taping his stick. Maurice takes the precaution of choosing the wood for his sticks himself. He checks the flexibility, the rigidity, the weight. He studies the grain of the wood. He's as cautious as the percussionist in a symphony orchestra. He measures the balance of handle and shaft. He examines the joints in the heel, its angle. It's from the heel of his stick that the Rocket fires his shots; he inserts the heel of his stick between the ice and the puck. Without those precautions, his stick would have no magic power.

Maurice also takes part in a far more secret ritual. At the beginning of the season, it is the veterans' duty to inculcate in the rookies the fundamental, sacred values that inspire the team in its search for victory. The first principle is self-denial. The rookie must give the team the total gift of himself. What finer symbol of that power than to sacrifice his penis! First the rookies are given psychological preparation administered with psychological subtlety by twenty or so hockey players who have been repeatedly knocked out, injured, dislocated in the wild pursuit of their ideal. Then the rookies are undressed for the grand removal. This is carried out with all the tact of nursing sisters. Next come the surgeon and his assistant all in white, complete with skullcap, mask and coat and with the necessary sharp instruments. When the rookie is sufficiently terrified, the part that's to be amputated is exposed. The surgeon's assistant, the Rocket, carefully shaves what there is to be shaved so that the surgeon, defenceman Doug Harvey, can cut "just a little bit," he testifies. The desire to play with the Canadiens is so powerful that no rookie has ever deserted.

Butch Bouchard, the captain, has retired from hockey. To replace him, his teammates choose the Rocket. He has to win. He has to play to win. To score goals. With a total of 460 goals scored during the regular season, he begins the ascent towards his five-hundredth. That will be a historic record. Score forty goals this year: it can be done. Keep the Stanley Cup in Montreal: we'll do it. This is going to be a good year!

When they see him invade enemy territory, people think that Maurice Richard is playing better than in the finest days of his youth. His technique, polished by long and rough experience, has been enriched by a profound understanding of hockey. Who could imagine that he's bothered by a pain in his elbow? He battles the pain by demanding even more of his left arm. But the pain paralyzes him. He goes to see a doctor. Fragments of broken bone are scraping against some nerves. An operation is urgently needed. Doctors always want to operate. The Rocket wants to play. Finally, at the end of November, he has to give in to the doctors. Then he changes his mind. What will happen to his objective of five hundred goals if he stops? The operation is a serious one. He hesitates. He needs his elbow for firing on the goal! But the elbow isn't working. The doctors are reassuring: "A small incision . . ." Everything was going so well.

Two weeks later he's back in the game. Has his elbow been damaged? The Rocket reassures fans by scoring a goal against the Maple Leafs; he also collects two assists. When the Canadiens and the Leafs are reunited the following week, the Rocket accomplishes two devastating goals. There's no doubt about it: the operation was a success.

Now Gordie Howe has equalled Nels Stewart's 324-goal record. Who is the better player, Maurice Richard or Gordie Howe? The debate goes on. In Montreal the matter is no longer discussed. Fans have calculated that to score 324 goals, it took Stewart 666 games, it took Howe 666—and the Rocket 526. Therefore Maurice is the best; but Gordie Howe is getting close. To hold on to his lead the Rocket has to run! To score!

February 1957 is a month of births for the Canadiens. Maurice's brother Henri announces the arrival of a little girl. One week later, Maurice and Lucille introduce their little Suzanne. Jean Béliveau also becomes the father of a little girl. Dickie Moore takes pride in the birth of a son. Just like victories, defeats and injuries, these births are shared with the fans. Jokes are made: all these babies are arriving at the same time, nine months after the Stanley Cup victory! They're proof that the Canadiens all celebrated in the same way! In churches, priests emphasize in their sermons that it is comforting to see our Canadiens respecting traditional family values, unlike the Communists, for whom sex is only a bestial act.

As for me, I'm interested not in the Canadiens' babies but in a newborn patriotic movement: *L'Alliance Laurentienne*. Its leader, Raymond Barbeau, must down a glass of honey before every speech. He's very smart. For every question he offers a reply that makes the questioner sorry he asked it. In his opinion, the future of the French Canadians can only be built in an independent country, *La Laurentie*. I read every newspaper article on the subject. Laurentia is the province of Quebec.

I think about it. Our people has suffered in Canada. It has suffered under French domination; it has suffered under English domination. My ancestors travelled the length and breadth of this country; they cleared it, they cultivated it. They contributed to the economic life of Canada. They took part in its political life. Must we leave Canada, as Raymond Barbeau preaches? When Maurice Richard loses a game, does he leave hockey? No: the next time, he scores a hat trick! No, Raymond Barbeau, I won't leave Canada for your Laurentia! You want to give me a little country, Raymond Barbeau. Thanks, but I already have a big one.

Late February, the Canadiens are struggling for first place in the NHL. On the twenty-eighth, the Canadiens shut out the Red Wings 3–0, with the Rocket scoring twice. Four days later, they crush Detroit 5–1. The Rocket has scored once.

On March 11, a strike begins in Murdochville, in the Gaspé. That's far away. Once again, it's a miners' strike. Gaspé Copper Mines is refusing to grant union accreditation to its workers. The next day, the eleven hundred strikers see eight hundred scabs arrive. Under police protection, they go down in the mine. Strikes bring terrible hardships. No one is safe.

The fans are worried as they follow the playoffs. The Canadiens will win the semifinals against the Rangers. They've already won three games; the Rangers only one. And tonight they're in Montreal. No doubt they'll prostrate themselves before the Canadiens.

Phil Watson has sworn to the press that his Rangers will mortify the Canadiens. Watson is soon disappointed. The Canadiens have a 3–0 lead. Have they become overconfident? The Rangers brace themselves. The game ends in a 3–3 tie. The Canadiens have nearly been defeated. In the locker room, Toe Blake demands of his players, "How will you explain to the fans if you lose? We were ahead 3–0. We thought it was all over and we could go home. We forgot that Watson's guys were still on the ice. Is that what you're going to tell the fans? We're going to go back home and we're going to come back to the game with the goods."

The overtime period begins. In the net, Gump Worsley stops up every crack. There's nothing abstract about the philosophy of the stocky, pudgy goalie: a puck is a javelin thrown at the goal; the goalie's job is to position himself in front of the javelin.

At the two-minute, eleven-second mark, Henri Richard fires the puck. Defenceman Lou Fontinato holds out his hand to catch it on the fly. It slides into his glove, then drops onto the ice. The Rocket scoops it up. He was there. What incredible intuition! He spots in advance how the play is going to unwind. Before any other player, he deciphers the logic from among the game's multiple complexities. With this information, he races to the spot where the puck will materialize and determines what comes next.

And so the Rocket takes the puck and shows up in front of Worsley. The goalie is waiting for the javelin. His equipment is obsolete. It's the same that he had at eighteen, when he was playing for Verdun. The Rocket knows Worsley: Worsley knows that he can guess his move before it starts. The Rocket fires. Worsley moves forward like a shield and throws himself onto his stomach. The Rocket hasn't really fired. It was a feint. Without haste, Maurice Richard shoots the puck over the supine body. It's a goal! The Rangers have been eliminated. Even the strikers in Murdochville are a little less unhappy.

The Bruins, reinvigorated, have defeated the powerful Red Wings in the semifinals, four games to one. Now Toe Blake gets his Canadiens ready for an abrupt final series. "Stay on the move all the time. Don't stop skating. You have to daze them. Grab hold of the advantage at the faceoff. Shoot as often as you can, but into the net." Every player must play to the limits of his strength and a little more. Every one of them has to help his teammate do what he does best. "You have to be hungry and thirsty. Those who aren't hungry and thirsty are losers."

For long hours, the Rocket waits for the night to end with his hands crossed behind his neck. Is he still capable of playing like in the good years? He has seen very good players give out after a dozen years. This is his fourteenth season. Can he play as well as his brother Henri, Béliveau, Geoffrion and Moore?

On Saturday, April 6, the Forum is full for the first game of the finals. The Rocket plays the way a musician might improvise a tune that makes the crowd dance. His spontaneity is flamboyant. His energy is devastating. As the game advances, it becomes even more dazzling. He invents complicated plays, yet his movements are impromptu. He goes at the opponents' goal like an animal going to the river to drink. Terry Sawchuk, who is resting, has been replaced by Don Simmons. In the second period, a backhand shot sends the puck grazing the goalie's skate and veering into the net. "Maurice Richard shoots—he scores." He isn't proud. A lucky goal isn't a good goal.

Almost right away he gets the puck back. The enemy surrounds him. He struggles to break away. Someone grabs the puck from him. He catches up with the enemy, spirits it away. Finally, after a rough scramble, he's back in front of Simmons. Too close to him, though. The Rocket turns to the left. With his right skate he brakes in a burst of white dust and lets himself fall onto his left knee. With his body leaning backwards, his knee sliding along the ice, he fires. In his eyes there's a slightly demented light. From that look, Simmons knows that the puck is already behind him. Goal number two for the Rocket.

A few minutes later he completes a hat trick. Three goals in less than six minutes! Never have the fans seen such fine hockey. Never has the Rocket been better! It's wild! And Maurice hasn't finished: in the third period he scores a fourth goal. The Bruins are stunned, 5–1.

The Canadiens' firepower is too powerful for them. In the next game, Jacques Plante doesn't let them score a single goal. In five games, the Canadiens take possession of the Stanley Cup.

Will the Rocket sleep better now? Eight goals in ten games. But young Geoffrion scored eleven . . . And he's been plagued by headaches ever since he collided with the Bruins' net. Newspapers, radio, television, all sing the praises of Maurice Richard: "amazing," "incomparable," "magnifique," "fantastique," "unique," "irreplaceable." Sportswriters empty out the storehouse of metaphors. One in particular stands out. At the top of his column the journalist wrote in big letters: MAURICE RICHARD. Then he left the entire space for his column blank and at the bottom, "When you've written the name you've said it all." This literary invention impresses me.

For some days now I've been wearing myself out on an essay I have to write about the seven proofs of the existence of God. I'm late. Now I know what to do. In the middle of the first page of my essay, I write in big letters: GOD. Then I staple together a dozen blank pages without writing anything else. At the very bottom of the last one I declare: "When you've written the name you've said it all."

The party fades away and normal life goes on with its woes great and small, everyday life where you don't often win, where you don't have a lot to celebrate. The debate over the Queen Elizabeth

Hotel does not subside. Fifteen hundred articles have now been written on the matter. A petition with 250,000 signatures of those who reject the name has been presented in the House of Commons in Ottawa. But the name will stay. It would be an insult to Her Majesty not to use her name after obtaining her gracious permission. Donald Gordon has permission to humiliate the French Canadians.

Finally it's the last night of boarding school on our hill in New Brunswick. We're gathered together under the starry sky of May, around a campfire. Before we go our separate ways with each of us following his own road into real life, we form a circle around the fire. Holding hands, we sing. Someone brings along a straw effigy of Donald Gordon. Submerged by our boos, it falls into the flames and burns as we applaud. No sooner has Gordon finished his career than we bring along another friend, Clarence Campbell. We don't allow him to stand trial. Fire!

Farewell, boarding school! We've become men. There's not one of us who still believes that he's Maurice Richard. We're just ourselves, very small on the hockey rink of the world.

═══

1957. Maurice's appetite is no longer just for winning. He's hungry for meat, for dessert. He's often hungry. In the summer he doesn't pursue a puck but he's still as hungry as if he'd played three periods; he eats and he puts on weight. Two hundred and ten pounds: that will be a burden to carry around on skates. He wishes he could burn off this fat. As often as he can he joins the Canadiens' baseball team. But the short run to first base won't make him thin.

Nor is it easy to lose weight when he travels to remote parts of the province of Quebec to referee wrestling matches. Maurice takes Lucille and the children to the Beauce, Lac Saint-Jean, Gaspé. In Jonquière, the large-mouth bass are biting and Maurice feels comfortable among the straightforward, unaffected people there. Sometimes Lucille and the children stay behind with the Bouchard family when he's on tour or when he goes on a fishing trip with his

new friends. People come from far away to see Maurice Richard in
the flesh with their own eyes. The referee's name figures promi-
nently on posters. Maurice puts up with a fair amount of fuss, but
then the time will come when he shows his fists and sends back to
his corner the bad guy who's gone too far. No bad guy is bad enough
to refuse to obey the Rocket's law. The children enjoy these trips.
The family drives through villages, stops for a picnic; they catch a
few trout in the river or the lake and cook them up. After their nap,
the children practise lethal holds on the international wrestling
champions and make them howl in pain. Then they get back on the
road to the next parish hall.

The summer's not bucolic everywhere. The Murdochville
strike has been going on for six months. Thanks to scabs, production continues. The miners' woes are worsening day by day. They
walk the picket line with their accusing placards. The bosses, with
full impunity, are uncompromising. Is our society helpless to settle
its own problems? Is it suffering from indifference to poverty?
Could it be that the government is better at protecting its rich than
its poor? What's happening in Murdochville has also happened in
Asbestos and Louiseville. And it could happen elsewhere. Worry.
Duplessis delivers powerful speeches against Ottawa, which is
oppressing the province of Quebec. Why doesn't he look after his
workers, who are truly oppressed?

On September 15, a procession of several hundred cars leaves
Montreal for Murdochville. The cavalcade, which grows longer from
village to village, follows the St. Lawrence River. In Quebec City, it
stops at the Plains of Abraham. For a moment, people stop and
reflect: what would have become of New France if Wolfe hadn't won
the skirmish in 1759? They imagine, they dream . . . Then, outside
the Parliament, union members and television stars set forth the
distress of the Murdochville strikers.

There has always been serious poverty in the Gaspé, but never
has it been so oppressive as it is in Murdochville. When Maurice's
father, Onésime, and his mother, Alice, immigrated to Montreal,

they dreamed of escaping their misery. The Murdochville strikers are so poor that they can't even dream any more.

Maurice Richard looks at his children. Every summer they go to the pure air of the country. They're dressed like a lawyer's children. Unlike him, they haven't experienced the hunger of the Great Depression. Often he tells himself that hockey has been good to him.

Toe Blake would have preferred to see him arrive at training camp not quite so heavy. The rookies surround him with admiration but it's the ambition of all of them to take his place. And so he works as hard to impress the boss as people do at twenty. He too has to impress the bosses. His records belong to the past. Only today counts. And tomorrow. Some members of Canadiens management consider that the Rocket should retire now, at the peak of his glory. They fear that if he waits around, he'll let his fans down. No one dares suggest this to Maurice. He can guess from their silences what they don't say. He isn't ready to go. He can still score goals. He's as fiercely determined as he was at the start.

At thirty-six, the Rocket now has to face up to Time. It's the greatest challenge of his life. He is playing against the time when he set his records, he is playing against the young Rocket whose acrobatics delighted the crowds. At thirty-six, he needs to be better than the young Rocket. He's playing against his own youth. He's playing against his age, against his weight, against his accumulated injuries; he's playing against the wear and tear on his muscles that, like the philosopher's bow, have lost some strength from being kept constantly taut. He is playing against his intuition, which is declining after it has invented so many spectacular goals. He is playing against his legend; he has to surpass his own history. Maurice is also playing against the future. And Time is guarding the net. It's against Time that he will score his five-hundredth regular-season goal. The Rocket isn't going to leave hockey. An old fisherman from his parents' Gaspé never leaves the sea because it's within him.

I'm a university student now, living in a small white room. On October 4, 1957, I read and reread, incredulous, stunned, the front page of the paper. What a tremendous conquest in human history. Earthlings have crossed a frontier that until now was inaccessible. So the comics of my childhood weren't fantasy. This is more important than the discovery of America! The Soviet Union has placed an artificial satellite in space. With its directional antennae and its 83.6-kilogram weight, it will circle the Earth the way our planet circles the sun at an altitude varying between 228 and 947 kilometres. Is Jules Verne's dream coming true? My head is filled with vertigo as I listen to our poetry professor, an old priest, discourse: "It has been given to me, who has lived in the time of the horse-drawn carriage, to see the invention of the atomic bomb, of television and of the artificial satellite . . . But I don't understand the good Lord, who has let the Communists get there first."

One of our classmates puts up his hand:

"The Russians aren't the first."

"No? Tell us then, who is first?"

"Us, the French Canadians. We've had a Rocket in orbit for a long time!"

═══

The Canadiens overturn everything that's in their way. In the season opener on October 13, they shut out the Red Wings 6–0. Terry Sawchuk, the best goalie in the NHL, is mortified! The Rocket and Dickie Moore both score hat tricks. For Maurice these are goals number 495, 496 and 497. Is it really time for him to take his leave?

Four days later, it's Henri's turn to mark his first NHL hat trick. Maurice is proud. His little brother is fast, tough, a fighter; like him, his only passion is scoring goals. On skates the will-o'-the-wisp is a bomb! The Canadiens have never been so powerful. With their line of fire, the Canadiens will keep the Stanley Cup. The Rocket's 499th goal. In the Forum, a euphoric din. Now the fans want number five hundred. They're ready for ecstasy. No sooner does his stick touch the puck than they're on their feet as if it were already in the net. They applaud. Shout. Urge him on. Insult his opponents. Threaten. Their feet are in the Rocket's skates. They are holding his stick, they're juggling with the puck. They're going to shoot. The Rocket is urged on by their voices as by a rolling tide. The Rocket has scored two goals and two assists, but he's missed number five hundred. The fans go home, let down.

On Saturday, October 19, more than fourteen thousand spectators are at the Forum waiting for an unforgettable party to begin! The Rocket will score his five-hundredth goal. Television technicians, with their cameras and their rolls of cable, get ready to transmit some historic images. It will be like a flash of lightning! If they miss it . . . They're nervous. Photographing the Rocket's puck is like trying to capture the passage of a bullet. The celebration will be easier to transmit but the shot . . . Premier Maurice Duplessis is there.

Maurice Richard is one of the first on the ice. He circles the rink. Doesn't take his eyes off the goalie. During the last playoffs, Glenn Hall was hit in the teeth by a puck. He hasn't fully regained his self-confidence. He is always dreaming about his farm in Saskatchewan. The Rocket's eyes don't let go of him; for him, the game is already under way.

Towards the end of the third period, Dickie Moore, in the Black Hawks' zone, scoops up the puck in a corner and passes it to Béliveau, behind Glenn Hall's net. Plagued, Béliveau breaks away and moves in front of the net. He looks for an opening. Glenn Hall closes the net. It's pointless to shoot. The Rocket is near the blue line. Béliveau sends him the puck. The Hawks are amazed by this pass. Why didn't Béliveau fire? As soon as the puck touches the blade of his stick, the Rocket sends it back as if it were a rebound, with a slapshot that rings out in the Forum. That sound is followed immediately by the silent undulation of the net as it's driven back by the puck. Usually, only the goalie can hear it. Tonight, the fourteen thousand fans hear the puck touch the net. The five-hundredth goal! Our five-hundredth goal! Under the force of his own movement when he fired, the Rocket takes a fall. He bounces back to give Béliveau a hug while the applause crackles for ten minutes.

We're champions! The organist, who has exhausted his repertoire of triumphal marches, improvises dance rhythms. For the fans, the game is over. Why go on? We've proven that we're the best!

Duplessis applauds. What magic word could he use in his speeches to stir up such a sea of patriotism? Montreal is no longer divided between English, French Canadians and immigrants. There are no more humiliated people. No more exploited people. There's no more Murdochville or Asbestos. No more voracious bosses. No more rich and poor. No more unsatisfied lives. The Rocket has brought about a revolution in the province of Quebec.

Jubilant, his teammates surround the Rocket with their masculine affection. Toe Blake comes running. The two men overcome their emotions, like men. Toe Blake has learned from his father what the mines of northern Ontario had taught him. The Rocket has learned from his father what the unproductive land of the Gaspé had taught him. People like them only shake hands at weddings, funerals and on New Year's Day. Toe and Maurice exchange a look. Each knows what the other is thinking. It was a fine goal: good work. Now the job is done. You don't talk about what's been done. Dick Irvin would have liked that goal. Poor Dick is far from the ice tonight. He has succumbed to bone cancer. Dick led them for so many years . . . It was he who invented the Punch Line. It's terrible, cancer. Poor Dick. From where he is now, he saw how the Rocket handled the puck. Dick Irvin certainly liked it.

The Rocket circles the ice, looks up at the stands. When the fans are touched by his gaze they sense that they're no longer the same: the Rocket has seen them. The Rocket salutes them with a wave of his hand.

After a game the Rocket usually confesses to the journalists that such-and-such a goal was just lucky or, speaking of another one, that he'd been sent "a real nice pass," or that he couldn't avoid sending that puck into the net. This modesty annoys some journalists. Tonight, he's enigmatic: "The most important goal is the last one."

At the university, future doctors, future lawyers, future politicians are lyrical. This five-hundredth goal by Maurice Richard excited me more than I'll admit to myself. Mon-

treal, where I've just arrived, is a foreign city to me. Everything
that I'm studying is foreign to me: the writers, their era, their country. Even my French language is foreign to me. In my village near
the Maine border, in the Beauce where I attended my first seminary,
or in New Brunswick, nobody talks the way they talk in my books
from France. But a puck isn't foreign to me. A rink is something I
know. To be surrounded by the snow-white winter, beneath a sky
made of the same ice as the ice on the rink, is something I know; to
feel small and want to become a strong man and shoot the puck into
the boards and make them ring out and then get the puck back and
flagellate the ice with skates that make me taller, make me go
faster, with shoulder pads that make me brawny—I know what that
is. I know what a grand dream hockey can be for a boy. None of my
books talk about it.

I'm touched by the Rocket's five-hundredth goal. At the
Widow's Tavern, where the students get together, I tell the future
doctors and future lawyers, "That five-hundredth goal may be the
only thing that belongs to French Canadians."

On November 3, another powerful piece of news comes to us
from behind the Iron Curtain. The Soviets have launched another
Sputnik into space. At 509 kilograms, much heavier than the first.
At 28,544 kilometres an hour, it's faster too. What's more, there's
an animal on board the satellite: a Laïka dog, a breed that resembles a Pomeranian. Her masters call her Curly. The papers have
christened her Laïka. Instruments are attached to her to assess
her biological behaviour. What does she think about in her air-
conditioned capsule? The sphere will travel for six months, then it
will disintegrate. How long can Laïka survive? What will she think,
all alone in outer space? What will her barks say to earthlings? After
a dog they'll send a monkey into space, then a man. To the moon . . .

The discussions at the Widow's Tavern go on. There's no limit
to what man can accomplish. The space to be explored is boundless.
Man's imagination is boundless. His curiosity too. One day our children will play hockey on the moon.

To my friends the future doctors, who are dissecting cadavers,
and to my friends the future lawyers, who do more talking than

thinking, I maintain that the strength of Maurice Richard belongs in the same category as that which drove Icarus to fly, Jules Verne to invent his moon rocket, the Russians to launch Sputnik and, soon, earthlings to fly to the moon. We have an urgent need to tear open the cocoon that envelops us.

On November 13, in Toronto, bad luck strikes the Rocket. He has just fired at the goalie; the puck rebounds, he rushes to get it back. Seeing that his goalie is in danger, defenceman Marc Réaume races up, throwing himself at the Rocket. The two athletes collapse on top of each other. They move to untangle their legs, their arms. Their muscles tense so they can get up and swing back into action. The blade of Réaume's skate weighs down but not on the ice; instead, like a knife, it penetrates the Rocket's sock and his Achilles tendon. Severs it. "When can I come back in the game?" The doctor thinks carefully. The Rocket is thirty-six. Hockey is a young man's game. Could it be that this accident is a way of telling him, "Enough!"?

"Maurice, you'll have to be patient."

Patient . . . Patient . . . The Rocket is sitting in his easy chair; his foot in its plaster cast is stretched out on a chair; his crutches lie on the floor next to him. Patience . . . The Rocket's life has stopped because hockey has stopped.

Elsewhere, life goes on. Hockey goes on. Hockey is changing. The world is changing. In the Bruins' lineup this January 18, 1958, there's a black player, the first to play in the NHL, named Willie O'Ree. Maurice tries to take a step. Even if he leans on his crutches, he can't stand up. The pain! Patience . . . He's not going to wait around praying to be healed. He's going to accomplish a miracle! The bear is irascible. He moans. He's rebellious. He rattles his cage. With his crutch, he goes around in circles. He hops on his good leg. "Maurice, you're shaking the house!" The Canadiens are playing tonight. His inner boiler is steaming with fervour the way it does before a game, but he can't take even one step. He sits back in his easy chair, lays down his crutches. Patience . . . Stay there, motionless.

Finally he takes a first step. Then another. Immediately, he puts on his skates. Limping, he skates. He gets to the blue line, goes towards the net. He is crippled but he's on his feet. He skates. He can increase his speed. He'd go faster if the pain didn't drive a nail into his leg every time his skate touches the ice. He'll put up with it. It's just a matter of getting used to it. To skate some more. Go faster. He simply has to learn how to glide better, to propel his body on the point of his skate without forcing his tendon. To impose his will on his muscles.

Despite his absence the Canadiens win several games. But the fans don't see the Rocket firing at the goalie. The fans aren't jumping to their feet to follow Maurice with his feet in his magic skates. Henri is the reincarnation of his brother in a smaller body. He's unbridled like Maurice. He does the job the Rocket would do if he could play. The Rocket is proud of him. But he wants to do his work himself! Henri is having a fertile period. The Rocket wishes he were playing with his brother but he's condemned to sit in a chair with his leg stretched out, reading over and over the newspaper stories about the deeds of those who are still playing hockey.

At the beginning of February 1958, the government of Canada, a minority government, votes to dissolve. An election will be held on March 31. Conservative prime minister John Diefenbaker, who needs the French-Canadian vote, makes them a promise: if he's brought back to power with strong support from the province of Quebec, he'll set up a simultaneous translation service for debates in the House of Commons. That way, French-Canadian MPs won't have to speak English to be understood by everyone.

That electoral twaddle has been heard before. Attention is now focussed on the Forum. Many rumours. Some claim they've seen Maurice without crutches. Others have seen him on skates. According to still others, the doctor has told Maurice that his leg no longer has all the muscles it needs. The Canadiens are winning; Henri is just as good as he is, maybe better. The time has come: the Rocket is about to announce his retirement. That's more important than Diefenbaker's declarations of love.

Then, on February 21, the news breaks. The Rocket is coming back! After a forty-three-game absence and even though his Achilles tendon was nearly severed, the Rocket is rejoining his team. When he leaps onto the ice in his usual way, the fans greet him as if he'd just scored his one-thousandth, his two-thousandth goal! Then the clamour dies down. All eyes are on his injured leg. It seems sturdy. Will the Rocket still be able to stun his opponents with his speed? Will he be able to come to a standstill in a cloud of icy dust? Will he be able to turn at an acute angle and continue as if he were going in a straight line? Is the Rocket still the Rocket?

He has already played this game in his head many times. He knows how the opponents will try to immobilize him. They'll hit his injured leg. Yes, there's still a little pain. Not much. And then there's the voice of the fans . . . This accident has obliged him to relive the cycle of a life. After the operation he was like a newborn, unable to move. He learned how to stand up, he took his first step, he learned how to skate. Now, two months later, he's out to conquer the unattainable.

The Rocket has received as many blows as an oak tree that's being felled. Tonight, the fans have come to see their wounded champion stand up again. He doesn't want to let them down. He gives his fans two goals! The Bruins' Harry Lumley, stunned, can't understand what happened. A few weeks ago the Rocket was an invalid. Two goals! After three months without playing. Two goals! His healing is miraculous. Will he leave his crutches with those of the miracle cures at the Oratoire Saint-Joseph? Tonight there was an epic beauty to his play.

In the crowd that leaves the Forum a TV actor, happy to be recognized, comments on the events to some female fans: "The Rocket is like a great actor; no matter how much pain he's suffering, when he steps onto the stage the pain disappears. Take me, for instance . . ."

In the locker room, journalists want their articles to reflect the frenzy of the game and they try to get hard-hitting quotes:

"Rocket, did that severed tendon cause a lot of pain?"

"No worse than anything else."

"Are you happy about your two goals?"

"The first one was pretty good but the second one was lucky."

"Are you starting to think about retiring?"

"I'm not all that tired."

He's never had a lot of trouble outsmarting Harry Lumley. Whether he was with the Red Wings, the Black Hawks, the Maple Leafs or the Bruins, Lumley has never really neutralized the Rocket. Maurice doesn't talk about that. Nor does he tell the journalists that he often thinks about Dick Irvin. His old coach must be pleased tonight. Maurice was like greased lightning, the way Dick liked to see his Punch Line play. The Rocket has won his game; Dick lost his. There are so many things that can't be understood.

The Rocket's magical return to the game, the Canadiens in first place, the prowess of Henri Richard, the many goals by Dickie Moore despite the cast on his wrist: this good news makes the politicians' propaganda impossible. How can anyone care about Diefenbaker's speeches?

═══

No sooner is the Rocket back in the game than the playoffs begin. In the first game of the semifinals, the Canadiens humiliate the Red Wings 8–1. The Rocket contributes two goals in under two minutes. He also gets two assists. In the second game, the Rocket contributes another two goals to a 5–1 victory. The next meeting is a closely fought game. It takes the Canadiens eleven minutes of overtime to snatch a 2–1 victory.

The fourth game in this semifinal series is the one-thousandth Maurice Richard has played since joining the NHL. The event doesn't seem to be turning into a celebration; the Canadiens can't get off the ground. The Wings are watching. At the beginning of the second period, the Red Wings gain a 1–0 advantage. Immediately the Rocket cancels it with one of his electrifying goals; he had fired the puck when, bulldozed by Bob Bailey, he'd fallen to his knees and was drifting along the ice. Three minutes later, Gordie Howe restores Detroit's advantage. With another goal Billy McNeill stabilizes the Red Wings' position. Will the Canadiens let their opponents rob the Rocket of his one-thousandth game? At the end of the second period, Detroit takes a 3–1 lead.

When the third period gets under way, the Rocket doesn't want the fans to remember only wonderful goals from the past. He wants his deeds tonight to become *new* memories, better ones. In the early minutes of the period he drives in a goal: 3–2. The Wings still have the advantage. Five minutes later, a goal by Dickie Moore ties the game: 3–3. In this, the Rocket's one-thousandth game, the Canadiens won't be completely humiliated. Forty-nine seconds later, loaded like a black cloud, the Rocket fires away: 4–3! To celebrate his one-thousandth game, Maurice Richard has given his fans a hat trick, a winning game and a place in the finals.

In the Red Wings' locker room, the odour of sadness is more acrid than that of sweat. To drive away the defeat, these athletes who move like killers are now sobbing like children. Terry Sawchuk confesses to the press that for every one of the seven goals with which the Rocket bombarded him, he used a different tactic. "I don't know how the Rocket does it; he's never the same."

The voices droning around us at the Widow's Tavern are talking about Maurice Richard. My friends and I, though, are concerned about the crisis in the universities. The federal government has voted grants to them. Duplessis is strongly opposed. Education, he proclaims, is a sacred responsibility of the province of Quebec. If the universities let themselves be seduced by federal gold, Duplessis will cut off their subsidies. We students are caught between these two governments who wish us well. The libraries are impoverished; the food is revolting; the professors mediocre; the laboratories wretched. On March 6, like the workers in Asbestos, Louiseville and Murdochville, the students go out on strike. *Le Chef*, Duplessis, is of the opinion that students ought to be studying, not getting involved in matters that are none of their business.

But the 1957–58 finals are beginning. To counter the Canadiens' firepower, the Bruins invent the Uke Line with three players of Ukrainian background: Bronco Horvath, John Bucyk and Vic Stasiuk. Their mission: to bombard Jacques Plante. But despite these kamikazes from the steppes, the Canadiens take the first game, 2–1.

In the second match, the Bruins push back the Canadiens and keep the Rocket far from the puck and the net. They win 5–2, a substantial victory. Will the Uke Line continue its ravages? Will the Bruins rob the Canadiens of the Stanley Cup? A 5–2 score: why didn't the Rocket do anything?

"He's not as young as he used to be, old Maurice."

"He's not all that old."

"For a hockey player, thirty-six isn't young."

His speed has diminished. In the past, he would hook the tip of his skate in the ice to send himself into orbit with a fantastic relaxation of his leg muscles. Ever since his tendon was severed, that movement has been unbearably painful. To project himself forward, he now has to support himself on the entire blade of his skate. The precaution slows him down.

But if Maurice Richard is slowing down, he's slowing down in his own way. In the third game of the semifinals, he stands out with two goals; Henri scores another. Jacques Plante withstands the Uke Line. A shutout: 3–0. Humiliated, the Bruins come back with vindictive fervour. They overpower the Canadiens, 3–0.

The Canadiens and the Bruins are now nose to nose, with each team having won twice. The team that loses the next one will be at a serious disadvantage. On April 17, the fifth game ends in a 2–2 tie. Neither team wants to give way to the other. The players confront each other like mountain rams. During the overtime period, the Rocket, who is twice the age of some of the rookies, is also twice as fast. At the faceoff, Henri Richard grabs the puck and passes it to Dickie Moore, who transfers it to the Rocket. Henri skates in front of the goalie and the Rocket has to hold back. To fool Don Simmons,

Moore pretends he's getting ready to receive a pass so he can make it swerve to Simmons. The goalie waits but the shot comes from the Rocket. It's the winning goal. In the Forum, where a damp vapour is floating, gathering in a sheaf, the Canadiens hug Maurice; they pummel him, flatten him under a thunder of cries and a shower of disparate objects. The Bruins retire to the locker room, sheepish, and don't recover. They lose the next game. The Stanley Cup stays in Montreal. It's their third Stanley Cup victory under Toe Blake.

Since his return to the game after his injury, the Rocket has scored thirteen goals in fifteen games. His obsession with firing the puck into the net is again unleashed. His power of concentration is still staggering, his energy torrential. He has an unwavering conviction that no situation is hopeless. It's when scoring a goal seems impossible that the risk becomes irresistible to him. Following the Rocket's recent exploits, some suggest that since he'll have to leave, he might as well leave with the Stanley Cup in his arms. But many are convinced that the Rocket will never stop. They need this upstanding hero when their political and religious leaders are crawling like little worms inside a rotten fruit.

Hydro-Québec has sold its gas distribution network to the Natural Gas Corporation. From this transaction some of Duplessis's cabinet ministers, friends of his party and promoters have realized an untaxable capital gain of nine million dollars. Public opinion is divided. For most people, Duplessis, a bachelor who is married to his province, can't have been dishonest. For others, these dishonest transactions are one more proof that this saviour of the people is nothing but a liquidator of its resources. Beneath the traditional Catholic virtue of the French Canadians, beneath all the Hail Marys declaimed by families, is hidden something that's not very attractive. This repressed corruption is beginning to seethe. Think of the riot at the Forum, of the numerous violent strikes . . . But those are pessimistic thoughts. We've won the Stanley Cup, life is wonderful. Thank you, Rocket!

Maurice Richard has been elected by the people and every politician wants to be seen shaking his hand. Maurice resembles

those people who do the difficult jobs: lumberjacks, labourers, fishermen, longshoremen, bricklayers. He has the rugged frankness of
those whose trades won't let them lie. Now and then politicians
like to drink from a spring of unrefined honesty. After our submissiveness of the past, in our present that is animated by the meagre
breath of our wheeling-and-dealing politicians, before the uncer-
tainty of the future, the heart of Maurice Richard is a lump of the
molten stone that's at the centre of the earth: the flame of life,
original and wild.

THE GODS OF OLYMPUS
DRIVE AWAY A MORTAL

1958. At the end of the election campaign, Diefenbaker wins 208 of the 265 seats in the House of Commons. For French Canadians, though, it is Maurice Richard who reigns. Now, at the beginning of the season, Rangers coach Phil Watson makes a prediction in the press: the Rocket will be forced to retire before the end of the season because he's far from being the player he once was.

What disrespect! Maurice will leave the ice when he wants to. Neither Watson nor anyone else is going to pick the date for his departure. He rages in silence. He'll make his reply with the puck. Of course the time will come when he'll close the door to the rink behind him. When? The question has been eating away at him for more than a year. It keeps him awake nights. He's never been a sound sleeper. Now he's disturbed by a question that's as persistent as a toothache: when will he retire? For hours he lies on his back gazing at the nighttime shadows on the ceiling. He can't bring himself to make a decision. His legs are no longer as strong as they were in his youth; sometimes they're better. Since the accident to his tendon he can no longer take off as swiftly as when he was scoring some fine goals. But he still wants to play. Besides, he's responsible for his family. The children are big teenagers now. He's not comfortable with them. He's afraid of them—he who isn't afraid of

Lou Fontinato or Hal Laycoe or Ted Lindsay. He loves his children. He'll encourage them when they play hockey. He reads to the youngest ones. If he knows something about it, he helps them do their homework at the kitchen table. But teenagers? He doesn't know the words that interest them. His own father, Onésime, was like him, not talkative, but life was different in those days. He wishes he were like Lucille; women know how to talk to children. For a man, it's hard. The older ones think that their father prefers the younger ones. He loves them all. And Lucille . . . How lucky he was to find a woman like her! He's responsible for a family. When he's finished with hockey, where will the money come from? The children are growing, they have hearty appetites. Right now, honours are descending on him like confetti, but when the fans don't see him on the ice any more, they'll quickly forget. Of all the things that exist in life, he knows only hockey. Without skates and a stick what can a hockey player do? Clad in his shoulder pads, shin pads, thigh pieces, couteres, looking lost in his armour, what can a knight do when he comes home after conquering the Holy Grail?

Phil Watson's remarks don't matter, but why does he feel so insulted? Maurice should ignore his chatter but he can't. He hasn't digested his supper properly. There are knots in his stomach. He has diarrhea. When he eats, nothing tastes good. He grumbles. Why does Watson's declaration upset him so much? His children are nervous because he's nervous; he doesn't like that. Lucille is good; she understands. But he knows that she wishes her husband weren't in such a foul mood.

The Rangers will be on the ice tonight. Driving the puck into Phil Watson's net would please Maurice as much as nailing his big mouth with a fist. Will his wrists have the strength he needs? Will he be able to shoot as precisely as he wants? Will he be able to break free of the traps that will be laid around him by the legs, arms, sticks and shoulders of the opponents? Ever since the talk around him has been about his imminent retirement, he's been badgered again by all these doubts. Phil Watson is accusing him publicly of being too old to play! The Rocket doesn't like scorn or contempt.

Not all that long ago he was too young to play. When he was a child playing on the street, the big boys would pass the puck back and forth as if little Maurice weren't even there. He made tremendous efforts. He wasn't too young when he landed the puck in the net. He'll score now, and then he won't be too old. If he doesn't score a goal, he's not alive. The Rocket will score a goal so he can live! And retire when *he* decides to.

To get ready to give Watson's Rangers a drubbing, he follows his usual timetable. Up at half past eight. To the Forum after breakfast. The opponents' strengths and weaknesses are analyzed, the tactics to be deployed decided on. After that come practices. Not only does the Rocket take part as if it were a real game, he extends it; he endeavours to shoot harder, faster; he repeats his feints, polishes them; he fine-tunes his shots on goal; he goes over his backhands. Just as a violinist dedicates himself to making all the music contained in his violin well up, he tries to extirpate all the power in his stick. Back home around three o'clock he devours a well-done steak, a potato, vegetables, tomato juice. For dessert, fruit salad or ice cream. After that he goes out for a walk. Back home again, he tries to nap. But he doesn't sleep. Too nervous. Too tense. Too preoccupied. He can see the Rangers in his head as if they were on the ice. Phil Watson, you talked too much!

Later, on the ice at the Forum at last, Maurice Richard gives his reply: two pucks in Gump Worsley's net. The Rocket isn't a player whose time is up. Worsley thinks that Watson should have kept quiet. The Rocket is let down. He wanted to stun Watson with a hat trick.

One afternoon, instead of being at the university, we're at the Widow's Tavern. We talk a lot more than we drink; words are free. Are we that noisy? Some customers, says the manager, are threatening to "haul us outside." We calm down. We've just reached an agreement on one point: as children, we all dreamed of playing hockey like Maurice Richard and no one in our group has ever seen the Rocket play in the flesh. Shouldn't we all go to the Forum? The Rocket won't be playing that much longer.

"We should've seen him play during his good years."

"Fifty years from now we'll look ridiculous when we admit that we weren't interested in seeing Maurice Richard play. The Rocket is immortal."

Our classmate's opinion carries a fair amount of weight. He knows about life. Older than the rest of us, he spent several years in the army. He's even visited brothels in Belgium. So let's go and watch an immortal player play! We hurry to the streetcar. God loves us tonight! Who do we see on a seat? Our classmate Marie. She's so pretty, so bright; she's read so many of the great immortal books. She never takes a step without an armful of books that she holds against her bosom where we don't dare to dream of resting our heads.

"We're going to see the Rocket at the Forum!" our veteran announces. "Want to come along?"

"Sorry, I'm going to see the Bergman."

"What's a Bergman?"

"A great Swedish filmmaker. Bergman is a genius."

If you'd known Marie you'd have followed her too, and you'd have endured *The Seventh Seal* in Swedish, without subtitles.

Phil Watson has predicted that the Rocket will knuckle under before the end of the season. The Rocket is glad to be in New York. He'll show Watson how he knuckles under. Since he has been playing with the Canadiens, in the regular season and playoffs, he has scored 599 goals. He'll score his six-hundredth against the Rangers. With his two-hundred-odd pounds he's a weighty ballerina. Here he comes. He feels slower; he puts even more energy into each of his bursts. Lou Fontinato is ready: big, strong, a fighter. The Rocket avoids the defenceman, passes him, but he's already gone too far to shoot the puck. All he can see is the side of the net. Gump Worsley seals every crack. Unhesitating, as if the manoeuvre has been rehearsed, without slowing down, while the Rangers are getting winded from pursuing him so they can squeeze him into the corner, he turns abruptly and goes behind the net. Worsley glides towards the other side to close the opening. Too late! From behind the net, propelling himself on his right leg, bending the left one as far as he can, driving the heel of his blade into the ice, he pushes his stick as far ahead of the goalpost as he can; the muscles in his left arm contract; with a backhand he sends the puck between the goalpost and Worsley's pad. "Maurice Rocket Richard shoots—he scores! His six-hundredth goal!"

Let's compare his deed with that of a motorcyclist who, while travelling along at sixty miles an hour, suddenly drops a loonie into a piggybank. Luck? No. We should be talking about a reflex. A hockey rink is like a chessboard. The pawns move in every direction; they're armed. The players move at high speeds. Imagine the astronomical number of possibilities that are multiplied to infinity. This is going on not amid the transcendental silence of a chess game but amid the animosity of a battlefield on ice. You have to guess through muscles that contract inside uniforms, and through gazes that stare in one direction, what the opponents' next move will be and assess what variations they'll apply to their tactics that you've decoded. A penetrating knowledge of the habits of every player, teammates and opponents alike, is essential. Through this rearrangement of lightning streaks, you have to decide at the speed of that lightning what your next move will be. Every fraction of a second the chessboard has to be reassessed. Already it has changed. Everything is changing constantly in this shifting violence. You have to start the next movement before you've decided what it will be. Without prodigious intelligence, no one would be able to outsmart five players who are all very determined to stop you from violating their net, who are protecting their goalie in front of a narrow goal. The Rocket's celebrated instinct is actually well-informed intelligence that his body transforms into action.

His six-hundredth goal! Driven forward by his own energy, the Rocket loses his balance. The opponents finally catch up with him because he's stretched out on the ice; they pile onto him as if they can still stop him from scoring that goal. When he finally extricates himself from the pile of Rangers, he smiles at the crowd, who give him an ovation though they've booed him so often. Behind the Rangers' bench, Phil Watson looks irritated.

It was such a beautiful goal that luck didn't dare to be absent on this November 25. It wasn't the sober goal of an old warrior whose body is cross-hatched with injuries and heavy with age. The body of the thirty-seven-year-old athlete is still inhabited by the soul of the young player who once scored fifty goals in fifty games.

===

When he was starting out, Maurice Richard was a mere mortal. Then he dashed off to conquer Olympus, where the gods reside. Those divinities tried to push him away by inflicting all sorts of wounds. Thanks to his bravery and his tenacity, the Rocket settled in among them. For that the gods have never forgiven him. The day will come when they'll drive this intruder off Olympus.

My friends laugh at my poetry. Am I right? Early in January the gods attack! During a game against the Maple Leafs, Maurice Richard, who has already injured his back, breaks a toe. A few days later he mutilates an elbow. On January 18, in Chicago, the Rocket is going towards the defence. Geoffrion passes him the puck; it ricochets off a stick. Geoffrion's shot was powerful. The puck hits the Rocket on his ankle. It's as if a scythe were slicing his foot. The blow landed on the spot where the skate offers no protection. The weak point in the armour that the gods on Olympus had been looking for. No pain has ever stopped the Rocket in his ascent towards a goal. This pain is hideous. He comes very close to the net. Defencemen Dollard St. Laurent and Al Arbour honour him with the ritual welcome. There's no strength in his ankle, which is numbed by the pain. The mortal collapses. Can't get up. The old warrior needs to be supported so he can leave the ice. And the Toronto crowd gratifies him with an ovation. Maurice thinks, a hockey player shouldn't be applauded because he can't stand on his feet.

People say that the Rocket is aging. That he's worn out from action. That there's too much fat on his bones. That he doesn't react as quickly as in the past to avoid blows. No one accuses the gods of Olympus except me, the poet.

His ankle is fractured. Toe Blake remembers. A few years ago a similar injury drove him out of hockey. Will an injury finally make the inevitable decision that the Rocket has been putting off? Maurice too remembers: Toe Blake, who didn't want to quit hockey, had to bid farewell to the Punch Line. They're both thinking the same thing. They don't say anything. Toe, who has lived with the Rocket's silence for so many years, knows that he thinks he'll be making a speedy return. In the past he always healed sooner than the doctor had predicted. Often he played better after an injury than before.

This season he has scored fewer goals, but they've been finer. Also, he scores when it's important to score. Yes, he'll tolerate a cast for a few days, he'll limp around for a while, and then he'll come back. Thus does he soliloquize to reassure himself. A prisoner of his easy chair, he finds it unbearable to waste all this time not playing. Look at him: a little old man with his crutches! He watches the time pass and time is in no hurry. Instead of sweating blood like a man, he's doing nothing useful. He waits. He reads and rereads the sports news. He listens to his records but his favourite country and western songs get on his nerves now. The house is cramped, suffocating. He feels like pounding the walls. He feels like cursing, but he holds back. Lucille is pregnant; soon there'll be another child. He knows that she understands his bad mood. She has a gift for comprehending his feelings, his thoughts, even when they're muddled. He needs air. He drives to the nearby rink where his children are playing; leaning on his crutches, he watches them. Perhaps his son will play for the Canadiens, like his father when he wasn't an invalid. He goes into the locker room to congratulate the future Rockets.

Announce his retirement from hockey? What will he do the next day? What will he do off the ice? The crowd applauds him when he's on skates, on the ice, but what will happen when he's in civilian's shoes? After he's gone the crowd will celebrate the younger players: Béliveau, Geoffrion, Moore and this Bobby Hull of the Black Hawks who's built like the bodybuilders you see in magazines. Maurice doesn't know how to do anything outside hockey. Go back to being a machinist? Work has changed. Maurice has changed. Leave the Forum and go back to the factory . . . Take off his Canadiens uniform and trade it for a machinist's overalls . . . Sell cars? He's done that; people would come to see him and leave with an autograph. He'd like to do something connected with hockey. His bosses aren't getting down on their knees to have him in their offices. Maurice is responsible for a family: six children soon. Why is he always worrying? Thinking about the future too much is like shooting into the net without having the puck on the blade of your stick. Too much worry is bad for the health. He's going to get better and start playing again. But anxiety is eating away at him. This time the future isn't the next game, it's the unknown. The gods of Olympus are satisfied. Afflicted with human concerns, the Rocket is merely a mortal in his easy chair.

Even though he's not with them, the Canadiens win victories. The team will likely win the Stanley Cup. His ankle will mend before the playoffs. He'll give his fans some goals the way they and he like them. The youngsters score goals. But nobody knows how to cook up a goal like the Rocket. Geoffrion maybe . . . Or Béliveau . . .

At the beginning of March, after six weeks of intolerable immobility, the time has finally come to break his cast. As soon as he's set free the Rocket will put on his skates. The doctor takes an X-ray. Just a precaution. The fracture hasn't healed yet. He'll need to be patient a little longer. The ankle won't heal any faster if he's impatient. The doctor sends him away to rest. The bone must not be submitted to any effort, any shock, or the break could widen.

Is this the end? He's not going to finish like this! The wrath of ten volcanoes shakes his soul. A phone call saves his family from a probable storm. The government of Czechoslovakia is inviting the Rocket to Prague, where a world congress on amateur hockey is being held. Stunned, incredulous, the Rocket flies to Czechoslovakia while the Cold War is raging. A French-Canadian Catholic is going to visit the Communists.

Some fans feel a certain concern. In those countries under Communist dictatorship a single word can send you to Siberia for fifty years. Or else you'll have to flee like many Czechs who have taken refuge in Canada. Maurice doesn't mince words; could the Communists keep him and exile him to Siberia? Will he find a church that's still open so he can go to Mass? On the other hand, hockey and Communism don't go together. Those countries can't turn out real players. Hockey is Canada's national sport; it's the fruit of our cold winters, our hard ice, our hearty food, our pioneers' temperament. Communist hockey . . .

The Communists are our enemies. During the Cold War our governments are making bombs that will destroy them. In their countries the same precautions are being taken. Visiting a Communist country is like visiting the devil. The Rocket is brave. Maybe he'll convert the Communists to French-Canadian Catholic hockey.

On March 10, under the roof of a great amphitheatre, fifteen thousand individuals, guided by the discipline of Party delegates, wait for the appearance of the greatest hockey player in the world, who has come from Canada. They've been told about his exploits. Some fans have read something about the Rocket in their newspapers.

At last, the master of ceremonies:

"And now, Mr. Maurice Rocket Richard!"

The crowd greets him as noisily as his fans in Montreal. But here he has stepped onto the ice without his skates. He's not wearing the Canadiens uniform. He's limping, leaning on a crutch. He's wearing a hat. *"Roketa! Roketa! Roketa!"* Just like Montreal. Yet he's in Communist Czechoslovakia! The voice of the crowd has given him a push that nearly knocks him over. The crowd is shouting like the crowd at the Forum. And there's a Cold War on. These people are Communists. Their warm welcome goes on and on. He hasn't scored a goal. All he's done is step onto the ice. Limping. He's embarrassed. To be loved so much, so far from home! Will he be able to hold back the tear that's prickling in the corner of his eye? Will he be able to hold back the sob that's gathering in his throat? He doffs his hat and salutes the crowd, bowing his head. The ovation starts up again. This wave of emotion turns his heart upside down. He wasn't prepared for such admiration so far from home, behind the Iron Curtain.

This international congress wants to promote international understanding. Two great sports heroes, one from the capitalist bloc, the other from the Communist bloc, walk towards one another, hands outstretched: Maurice Richard and Colonel Emil Zatopek. Before he joined the army, Zatopek was a fabulous runner. He set a record for the ten thousand metres at the 1948 Olympic Games in London. In 1950 he improved on that record. At the Helsinki games in 1952, he won three gold medals. Zatopek is the Czechs' Rocket. The two men approach one another, open their arms, embrace. Two legends, two sports, two countries, two philosophies, two political regimes embrace.

During his trip Maurice is introduced to groups of players, coaches, hockey league organizers. He tells them how he learned to play on the icy streets near his house. He explains the National Hockey League to them. He describes his training. He relives certain episodes, explains how he outsmarted one goalie or another.

A few days later he returns to his free country, weighed down with gifts and memories. The government of Czechoslovakia has given him an automobile, a Skoda convertible.

No one in the province of Quebec is unaware of Maurice's triumph on the other side of the Iron Curtain. So Communists aren't always sentenced to hard labour. So they're allowed to play hockey. And on top of it, they don't produce only weapons; they also know how to build cars. Sports cars. I, the poet in a capitalist land, bought myself an old English Hillman yesterday for three hundred dollars, which breathed its last in the hills of the Eastern Townships. I abandoned it sadly, as if I'd been rejected by my first love.

Back home, the Rocket rushes to see his doctor. He can't wait to get back into his skates. He feels a lot better. The doctor examines him, then advises him to rest a little longer: "An ankle's a delicate thing. It's complicated." He notes a slight improvement. Maurice confesses that he still suffers from a slight throbbing pain. It's the reason he limps. At the end of March 1959, it's obvious to everyone: the Rocket won't be playing again. Fortunately, the Canadiens are doing fine. They win the semifinals against the Black Hawks.

Spurred on by Punch Imlach, the Leafs have become strong again in front of their goalie Johnny Bower, the man whose face is marked with 250 stitches, whose fingers have been twisted by pucks that explode like grenades. Imlach uses shock tactics to kindle his players' enthusiasm, so it's said. One day he spilled a bucketful of banknotes on the floor: "Win the Stanley Cup and you'll have even more!" His methods of persuasion seem to work. The Leafs didn't make the playoffs last year and here they are in the finals against Montreal at the Forum.

Toe Blake opens the gate. The Rocket appears on the ice. No one was expecting him. The fans leap to their feet. The Rocket will win the Stanley Cup for them! But alas, the old champion who steps back into the arena can't hide the fact that he's wounded. One foot hesitates. He skates with a difficulty that only he can know. Maurice isn't the Rocket tonight. Toe Blake gazes at the champion with a certain sadness. The hungry old tiger has grimaced: he shouldn't have jumped onto the ice. This morning during warm-up Toe noticed the stiffness in his ankle, which weakens his skating. The Rocket was aware of it too. It's not his first encounter with pain. He's experienced. He knows it will be forgotten with the warm presence of the fans around the ice, the puck to be captured, the opponents to overthrow, the net down there to be smashed in. He's been afflicted with suffering keener than this and hockey has always healed him.

The puck slides towards the blue line. He races after it. Toe Blake is watching. The skate on his injured foot is unsteady. The hesitant movement of his skate doesn't correct itself. The Rocket's muscles fear the burn that is caused by the thrust of the skate. He tries to relieve it: with every thrust he takes a precaution. But Maurice isn't ready to confront the Maple Leafs. In the locker room Toe Blake didn't have the courage to stop him. He should have. He regrets having wanted to please his old friend. But could he stop his partner on the Punch Line from putting on his skates? Could he keep the best hockey player of all time on the bench like a rookie he didn't altogether trust?

The Rocket reaches out to grab a pass. His pain persists. He absorbs the crush and the bodychecks. The other side's blue line is so far away! The Leafs are skating fast tonight. He glances at the coach. He wishes Toe Blake would call him back. The coach looks away. He doesn't want to humiliate the Rocket. He gives him another few seconds to play hockey as he wanted so badly to do. The young players see a great champion, despite his age, despite his records, despite his injuries, being consumed by the game. Out of breath, with that red-hot nail going through his ankle and the pain that reverberates in his leg, Maurice is playing to convince the bosses that he still has a place with the Canadiens. Finally, Toe Blake recalls him. He has to do it.

Maurice has not worked wonders. It was his first try. A warm-up. The fans haven't seen the real Rocket yet. It will be different next time. He knows that he can skate. Endure a bodycheck. Next time he'll give them a goal. Toe Blake wants to win this game. He's in no hurry to use his lame champion. The Rocket waits. Toe avoids looking at him. He's uncomfortable; the other players are aware of it. He pretends to forget him. You don't forget the Rocket. The game goes on and the Rocket, on the bench, waits for a sign from the coach. The crowd applauds the Canadiens and the Rocket isn't playing.

Out of respect, out of friendship, Toe Blake finally sends him back into the game. The champion doesn't want to give up. Johnny Bower is waiting for him at the other end. The goalie follows the puck so attentively that his eyes are worn out like the eyes of an old monk who has read too many manuscripts. The Rocket has often outsmarted him. Tonight, Bower notes, the Rocket's a little slow. Could it be another of his tricks? Out of respect, out of friendship, Toe Blake recalls the Rocket. At the end of the game the victory goes to the Canadiens. He was of no use.

He dons his uniform for the next game too.

The fans notice that he doesn't work any miracles.

He also plays a little during another game.

His leg no longer holds him up.

He's incapable of scoring a single goal. His six-hundred-odd are only memories. Smoke and mirrors? Statistics. The goal that he's unable to score erases all the others. This player wearing number nine is not the Rocket. The crowd grumbles when he touches the puck.

"Give 'em hell, old man! You can do it!"

The Canadiens bring the Leafs down in five games. For the fourth consecutive year they win the Stanley Cup. That record used to be held by the Ottawa Silver Seven (from 1903 to 1906). Maurice Richard slips away from the journalists. He hasn't accomplished anything; why should he answer their questions?

The hero of the playoffs is Marcel Bonin. As a child he used to listen to Maurice Richard's prowess and dazzle described on the radio. Playing with a stick and a frozen horse turd he would imitate Maurice Richard. Now, still amazed, he's playing at his side. He still dreams of playing like him. With superstitious admiration, Marcel Bonin borrowed the Rocket's gloves and scored ten goals in eleven games!

I have no interest at all in the Stanley Cup parade. I'm in love. My muse and I walk hand in hand along St. Catherine Street in Montreal, in the hope of spotting Fidel Castro's bearded revolutionaries on a visit. The newspapers photograph the slightest move by these great patriots. A poor poet, I donate a few cents to a charity that buys toys for Cuban children.

On Mountain Street we spy a dozen of Fidel's revolutionaries in combat dress, beards wild. We quicken our pace to get close to them. To get close to the Revolution. We repeat the words that Fidel Castro said into the microphone of the journalist René Lévesque: "I want to eliminate poverty and ignorance and create a humanistic democracy."

══════

1959. Wherever he goes, honours rain down on the Rocket. He is one of the dignitaries invited to a dinner with Queen Elizabeth. He receives honorary distinctions. Shouldn't he retire now at the peak of his glory?

His body is heavier again. The Canadiens' management insist that he lose weight so he can get back his agility and reduce the risk of accidents. Why is he hanging on? Won't he let his fans down when he no longer resembles his legend? On the ice, the Rocket made decisions at the speed of light; now he's indecisive, hesitant, like some junior employee.

He was promised a job at the Forum. Such responsibility frightens him. Hockey is his territory, his life. He needs that hostile ground. The only thing he knows how to do is to overturn obstacles, clear a path for himself through traps to get to the goal. For years he has been consumed during a game and then, like the phoenix, has been reborn from his ashes in the next one. He's not going to sit at a desk and watch the time pass on sheets of paper. He's afraid of that.

On this occasion, Time is on the defensive, determined not to let him pass. His children don't want him to give up hockey; it's fun to go to the Forum. Little Normand doesn't want his father to stop; he's the champion and he isn't old. Most of all he likes attending the Canadiens' practices. All the players know him. He learns their tricks to help him play better. Lucille hopes that her husband will make up his mind. She doesn't like to see him torn like this. This isn't her man. She'd rather he was on the ice with sweat running down his forehead, worn out, his face scarred, than see him daydreaming in a chair.

He'll play again. If his playing days are over, as he has read in the sports pages, why does Phil Watson want him in New York? Why does Punch Imlach want him in Toronto? Why does Muzz Patrick want him in Detroit?

Toe Blake analyzes the statistics. Last season the Rocket only took part in forty-two games. He accumulated seventeen goals. It's far from a historic record but let's compare: during the same season Gordie Howe, playing in seventy games, scored a total of twenty-eight goals. The numbers show that the Rocket's career isn't over.

On August 30, 1959, at 4:12 P.M., the Papineau streetcar is completing its final run. It's Maurice's local streetcar, the streetcar of his youth. This is big news in Montreal. They're talking about it on the radio, in the newspapers. This streetcar won't be running any more. Montreal is becoming modern. Life is changing . . .

Is there still a need for the Rocket? In the fall of 1959, the Forum would be sold out, even if the Rocket weren't there. Because of the electrifying excellence of their game, the young players are giving fans the strong emotions they need. The Rocket likes these youngsters who wanted to resemble him, who *do* resemble him. Everything he's managed to do on the ice he has accomplished through action, with the intelligence of an animal capturing its prey. Something clear and obvious forced itself on his muscles. That's how he made his decisions in front of a goalie. In front of the door that is opening on his retirement, nothing is clear or obvious.

On September 7, a seismic shock jolts the province of Quebec: the death of Duplessis. It marks the end of fifteen years of domination. *Le Chef* had built a powerful machine that imposed his own form of justice: favours to those who supported his party and punishments to those who protested. Those who ventured to contradict his opinions were accused of being perverted by Communism. For some intellectuals he was merely a shameless demagogue who took advantage of the favourable economic picture in America. He was adulated as a little dictator. And as a little dictator he was feared.

At his funeral in Trois-Rivières, his coffin is honoured by more than sixteen hundred wreaths from grateful friends: contractors, politicians, bishops, directors of religious communities, village mayors. When Duplessis is laid to rest it is a certain past that is being buried. Even his adversaries feel a little sad. Was there a French Canadian who didn't shiver a little when Duplessis sang the praises of provincial autonomy? Or who wasn't proud to wave the fleur-de-lys flag that he gave his province?

He was one of the Rocket's devoted fans. He went regularly to see him play at the Forum and sometimes in the United States. Now and then he'd send him a note of congratulations. Duplessis was the champion of autonomy. The Rocket was the champion of hockey. "When I'm in my coffin, it'll be too late to play hockey," the Rocket muses. Now is the time when he should be playing. A man isn't old at thirty-seven. His broken ankle has healed. He has to stop hesitating. Stop worrying. And play. He will devote to hockey the energy that he's burning in self-doubt.

Four days later, Paul Sauvé succeeds Duplessis. Most urgently, he tackles corruption in the civil service. If civil servants are properly paid, he thinks, they won't be tempted to add to their earnings by cashing in on favours granted. Paul Sauvé announces as well that his government will work towards "the development of Canada while guaranteeing its full flourishing to Quebec."

During the summer, Maurice did a lot of walking; he played golf and baseball. He brought his weight down to 185 pounds. Last season he didn't make the slightest contribution to the Stanley Cup victory. But he's not going to be useless any longer. This season he'll prove to his fans that the Rocket is still the Rocket. Canadiens management has come up with an idea that excites his will. His young brother Claude has been invited to training camp. Frank Selke and Toe Blake are watching him. Mr. Selke would like to offer the fans a Richard Line that would toss dynamite at enemy goalies' pads.

At training camp, the Canadiens' rink is flooded with new recruits who are determined not to leave it. It doesn't bother them to try to expel the old players. Sam Pollock's farm teams are an inexhaustible source of youth and talent. Hockey is changing.

A new machine has arrived. With an amused smile, Maurice sees it go onto the ice. Between periods it's no longer necessary to unwind hoses like anxious firemen to flood the scarified ice. The Zamboni, a kind of big tractor, works like an enormous paintbrush to smooth the ice and make it sleek. The water in the hoses used to freeze in droplets. The Zamboni rubs away those tiny rough surfaces. Polished ice offers less resistance to skate blades. Players skate faster. The Rocket likes that.

Skates are no longer made of leather; now the boot is moulded in plastic. You have to get used to it. The foot is less comfortable in plastic than in leather. But it gives better support. There are fewer vibrations in the feet. And less energy is used up on the thrust of the skate.

Trains are a thing of the past now. The Canadiens nearly always travel by plane. The players often enjoyed themselves on the train but the long journeys were tiring. The beds were too short. The athletes were shaken up with every turn of the wheels. Less tired now, they'll play livelier hockey. Some fans wonder in fact whether all this comfort will make the players soft.

Even the sticks are improved. They're lighter. Too light, the Rocket thinks. These new sticks are supposed to increase the power of his shot. Fiberglas makes them more rigid. How can you extract all the power from this new stick? The Rocket experiments. He spends long sessions firing again and again. The greatest hockey player in the world is working on improving his shot.

On September 19, during a game outside of competition, Toe Blake tries out the line with the three Richard brothers. What a find: the old champion battling against time; Henri with his smaller, lighter body, who is repeating the Rocket's feats; and young Claude, for whom the ice is like a new slate on which nothing has yet been written. He seems as talented as his brothers. The line of three Richards: the past laden with memories, the present laden with electricity and the future laden with hope. The Canadiens will go on being strong for a long time. For a long time the Stanley Cup will stay in Montreal, in the province of Quebec!

Each Richard is measured against Maurice. In the minor leagues as well as in the NHL. Even Maurice's children when they play in park leagues pay a price because their father is the Rocket. They have to be more talented than the others; they're watched more closely than the others, attacked more than all the others. Claude knows that no one has much patience with a Richard who doesn't work a miracle when he touches the puck.

On the Richard Line Maurice is brilliant. He's proud of his young brother, who is hardly older than his daughter, Huguette. Sensing his nervousness, Maurice reassures him: "Even with the Canadiens, hockey is still hockey." Then he smiles: "A little faster, a little tougher, a little better . . ." He hasn't forgotten the first game he played with the Canadiens, when he went onto the ice beside the great Toe Blake. It's like yesterday . . . or the day before.

During this first game with the Canadiens, Claude can't put the puck in the net. The next day he's sent back to Ottawa, to his junior team. This decision leaves Maurice with a bitter taste. He's convinced that Claude has the necessary talent. Why is management refusing to let him have another try? "Give him another two or three games and he'll find the back of the net." Claude's failure is a failure for the Rocket. Management would like to get rid of the old Richard, but he is resisting. So they're taking it out on the younger Richard. Maurice has his past; they can't deny him that. His young brother has only a future. And they haven't given him enough time to prove that he can become a Canadien. He's a Richard. Like Maurice, like Henri.

Maurice signs his contract. What are his objectives? ask the journalists. "I'd like to score a few goals, if I don't get injured." The Rocket's modesty is legendary: "Score a few goals . . ." The athlete who speaks those words is not the Rocket. His objectives have never been modest. He's a tired man, filled with self-doubt, disgruntled. The Richard Line could have been even better than the Punch Line. "Score a few goals": that's the ultimate resistance by the old soldier who will leave his trench as soon as he's flattened a few enemies— the last ones. Then he can proudly go home, if he's not injured.

During the first years of his career, some considered the Rocket too frail to play with the Canadiens. Today, they've decided that he's finished. He was injured so often when he first started out. Scoring goal after goal as he conquered hockey, he developed an attitude of invincibility. And if injury struck him down, the miracle of healing would soon be accomplished. To promise his fans a few goals on condition that he isn't injured: that's not the Rocket. The old champion is as much afraid of playing the game as he is of leaving it.

Hockey is changing. Of all the goalies Maurice has known, Jacques Plante is the best, but he knits, and he writes poems. Yet he's not afraid of the puck. He takes pleasure in keeping it out of his net, in grabbing hold of a wandering puck and sending it to a teammate who's ready to attack. Goalies in the past weren't good skaters. The great Georges Vézina, for instance, learned to skate after he'd become a good goalie. Before that, he played without skates! Plante skates like a forward. In fact he's often taken for a forward. The Rocket considers such manoeuvres risky. But opponents are frustrated by this goalie who doesn't do anything the way other people do. Like him, Jacques Plante is a lone wolf, contemplative, before and after a game. He respects Plante in spite of his strange little ways.

At the beginning of November, Jacques Plante decides to appear before the crowd in the protective mask he sometimes wears during practice. The fans will wonder if he's suddenly scared of the puck. Is it because a few days ago he got one right in the face? Frank Selke is convinced that the fans won't care for this masquerade. They like to see the faces of their Canadiens. "A man has to be able to look at the puck face to face." Toe Blake tries to talk him out of hiding behind this protection. Does Plante contravene any regulation? The oldest fans recall Clint Benedict of the Montreal Maroons; in his day, nearly fifty years ago, he used to wear a mask. The Rangers' Gump Worsley laughs at Plante. "A goalie in a mask is a chicken. The only mask I wear is my face." In response to his detractors Plante, in his mask, lines up eleven consecutive victories.

Hockey is changing. Players aren't embarrassed to wear protective helmets. Soon another goalie, the Bruins' Don Simmons, also turns up with a mask. The Rocket, who has taken so many blows and returned them, wonders if these youngsters are tough enough to play the game. Will they be asking next for a puck made of softer rubber? Aren't they excited at the prospect of presenting themselves to danger with chests offered and faces bare? Hockey is changing . . . Hockey is changing but the danger is still there. The danger—that's what it's worthwhile to pass through in order to arrive before the goalie, breathless and sweating, and to fire a shot laden with all the fear in his soul. When the fans shout, they're expressing the ecstasy of the players. That is what Maurice can't leave.

In Detroit on November 26, the Canadiens are finishing the game with a 4–2 lead. Barely a minute and a half left to play. The entire team is positioned on the defence line. They just have to protect the victory. The Red Wings work to open that rampart. To shake up the Canadiens' certitude. And to take advantage of a moment's confusion to score at least one goal. Murray Oliver sneaks into their zone. The puck comes towards him. With a little luck he could scoop it up and score. The Rocket plunges in to block his trajectory. Has he calculated his move badly? He hasn't calculated anything at all. He has done what he was supposed to do: stop the puck. It hits him in the face. Hard. He gets up. Dazed. He feels as if he's been hit with an axe. He can't stand up. His legs are wobbly. Someone holds him up. The champion leaves the ice as if all at once he's forgotten how to skate. His cheekbone has been fractured. The jealous gods of Olympus are striving to make the Rocket tumble to the earth where humans walk.

Drugs don't deaden the pain. The journey to Montreal is endlessly painful. Applying ice to his cheek is useless. The pain burns. He thought he'd made the acquaintance of every kind of pain, but this is one he's never encountered. It's the most pitiless, the most intense. It's torture. This time the Rocket has reached the end of his dazzling breakaway. Before him stands an implacable goalkeeper: Time. It's the end of the grand game that has been his life.

But it's not over! He hasn't scored all the goals he wanted to score. There are still breakaways to invent. Opponents to mystify. Pucks to catapult. Battles to end. Shivers to give to the crowds. The Stanley Cup to offer to the fans. These thoughts don't ease the pain. The train trip is endless. Is it his last one with the Canadiens?

As usual, Lucille is waiting for him at the Central Station. During all these years she has stayed at home with the children when the Rocket was setting fire to the great rinks of America. She followed her man's action without being too frightened at seeing him get involved in the brawls that terrified her children. She had confidence in him. She was sure that a fist in the right place would get him out of trouble. Yet it's always shattering for her to see him come home injured. Why does he have so few defences against bad luck?

People recognize the Rocket's wife. They scrutinize her. Whisper. Don't dare to disturb her. Disturb her a little. Maurice appears.

This time he looks like a champion who's been hammered. They embrace discreetly. Lucille hardly dares to touch the puffy face, the bruised skin. She hopes that it was his last game but she doesn't say a word. Maurice will make up his own mind. Or has the puck made the decision for him, though he tries to reject it? With what words will they break the silence that's stifling them? "It hurts a little," the Rocket complains. They don't need to say any more. Suddenly tears express what they're thinking. The unshakable Rocket, the dazzling Rocket, the best hockey player in the world, the Rocket who avenges French Canadians for historical injustices, today is lost like someone who doesn't know what to do with his life: "That's not the way I would have liked to finish."

The doctor's office. Through his grim thoughts, the Rocket hears: "You'll be back in the game in a month if everything goes as it should." So it's not over! The champion gets up. He realizes that he wasn't as badly shaken as he thought.

In three weeks he'll be on the ice. In two weeks. He waits for the nights to end. Shouldn't he be announcing his retirement? In one week he'll jump onto the ice at the Forum. The fans will celebrate his return. And wait for his next goal. As he lies there sleepless, thoughts about a bleak future clash with visions of imminent breakaways towards the other side of the blue line.

During cold December days in Montreal, you stay warm inside. Especially when you've got nothing to do except wait. Idle, you distract yourself by nibbling something. Maurice has so much energy. So much appetite. The time passes so slowly. Snacks. Tries to take a nap. It's a much heavier Rocket who shows up in the Canadiens' locker room at the end of December.

The Canadiens are a superb team. Jean Béliveau, Boom Boom Geoffrion, Henri Richard, marvels of speed and elegance, blast away at the opponents' nets. Marcel Bonin offers less artistic beauty, but he's as solid as an eighteen-wheeler. He scores goals as if he were rolling over his opponents. Off-season, he's a wrestler; his opponent is a bear. And if the bear is too polite, if the confrontation lacks excitement, he chews glass.

Maurice finishes his fifty-one-game season with nineteen goals. Many players would be happy with such a performance. For the best hockey player of all time it's mediocre. Some journalists say so. Have the journalists already forgotten his accomplishments? It's easy to tap a typewriter. Do those scribblers have the faintest idea of the effort it takes to score just one goal? Scoring a goal is winning against the impossible. The impossible is always there at the end of the rink, in the enemy net. The Rocket isn't going to withdraw from the battle. But memories aren't enough. In hockey only the present moment counts. With his stick on the puck he must bestow on that moment the dazzle of lightning.

Even the fans are changing. He no longer senses them shiver when he juggles with the puck. "Give 'em hell, Maurice. You've still got it in you!" He no longer feels, as he did in the past, urged on by the fans who see Maurice Richard playing in slow motion. They're dazzled now by other players. But Maurice can't quit.

In the semifinals the Canadiens eliminate the Black Hawks in four games. The Rocket isn't at the party. His shots are no longer frightening. The goalie sees them coming.

As the fans hope, the Canadiens meet the Leafs in the finals. According to predictions the Canadiens should guillotine the Leafs in four games. The Canadiens will dominate them completely. The Stanley Cup will stay in Montreal.

Last year, because of his injury, Maurice Richard didn't score a single goal during the playoffs. This year is he condemned to watch the young players? In the third game, near the end of the second period, the Canadiens are leading 3–1. Phil Goyette widens that lead to 4–1. One minute and four seconds later, the crowd at the Forum holds its breath before a stirring magic. Even though it's no longer necessary, the old Rocket has metamorphosed into the young Rocket. The wings of Mercury have grown back on his skates. The young Rocket soars with that will he has to knock down cliffs, to break the sound barrier, with the ineluctable certainty that he's about to score a goal. The young Rocket seems to be dancing on the surface of the ice, but there's a sound of ice grating as it's lacerated by his skates. The ice hisses as if it were melting under the fire of his blades. His pursuers seem to be suffering from sudden old age. He enters the adversaries' zone as if the defence had opened the door. When he gets to the goal, he sketches a feint, a streak of lightning blinds Johnny Bower—and the puck is inside the net. Without giving the goalie time to understand that he's been outwitted, the Rocket fishes back the puck with the tip of his stick. The fans give him the kind of ovation they used to give the young Rocket.

Why did he insist on hanging on to that puck? asks the failed-poet-turned-sportswriter. "I kept the first puck I put in a net in the NHL. I want to keep my last one too."

The Stanley Cup celebrations are mingled with hopes stirred in the province of Quebec by the new leader of the Liberal Party, Jean Lesage: "It's time for a change!"

His party is elected with a slim majority and the new government is sworn in on July 5. In the days that follow he makes more decisions than all the other governments since the turn of the century. He takes responsibility for education away from the Catholic clergy. To clean up corrupt government business he requires all departments to proceed by way of public bids: before a contract is awarded, the merits of each tender must be studied. He announces his determination to protect the French face of Montreal. He enters into a dialogue with the federal government to set up hospital insurance. He issues a directive that all government cheques will now be addressed directly to the recipients, without passing through the hands of his MLAs' political organizers. Finally, Jean Lesage ensures that "We do not intend to lock ourselves inside an isolation that would be as illusory for one member of our Confederation as it would be harmful to the country as a whole." In a few days the province of Quebec has become a different province. People feel the way they do after a goal by the Rocket.

Does anyone remember that before any politician, the Rocket taught us about effort, honesty, pride, liberty, the honour of not feeling inferior, relentlessness in the face of obstacles, the excitement of overcoming the impossible?

No one thinks about that.

No one.

No one. Not even me, the poet, in a little room with flowered wallpaper. I am surrounded by books. I'm in love. And the great immortal authors never mentioned hockey. And the painters I know have never painted hockey players . . .

═══

1960. Over the summer Maurice has put on more weight. Every bright day brings him closer to that dark day when he will have to leave hockey. He's never conceded the puck to an opponent without a struggle. This time it's not just the puck that's being fought over, it's the game of hockey. He can't sleep. So much thinking has made him more tired than he was before the holidays. Four or five hours is all he can bear. The rest of the night he thinks. And tries to digest his food. He eats too much, he knows that, but he's hungry. Afterwards he has a stomach ache. It feels as if he's swallowed nails. And then he's in a bad mood.

If he goes for a walk he comes home tired. How will he skate this fall with legs that don't even want to take a little walk? There's a good reason why his results are mediocre. He won't be able to skate any more. That's not true. He will skate. He recalls his last goal, against Johnny Bower. How many young players with their good legs can score such a fine goal?

Leave now? He's saved some money. Not much, because he has a lot of time ahead of him. He's responsible for a family. Teenagers. Younger growing children. People advise him to start a business. He can't see himself behind a counter. What does he know about business? He's sold cars in the summer. It wasn't his favourite activity. He didn't feel like giving customers a spiel like other salesmen. You have to know about business. The only thing that he's learned is hockey. And it's enough; he'll turn up at training camp. He'll convince Toe Blake and Mr. Selke that the Canadiens still need the Rocket.

Invest his savings in a business? A tavern? A restaurant? He's seen others being completely stripped of their savings that way. On trains and planes, he has read magazines about business, but he doesn't have a head for such things. There's nothing like hockey.

And when he can't play any more? He'll play this year. He'll lose weight. He'll work on the muscles in his legs. He just has to start skating again. Speculate on the future . . . That makes him worry. Work in an office? Mr. Selke offered him a job. He can't stay cooped up in an office. "Come in the morning, open the venetian blinds. Close them at night when I leave. I can't do that."

He is terrified by a future without hockey. Without his Canadiens uniform he'll look like those priests who, after living in a soutane, find themselves in a place where there's no longer such a thing as Mass. The Rocket has lived his life surrounded by his fans. And now this lone wolf is afraid of ending up on his own.

Gordie Howe has become a better hockey player than he is; his brother Henri, Béliveau, Geoffrion, Bonin—all are greater than he is. And Bobby Hull . . . Hockey has changed, the world has changed and the Rocket has got older. He doesn't know where to go. On September 12, for the nineteenth time, he turns up along with the young rookies at the Canadiens' training camp.

As soon as his skates touch the ice, Maurice can feel the rust in his joints. He's slow. He's heavy. The muscles in his legs are like old elastics. Even his instincts are hesitant. In the past, he knew before he thought. Now he thinks and he no longer knows. He shouldn't have come to this camp. Yet his shot is still authoritative. He's spent the summer harping on the notion that he is no longer the man he used to be. Maybe he's convinced himself? In the past, the greater his self-doubt, the more goals he scored. It was by sheer effort that he drove away doubt. His muscles are soft. Does he still have the will to play? Not wanting to retire is one thing; wanting to play hockey is another. By the end of the workout his face relaxes. The Rocket really does want to play hockey.

The next day he comes back, not so tense. Today he's going to play for the sake of playing. Waves of pleasure pass through him when the puck lands inside the net. "It's just a practice, Rocket!" Like the rookies, the old champion wants to be worthy of his place on the team.

"Rocket, Mr. Selke wants to see you."

The Rocket takes off his uniform and goes up to the general manager's office.

In the immortal books that I read, hockey does not exist. The characters don't play sports. You never see a crowd gather to watch great games in which the dark forces of life confront one another. Now, at the end of summer, I'm reading an account of the last day of an old Spanish count. Pride keeps him as straight as a capital I. When he wakes up, the light is unbearably beautiful on the hills of Estremadura. The greatest passion in his life has been for women. When he's really truthful, he admits that his great passion was actually for horses. On the day in question he asks his servant to dress him in his finest outfit. He asks his armourer to bring his finest revolver. He asks his stableboy to make ready his finest mount.

And the old count tours his property, gazing at everything that has been done. On his way home he stops at the most charming inn in the region. He requests the finest room. He asks for the most beautiful girl. He has the best wine sent up.

After the siesta, he gets back on his horse and stops at the church, where he recites the most beautiful prayer he knows. Then he leaves the most generous alms in the poor box. And his fine horse takes him back to a tree that has a hole in it as if its heart has been torn out. It's there that the old man has left his revolver. There, his life ends.

I think about that story on the morning of September 14 when I see on the front page of the paper the Rocket's face marked with emotion. He announces that he is "no longer an active member of the Canadiens hockey club."

Time has won. The Rocket accepts defeat. The hero of my childhood has been beaten. I have become a man.

"And now, what will I do . . . ?" That's a song you can hear on every radio, every jukebox this summer. I also think about a poem that tells of a bird with a tremendous wingspan. When it flew in the sky with its wings spread wide, the albatross was majestically beautiful. Back on the ground, because of its cumbersome wings the albatross looked miserable. Majestic in the sky; awkward on the earth. Thus did a poet describe the poet.

With his great wings spread on the ice, Maurice Richard was beautiful. Can anyone imagine him on the earth with people who sell insurance, beer, heating oil, hair care products, with people who work in offices?

The failed-poet-turned-sportswriter was favoured with a burst of inspiration: "The Rocket crossed the ice the way a meteor crosses the sky." When I'm old, will I talk about the Rocket the way my grandmother talked about Halley's comet? In our memories the Rocket will never stop skating, never stop scoring goals. We will hear, "Maurice Rocket Richard shoots—he scores!" till the end of our lives.

May 27, 2000. I've just put the final period on the final paragraph of this book. This afternoon on the radio I heard: "It's a matter of time for the Rocket." I stare at that period on the screen. Have I really finished? The phone rings. "You must have heard the news?" I tell the journalist, "I don't think I have anything to say." But I know what I'm thinking: we have been, we will be better men because the Rocket crossed through our childhood.

INDEX